Interventions That Work

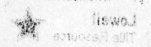

Interventions That Work

*A Comprehensive Intervention Model
for Preventing Reading Failure
in Grades K–3*

Linda J. Dorn
University of Arkansas at Little Rock

Carla Soffos
University of Arkansas at Little Rock

PEARSON

Boston   Columbus   Indianapolis   New York   San Francisco   Upper Saddle River
Amsterdam   Cape Town   Dubai   London   Madrid   Milan   Munich   Paris   Montreal   Toronto
Delhi   Mexico City   Sao Paulo   Sydney   Hong Kong   Seoul   Singapore   Taipei   Tokyo

Vice President/Editor-in-Chief: Aurora Martínez
Editorial Assistant: Meagan French
Marketing Manager: Danae April
Production Editor: Karen Mason
Editorial Production Service: Schneck-DePippo Graphics
Manufacturing Buyer: Megan Cochran
Electronic Composition: Schneck-DePippo Graphics
Photo Researcher: Deborah Schneck
Cover Designer: Jenny Hart / Elena Sidorova

Credits and acknowledgments borrowed from other sources and reproduced, with permission, in this textbook appear on appropriate page within.

Photo Credits: pp. iii, 1, 2, 3, 5, 7, 20, 38, 53, 76, 89, 99, 121, iStockPhoto; pp. 17, 42, 44, 51, 55, 61, 64, 65, 66, 72, 75, 83, 88, 105, 112, 113, Linda Dorn; p. 90, PAL image.

10 9 8 7 6 5   EBM   14

www.pearson.com

ISBN-10: 0-13-245875-6
ISBN-13: 978-0-13-245875-7

About the Authors

Linda Dorn

Linda J. Dorn is a Professor and graduate coordinator for the doctoral program in reading education at the University of Arkansas at Little Rock. She is Director of the Center for Literacy where she coordinates the development and implementation of five literacy initiatives, including the Partnerships in Comprehensive Literacy (PCL) Model and the Comprehensive Intervention Model (CIM). She has co-authored four books, including *Apprenticeship in Literacy: Transitions Across Reading and Writing,* numerous book chapters, scholarly articles, research reports, and professional development videos including the Interventions That Work series. Her upcoming publication with Carla Soffos is focused on interventions that work for adolescent struggling readers.

Carla Soffos

Carla Soffos is a literacy coach and Reading Recovery teacher leader at the University of Arkansas at Little Rock. She has twenty-six years of experience in education, including teaching at the primary grades and literacy coaching in grades kindergarten to eighth. She is co-author with Linda J. Dorn of three books, *Shaping Literate Minds, Scaffolding Young Writers,* and *Teaching for Deep Comprehension* and several professional development videos, including the Interventions That Work series. Her upcoming publication with Linda Dorn is focused on interventions that work for adolescent struggling readers.

Contents

Appendices
(also included on CD in back of book)

Figures and Tables

Chapter 4   Assisted Writing Intervention

Chapter 5   Guided Reading Plus Intervention

Chapter 6   Learning about Letters and Words

Chapter 7   **Implementing the CIM as an RtI Method**

Preface

The research on early intervention is clear. We know that most reading difficulties can be prevented through high-quality instruction. However, this is not as simple as providing a student with extra support; instead, it requires a diagnostic process to determine the problem and to use the student's strengths to scaffold the weaknesses. Unfortunately, many schools are lured into using packaged programs as quick fixes. This solution is flawed because a packaged program is not personalized instruction nor can it identify what a student knows; therefore, it can only take a prescriptive approach to remediate weaknesses. Duffy and Israel (2009) wrote "one of the major reasons instruction cannot be packaged and prescribed in advance is the growing understanding that 'being explicit' does not mean students are passive recipients of explanations" (p. 671). We know that thinking is an active process and that learning is co-constructed during meaningful interactions with more knowledgeable persons. The teacher is the most critical person in shaping the student's literate knowledge.

The Comprehensive Intervention Model (CIM) emphasizes teachers as the agents of literacy improvement, and that scripted programs are counterproductive to teacher and student development. The CIM framework includes a combination of: (a) high-quality, differentiated classroom instruction; (b) a portfolio of research-based interventions; (c) a seamless assessment system at an individual and system level; and (d) school-embedded professional learning for increasing teacher efficacy and building capacity in schools.

Since 1991, we have collaborated with teachers in the development, implementation, and refinement of the small-group interventions. We observed the diverse needs of struggling readers, and we created a portfolio of interventions for accentuating particular literacy areas. Each intervention includes authentic reading and writing opportunities that mirror high-quality classroom instruction. The CIM stresses instructional congruency and seamless assessments across classroom and supplemental programs with built-in structures for promoting collaboration among teachers.

In Chapter 1, we introduce the CIM as a Response to Intervention (RtI) process. With the passage of the Individuals with Disabilities Education Act (IDEA) in 2004, schools can evaluate a student's responsiveness to intervention to determine whether a student should be considered learning disabled. The CIM uses a four-tiered, layered approach as a problem-solving process for monitoring a student's response to intervention. All interventions are delivered in a 30-minute framework that includes a reading phase (Day 1) and a writing phase (Day 2). The different interventions can be layered or mixed to promote the student's acceleration in reading.

In Chapter 2, we present the components of a comprehensive assessment system (CAS) as an RtI process. One goal of RtI is to develop more valid procedures for assessing and identifying students who are at risk of reading failure. Intervention and assessment are dynamic processes; for instance, the teacher designs a responsive intervention based on the student's strengths and needs, then assesses the student's capacity to learn from instruction. If a student is not responding to intervention, the problem is with the teaching, not with the student. Therefore, assessment is a reciprocal and recursive process: the student's learning provides a mirror on the teacher's instruction. The CAS offers teachers a process for examining teaching and learning through multiple measures and across different contexts (classroom and intervention).

In Chapter 3, we advocate for a differentiated framework for meeting students' needs in whole-group, small-group, and one-to-one settings. The workshop approach presents a predictable structure for organizing classroom instruction, while delivering interventions within this framework. In a writing workshop, the classroom teacher meets with an individual or small groups of students, and the intervention teacher provides a writing process intervention to the most needy students. A writing continuum is used to monitor the students' progress over time.

Chapter 4 describes how a writing intervention can be used to increase reading achievement. The assisted writing (AW) intervention includes two types: interactive writing (IW) and writing aloud (WA). The IW intervention is designed for emergent and beginning early writers; and the WA intervention is for writers who need assistance with the writing process. Teachers make decisions about the most appropriate intervention to match the student's needs.

In Chapter 5, we present the Guided Reading Plus (GRP) intervention at the emergent, early, and transitional levels. During phase one (reading phase), the teacher provides targeted instruction in word study, followed by opportunities for the students to apply word-solving strategies during their guided reading component. During phase two (writing phase), the teacher prompts the students to write about the reading from the guided reading discussion. The GRP intervention aligns with high-quality classroom instruction, while providing targeted instruction in word study, strategy use, and writing about reading.

Chapter 6 focuses on the word study component of the assisted writing and guided reading plus interventions. We present change over time in the development of the phonological and phonemic systems, along with instructional activities that align with the processing continuum. The goal of an effective word study component is achieved when students use strategies to solve words quickly and efficiently during reading and writing.

In the final chapter, we present case studies of five schools that are implementing the CIM as an RtI method. The literacy coaches in the Russellville School District in Arkansas share how they used the ESAIL (Environmental Scale for Assessing Implementing Levels) to assess the school's literacy environment and to develop a professional development plan. Next, two literacy coaches from Washington School for Comprehensive Literacy in Sheboygan, Wisconsin, describe their comprehensive assessment system and the assessment wall. The staff at the third school, Anne Sullivan Elementary School in Green Bay, Wisconsin, presents details for organizing and managing RtI teams across the school. Fourth, the literacy coaches from the Council Bluffs Community School District in Iowa describe their RtI process for creating a seamless, data-driven approach for identifying students for special education and monitoring their progress across classroom, supplemental, and special education programs. Finally, the teacher leader and literacy coach from Spokane Public Schools, Washington State, present their RtI plan for reducing referrals to special education, while using professional development as a tool for increasing teacher knowledge and promoting instructional coherence across the district.

Throughout the book, we have tried to emphasize the teacher as the heartbeat of the CIM. The teacher must understand how students learn and be able to provide the best instruction possible. Further, an intervention model must be based on what we know about high-quality classroom instruction. Our final message is that it takes a team of teachers working together to ensure the literacy rights of the most struggling learners. The book is organized to provide teachers with tools for implementing a responsive intervention for preventing reading failure in the early grades.

Acknowledgments

We are indebted to many people for their contributions and support of our work. These individuals exemplify the spirit of collaboration in achieving a common goal. For us, the goal has been to create a comprehensive intervention model that is grounded in evidence-based practices, authentic experiences with struggling readers, and learning situations among teachers. The book would not be possible without the influence of the classroom teachers, literacy coaches, interventionists, and administrators who welcomed us into their schools and contributed real-world resources to the chapters. To this entire group, we say thank you.

We owe special acknowledgment to Sonya Smith and Alisa Paladino, Reading Recovery and CIM teachers in the Conway School District, Arkansas. These two teachers epitomize what it means to hold a tentative theory that is open to revision based on student learning. They have welcomed constructive feedback as we have collaborated to refine the Guided Reading Plus and assisted writing interventions. Also, we acknowledge Vicki Altland, literacy coach in the Conway School District, for her insights and feedback on the seamless assessment system. She is the impetus behind the assessment portfolio and the development of an assessment wall for progress monitoring on multiple measures. Also, thank you to Heather Nutt for her contributions to the writing chapter.

In the final chapter of the book, we invited five schools to describe their implementations of the CIM as an RtI method. These individuals were amazing: they compiled resources, secured permissions, and submitted their work within a short time line. Thank you to the literacy coaches in Russellville School District in Arkansas: Freda Ellenburg, Lori Ferren, Suzanne Gray, Jeanine Humphrey, Lisa McElroy, Kim Meatheany, and Elizabeth Mullins. Also, we appreciate the support of the Russellville principals: Paula Gallagher, Cathy Koch, Mark Gotcher, Tami Chandler, Don Dodson, Brenda Tash, Sheri Shirley, and D'Anne Barrow, Curriculum Director. Thank you to the literacy team at Washington Comprehensive Literacy School in Sheboygan, Wisconsin: Katie Meyer, literacy coach; Brian Reindl, literacy coach; and Karl Bekkum, principal. Our appreciation is extended to the Council Bluffs School District leadership team: Dr. Martha Bruckner, Superintendent of Schools; Dr. Ann Mausbach, Executive Director of Curriculum and Instruction; Julie Smith, Supervisor of Elementary Education; Kari Means, district Strategic Processing Coach for special education; and Melissa Chalupnik, district literacy coach. Also, we thank the staff at Anne Sullivan Elementary School in Green Bay, Wisconsin: Kay Savela, district literacy coach; Michael Fraley, principal; Lori Cathey, bilingual instructional coach; Kortney Cherveny, literacy coach; and Angela Hager, literacy coach. Finally, we offer appreciation to the leaders in Spokane Public Schools, Washington State: Molly Bozo, Reading Recovery teacher leader and CIM Coach; and Linda Wert, Special Programs Coordinator. Without the contributions of all these dedicated and visionary leaders, this book would be missing an important section—the application of the CIM to the school context.

Also, we would like to express our special appreciation to our colleague and friend, Janet Behrend, University of Arkansas at Little Rock, for her hard work and commitment to the CIM. Janet was instrumental in creating resources and in training Reading Recovery teacher leaders in the small group interventions. We would also like to acknowledge Thomas Gunning for his feedback on the word study chapter and Lance Gentile for his feedback on the language development section of the Writing about Reading checklists. The work of these two scholars has been influential in our small-group interventions, and we are grateful for their insights in these areas. We would like to thank our reviewers for their helpful feedback: Pam East, Conway School District, Conway, Arkansas; Joyce Hemphill, North St. Francois County R-1 School District, Bonne Terre, Missouri; Mary Ann Poparad, National-Louis University, Lisle, Illinois; and Karen J. Scott, Ozark Missouri Public Schools, Ozark, Missouri. Finally, we would like to extend our special thanks to the Pearson editorial team: Aurora Martínez, Meagan French, Deborah Schneck, Karen Mason, and the behind-the-scenes staff who devoted their time and talent to our work. We appreciate your commitment to producing a high-quality publication.

In closing, we extend a special acknowledgment to our family and friends who have stood by us during the two years of writing this book.

Linda J. Dorn
Carla Soffos

Foreword

Schools across the United States are developing the structure of their Response to Instruction (RtI) initiatives. Some states' education agencies have already set deadlines and criteria for such initiatives. Unfortunately, few, if any, state education agencies have offered schools any RtI framework that is likely to dramatically reduce the number of children who struggle with learning to read and write. Far too many of the professional texts now available on the topic of RTI focus almost exclusively on implementing a progress monitoring plan with little said about the instruction that will produce the progress to be monitored. What we do know, however, is that there is not a single commercial reading or writing program with research evidence that supports its use in an RtI initiative. Of the 150-plus reading programs studied, only a single reading "program," Reading Recovery, was found to have "strong evidence" of its positive impact on accelerating reading development. You can go to the website of the federal What Works Clearinghouse (www.wwc.ed.gov) to see the sorry results the other commercial programs have produced.

But Reading Recovery is different from other commercial reading programs in that the primary function of the Reading Recovery program is long-term professional development that builds the expertise that early literacy teachers need to work effectively with the children experiencing the greatest difficulties in acquiring literacy proficiency.

Now Linda Dorn and Carla Soffos have taken much of what we have learned from Reading Recovery and expanded upon it. *Interventions That Work: A Comprehensive Intervention Model for Preventing Reading Failure in Grades K–3* is a useful and powerful text for anyone interested in the details of good reading instruction in an RtI initiative. This book presents the Comprehensive Intervention Model (CIM) as one RtI plan. CIM involves leveled book-reading along with interactive writing activities. The details for implementing each of the components needed in an effective RtI effort are the essence of this text. What I especially appreciate is how it links intervention lessons with the lessons children are receiving in their classrooms. After having reviewed a dozen or more RtI efforts that put struggling readers in two (or sometimes three) strategically incompatible reading programs, reading the descriptions of coherent literacy lessons for struggling children offers hope for our struggling readers.

But perhaps what makes this book unique is its focus on systemic reform activity. In other words, the RtI process involves whole school reform. This means that virtually all the professional personnel in a school will be involved in creating the

CIM plan. Much emphasis is given to providing professional development so that all classroom teachers will be offering high-quality and effective Tier 1 reading and writing lessons to every child in their classrooms. No RtI model can possibly produce the intended effects without ensuring high-quality classroom reading and writing instruction for all children. Thus, the need for professional development that (1) enhances classroom teachers' expertise about effective reading and writing lessons and (2) fosters a school-wide belief system that classroom teachers play the most important role in RtI.

I recommend that readers begin with the final chapter of this text. I recommend this because that chapter presents five school district case studies of the implementation of the CIM plan, illustrating all the ways this model can be flexibly implemented to achieve the primary RtI goals of (1) improved reading and writing performance, especially among those children at risk of experiencing literacy difficulties and (2) a substantial reduction of children identified as pupils with disabilities. After completing the final chapter, readers can return to the beginning of the book and learn the details of each of the components of the CIM plan and details about the nature of high-quality reading and writing lessons.

In an era when most schools I have visited are implementing a haphazard RtI process with few elements one could find in the research, it is a real win for the profession that this book exists—a real win because it is so practical and so completely based in the research evidence. If all schools used a version of the CIM plan in designing their RtI initiative, the promise of RtI could be fulfilled.

Dick Allington
University of Tennessee

Interventions That Work

A Comprehensive Intervention Model

The future of our society depends on a literate populace—a culture of learners who understand how to solve problems, seek solutions, communicate effectively, and construct meaning. If a student is struggling in literacy, it is critical to provide an appropriate intervention as soon as possible. Furthermore, an intervention for reversing reading failure must be grounded in a model of effective, strategic reading.

Research indicates that the struggling reader has developed an inefficient system for solving problems during reading (Paris, Lipson, & Wixcon, 1994; Harris & Pressley, 1991).[1] This inefficiency has led to unthinking, guessing reactions that are in contrast to the reflective and intentional thinking that is associated with good readers. Strategy-based interventions are designed to foster the development of self-regulated processes, that is, the student's capacity to use knowledge, skills, and strategies for solving problems, generalizing information, and constructing new learning.

Good readers use strategies to initiate efficient problem-solving plans, monitor their actions, and redirect their thinking when meaning is threatened. This higher-level thinking is related to three psychological functions (Luria, 1980; Vygotsky, 1978):

- Conscious awareness (I know what I know)

- Selective attention (I can focus on what is important)

- Voluntary memory (I need to remember this)

An intervention must enable poor readers to develop these higher-level psychological processes, thus promoting their ability to use efficient and flexible strategies for learning. Research-based interventions have shown that struggling readers can acquire efficient strategies for self-regulating their reading.

The purpose of this chapter is to present the Comprehensive Intervention Model (CIM) as a Response to Intervention (RtI) method for preventing reading difficulties. First, we describe how strategic activity and transfer are the ultimate goals of any intervention. We move to an overview of RtI, including a description of the four-tiered model of layered interventions, and an explanation of how interventions are delivered in two waves of literacy defense. We conclude by describing how the CIM uses a portfolio of interventions to meet the diverse needs of struggling readers.

 **Constructing Knowledge**

Learning is an active and constructive process that is stimulated by opportunities to acquire new knowledge in collaboration with others. From an intervention perspective, the teacher creates a supportive context (an intervention group) and uses meaningful tools (books, writing, etc.) to engage the reader's mind in constructive activity. Constructive activity is cognitive—an intentional and strategic process for accomplishing a particular task. Strategies can be defined as neural actions for assembling, integrating, and monitoring information for constructing new knowledge. It is essential for teachers to understand what students already know (background knowledge) and be able to prompt for strategic activity (problem-solving knowledge) that links the known and unknown information.

The brain processes information at two levels. The lower level (back cortex) is involved in storing and processing long-term memories (prior knowledge) and the higher level (front cortex) is involved in decision-making activity (see Figure 1.1).[2] During an intervention, the teacher uses prompts that activate students' minds to connect the lower and higher level processes for constructing new knowledge. This inte-

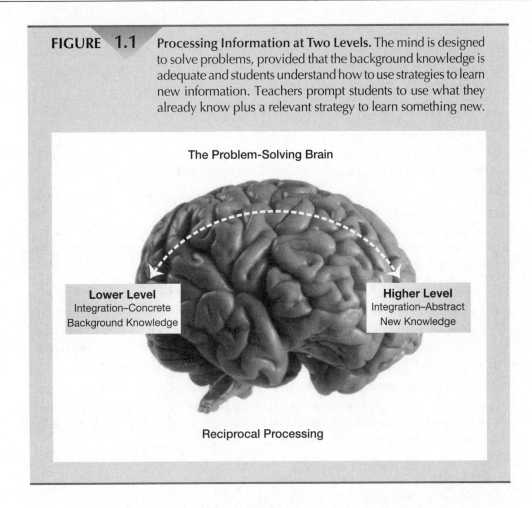

FIGURE 1.1 **Processing Information at Two Levels.** The mind is designed to solve problems, provided that the background knowledge is adequate and students understand how to use strategies to learn new information. Teachers prompt students to use what they already know plus a relevant strategy to learn something new.

The Problem-Solving Brain

Lower Level
Integration–Concrete
Background Knowledge

Higher Level
Integration–Abstract
New Knowledge

Reciprocal Processing

gration occurs in the motor cortex where students use physical actions (speech and writing) to generate and test information. In the process, ideas are transformed into words; and meaning becomes more precise. At the same time, the teacher creates flexible opportunities for students to transfer their knowledge, skills, and strategies in different contexts and across changing purposes.

Teaching for Transfer

The ultimate goal of an intervention is to empower students to regulate their learning for task-specific purposes. Students must understand that knowledge can be transferred to different contexts and for different purposes and goals (McKeough, Lupart, & Marini, 1995). Too often, we find students who do not understand that knowledge is generalizable; consequently, they view each learning opportunity as a novel experience. When teachers teach for transfer, they enable students to use what they know to learn new information; and teachers collaborate with one another to promote the student's transfer of knowledge across multiple settings. Self-regulation and transfer are dependent on the reader's control of three knowledge sources (Meichenbaum & Biemiller, 1998; Paris, Lipson, & Wixson, 1994):

- *Declarative knowledge:* Knowledge of the literacy task
- *Procedural knowledge:* Knowledge of steps/procedures for carrying out the literacy task
- *Conditional knowledge:* Knowledge of flexible strategies for performing the literacy task in varied contexts and for different purposes

The CIM includes a framework for aligning instruction across classroom and supplemental settings. Transfer is facilitated as the student learns the new task in an environment with reduced distractions and tailored support, then applies the knowledge to an environment with normal distractions and distributed support. In the CIM, the following steps are used to promote transfer.

- The teacher instructs the student in a small group within the classroom setting.
- An intervention specialist provides highly tailored support, precision teaching, and expert scaffolding to the student. The intervention occurs in a setting with limited distractions, thus enabling the student to develop conscious awareness, selective attention, and strategies for problem solving in connected texts.
- Classroom and intervention teachers observe the student's ability to transfer knowledge across the two contexts. If transfer is not occurring, the teachers examine instructional factors (e.g., text levels, teaching prompts) that could impact the student's ability to generalize knowledge.

 ## Response to Intervention

Response to Intervention (RtI) is a comprehensive assessment and intervention process for identifying students with literacy difficulties and providing targeted interventions to prevent reading failure (Johnston, 2010; Lipson & Wixson, 2010). The first step in prevention is to ensure that all students receive a high quality general education program. Therefore, if more than 15 to 20 percent of the student population is experiencing difficulty in reading, the school needs to examine the classroom curriculum. Some questions to begin the discussion are:

- Is the curriculum based on evidence-based practices?
- Is instruction differentiated to meet students' needs?
- Is assessment built into the curriculum?
- Do students have adequate reading materials to address the diversity of student learning?
- Does the teacher understand the developmental continuum of reading and writing processes?

School teams can use a modified version of the Environmental Scale for Assessing Implementation Levels (ESAIL) (2005) to assess the school's learning climate and literacy curriculum (see Chapter 7 and Appendix G1 on pages 187–192).

These resources recognize that the first line of defense for preventing reading difficulties resides in the classroom.

A Tiered Approach to RtI

The CIM is grounded in the philosophy that struggling readers need consistent instruction that is layered across classroom and supplemental programs. Students with reading difficulties should engage in the same high-quality curriculum as their classmates, although teachers should differentiate the content by providing extra time, adapting specific methods of teaching, and providing additional adult assistance. The CIM interventions are designed to offer "positive differentiation" (see Gindis, 2003) by varying the degrees of intensity and the duration of services.[3]

The CIM uses a layered approach within a four-tier framework for aligning classroom instruction, supplemental interventions, and special education (Dorn & Schubert, 2008; 2010). The interventions are not delivered in a rigid, lock-step manner; instead, the RtI team makes data-driven decisions about the most appropriate intervention (based on intensity, duration, size of group, teacher expertise) for meeting the unique needs of the individual learners. Three sets of knowledge related to poor readers should be considered:

- Poor readers must unlearn inefficient and inappropriate responses that are preventing them from making literacy progress. Unfortunately, many of these responses have become habituated reactions to problems, thus interfering with the new learning. The situation can be further exacerbated by inappropriate interventions delivered by unqualified staff.

- Poor readers must make giant leaps in their learning in order to catch up with their grade-level peers. This can be an upward struggle for low-ability readers. As classroom instruction improves in quality, the reading levels of average readers may also increase; and the achievement gap between the poor and average reader could actually widen. When this occurs, the student may need a temporary intervention to close the gap.

- Poor readers must maintain their gains after the intervention has ceased, often in spite of other social issues that can impact literacy. This implies that struggling readers need sensitive observation and flexible support for at least one year beyond the intervention period.

The CIM includes multiple layers of intervention to promote and sustain reading progress over time. If the student is not responding to intervention, the problem may be with the teaching, not with the student. This diagnostic model requires teachers to use data in systematic ways, including observations of how students are learning on different tasks across changing contexts (classroom, Title I, special education). The layered framework views all teachers as intervention specialists, including classroom teachers, supplemental teachers, and special education teachers (see Figure 1.2).

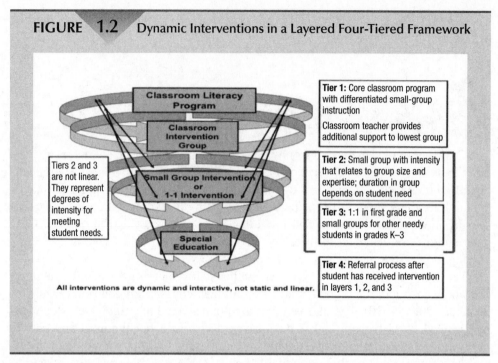

FIGURE 1.2   Dynamic Interventions in a Layered Four-Tiered Framework

Reprinted from A Comprehensive Intervention Model for Reversing Reading Failure: A Response to Intervention Process, by L. J. Dorn and B. Schubert, 2008, *Journal of Reading Recovery, 7*(2), 29–41. Reading Recovery Council of North America. Reprinted with permission.

Two Waves of Literacy Defense

A comprehensive approach to RtI requires a framework of unique and well-developed interventions that meet the diverse needs of struggling students across the grades. The CIM is conceptualized as "Two Waves of Literacy Defense" with the first wave taking a preventive stance with K–3 interventions (Dorn & Henderson, 2010a; Dorn & Schubert, 2008). The premises of early intervention are logical:

- Intervene as early as possible before confusions become habituated and unthinking reactions.

- Provide intensive, short-term services that focus on problem-solving strategies in continuous texts.

- Make data-driven decisions about the intensity of interventions, the duration period, and the need for follow-up support.

The second wave of literacy defense occurs at the fourth- to twelfth-grade levels. With appropriate interventions, readers at risk in the upper grades can become successful readers. However, the interventions may take longer, because the students have habituated unproductive reading practices that can create resistance, passivity, and lack of motivation. To address these challenges, schools must redesign their general education programs in three significant ways. They must:

- Create a classroom model of differentiated instruction.

- Place an emphasis on reading comprehension in the content areas.

- Provide interventions, including small group and one-to-one, for the students who are still reading below grade level.

First Wave of Defense

The goal of intervention is to increase the overall literacy achievement by the end of third grade and to reduce the number of children identified with learning disabilities within 1.5 percent or less of the general population. Toward this goal, struggling readers are provided with multiple layers of intervention. To illustrate, at Tier 1, the classroom teacher provides the entire class with a 90-minute literacy core of differentiated instruction: whole group (spelling/word study, shared reading, interactive read-aloud, strategy-based minilesson); small group (guided reading, literature discussion, assisted writing); one-to-one (reading and writing conferences); and independent (easy or familiar reading, word study, writing in response to reading). For struggling readers, the teacher provides an additional classroom intervention; for example, she might add a word study intervention and a writing-about-reading intervention to the traditional guided reading lesson (see Figure 3.1 for sample schedule).

Concurrent with Tier 1, the lowest students may also receive a Tier 2 small-group intervention or a Tier 3 one-to-one intervention with a reading specialist. In some cases, a student might receive three interventions at the same time. If a student is not progressing at the expected rate, the classroom teacher, in collaboration with the school's intervention team, may initiate the referral process for special education. In Tier 4, the special education students continue to receive Tier 1 classroom instruction to meet their literacy needs, and the classroom teacher and special education teacher collaborate on a seamless approach across the two contexts. The expectation is that the special education students will continue to make good progress with the potential to reach literacy proficiency over time.

Second Wave of Defense

In the second wave of literacy defense, Tier 1 instruction uses a workshop framework for differentiating instruction, including small groups and one-to-one conferences (see Figure 1.3). Interventions focus on comprehension of content-area text through strategy-based instruction. In Tier 2, struggling readers receive supplemental small-group instruction from intervention specialists. Tier 3 interventions include individual or small groups of three students or less, and are provided to students who are reading below grade level. In schools with literacy coaches, the coaches might spend up to 40 percent of their time providing Tier 2 and Tier 3 interventions to the students who need it most. Special education teachers provide Tier 4 intervention in collaboration with Tier 1 classroom intervention to provide a seamless transition for learning disabled students.

| FIGURE 1.3 | Two Waves of Literacy Defense |

First Wave of Literacy Defense

Literacy Goal: To increase literacy achievement by the end of third grade and to reduce the number of children identified with learning disabilities within 1.5 percent or less of the general population.

Therefore, to promote accelerated learning (in contrast to remediation), students might receive multiple layers of interventions at the same time. Tier 1 classroom instruction includes two levels: differentiated core instruction, plus a classroom intervention for students who are not responding to the core instruction. Some low-performing students also receive supplemental intervention from a literacy specialist at the same time. Supplemental interventions are provided based on intensity, expertise, and student needs. Referrals to special education are based on students' responses to intervention in Tiers 1, 2, and 3.

	Tier 1 (includes core instruction, plus classroom intervention)	Tier 2 (supplemental group)	Tier 3 (supplemental instruction)	Tier 4 (special education in literacy processes)
Levels of Intensity	Classroom Teacher (Differentiated Instruction)	Intervention Specialist (Small Group, 1:3, 1:4, 1:5)	Intervention Specialist (1:1, 1:2, 1:3)	Special Education Teacher (Small groups or 1:1)
Layered	Tier 1 only	Tier 2 plus Tier 1	Tier 3 plus Tier 1	Tier 4 plus Tier 1
Kindergarten Interventions	Provides all students with differentiated instruction, including whole group, small group, and one-to-one, plus provides low-performing students with an additional classroom intervention in emergent literacy foundations.	Provides additional small-group intervention in assisted writing.	Provides more intensive small-group intervention in assisted writing.	
First-Grade Interventions	Provides all students with differentiated instruction, including whole-group, small-group, and one-to-one, plus provides low-performing students with an additional classroom intervention in assisted writing, word study, reading response log, or writing process.	Provides additional small-group intervention in assisted writing, Guided Reading Plus, or writing process.	Provides one-to-one instruction (Reading Recovery) to the students who need it most. Provides small group instruction (1:2 or 1:3) in assisted writing, Guided Reading Plus, or writing process to other students who need it.	For students who received Tiers 1 and 2 in kindergarten and Tier 1, plus Tier 2 or Tier 3 in first grade, the classroom teacher might start the referral process for children who are not responding to interventions. Data from previous interventions are used to plan next steps, and intervention is aligned with Tier 1 instruction.
Second-Grade Interventions	Provides all students with differentiated instruction, including whole-group, small- group, and one-to-one, plus provides low-performing students with an additional classroom intervention in assisted writing, word study, reading response log, or writing process.	Provides additional small-group intervention in assisted writing, Guided Reading Plus, or writing process group.	Provides more intensive small-group intervention in assisted writing, Guided Reading Plus, or writing process group.	If student does not respond to Tier 1, plus Tier 2 or 3, the classroom teacher starts referral process for special education. Data from previous interventions are used to plan next steps, and intervention is aligned with Tier 1 instruction.

FIGURE 1.3	Two Waves of Literacy Defense (continued)

| **Third-Grade Interventions** | Provides all students with differentiated instruction, including whole-group, small-group, and one-to-one, plus provides low-performing students with an additional classroom intervention in assisted writing, word study, guided reading, reading response log, or writing process. | Provides additional small-group intervention in assisted writing, Guided Reading Plus, writing process, or comprehension focus group. | Provides more intensive small-group intervention in assisted writing, Guided Reading Plus, writing process, or comprehension focus group. | If student does not respond to Tier 1, plus Tier 2 or 3, student is placed in special education. Data from previous interventions are used to plan next steps, and intervention is aligned with Tier 1 instruction. |

Literacy Goal: In the First Wave of Literacy Defense, 98 to 99 percent of struggling learners who received Tier 1, plus Tier 2 or 3 interventions will have achieved literacy proficiency by the end of third grade. This goal recognizes that 1.5 percent or less of the general population may be diagnosed with a literacy disability. In Tier 4, the students in special education will continue to receive Tier 1 classroom instruction to meet their literacy needs, and the classroom teacher and special education teacher will collaborate on a seamless approach across the two contexts. The expectation is the special education group will continue to make good progress with the potential to reach literacy proficiency over time.

As students move into the upper grades, a second wave of intervention is designed to ensure that struggling readers receive Tier 1 classroom support in small group or individual interventions, plus supplemental support, as needed, by literacy specialists. Tier 3 intervention is provided to students who are reading at or below basic levels. This intervention can be provided by literacy coaches, ELL teachers, and reading specialists.

Second Wave of Literacy Defense

Literacy Goal: To increase literacy achievement for all students with simultaneous interventions that focus on research-based, problem-solving strategies for reading and writing in the content areas.

Therefore, classroom teachers in the content areas acquire knowledge of reading strategies, as well as management techniques for differentiating instruction to meet the needs of struggling readers. In Tier 1 classroom instruction, students receive whole-group, small-group, and one-to-one support within a workshop framework. In Tier 2 intervention, struggling readers receive supplemental instruction provided by literacy specialists, interventionists, or literacy coaches. In Tier 3 intervention, students who are reading below the basic level receive more intensive instruction during 1:1, 1:2, or 1:3 interventions. Special education teachers provide Tier 4 support in collaboration with Tier 1 classroom intervention to ensure a seamless transition for learning disabled students.

Tier 1 (classroom intervention beyond core program)	Tier 2 (supplemental group)	Tier 3 (supplemental instruction)	Tier 4 (special education in literacy processes)
Classroom Teacher (Differentiated Instruction)	Intervention Specialist (1:3, 1:4, 1:5)	Intervention Specialist (1:1, 1:2, 1:3)	Special Education Teacher (Small Groups)
Tier 1 only	Tier 2 plus Tier 1	Tier 3 plus Tier 1	Tier 4 plus Tier 1
Provides all students with differentiated instruction within a workshop framework, including whole-group, small-group, and one-to-one. Struggling readers receive classroom intervention in small group or individual reading/writing conferences.	Provides small-group supplemental intervention for students who are reading below grade level.	Provides more intensive intervention for students who are reading at or below basic level in reading and writing.	Provides small-group intervention that aligns with classroom support for students with learning disabilities.

Reprinted from A Comprehensive Intervention Model for Reversing Reading Failure: A Response to Intervention Process, by L. J. Dorn and B. Schubert, 2008, *Journal of Reading Recovery, 7*(2), 29–41. Reading Recovery Council of North America. Adapted with permission.

The Comprehensive Intervention Model (CIM)

For decades, many schools have used a discrepancy model for identifying students with learning disabilities. This deficit approach assumes that the problem lies within the child, while ignoring the fact that external factors (e.g., flawed assessments, inappropriate materials, limited opportunities, poor instruction) may be the root cause of reading difficulties (Spear-Swerling & Sternberg, 1996).[4] As a result, many children are identified as learning disabled based on a defective system (Aaron, 1997; Allington, 2002).

Marie Clay (1987) has argued that learning disabled and low-achieving readers are indistinguishable groups. She insisted that there is no evidence to suggest that children with learning disabilities should be taught any differently than children with reading difficulties. Many of the programs developed for poor readers, generally by specialists in the field of reading, might also be highly appropriate for children with reading disabilities.[5]

Numerous studies of small-group interventions have demonstrated their effectiveness with struggling readers (e.g., Goldenberg, 1992; Graham & Harris, 2005; Scanlon & Anderson, 2010; Saunders & Goldenberg, 1999; Vellutino & Scanlon, 2002). Three state-level studies in Arkansas provide support for a comprehensive literacy model that includes both Reading Recovery and small-group components (Dorn & Allen, 1995; Harrison, 2003; James, 2005). These studies found that Reading Recovery and small-group programs are complementary interventions that recognize the diverse needs of struggling readers and provide varying degrees of intensity.

The small-group interventions in the CIM were developed by examining research on successful literacy practices and refined through partnerships with teachers in the schools (Dorn, French, & Jones, 1997; Dorn & Soffos, 2001a; 2005a). All interventions are structured around predictable lesson components and established routines with daily instruction. Within this framework, teachers employ data-driven, decision-making processes, including selecting books, prompting for strategies, and teaching for independence and transfer.

CIM Portfolio of Interventions

The CIM portfolio includes a collection of seven evidence-based interventions for kindergarten to middle school:

1. Reading Recovery

2. Guided Reading Plus group

3. Assisted writing—interactive writing group

4. Assisted writing—writing aloud group

5. Writing process group

6. Comprehension focus group—genre units of study

7. Comprehension focus group—content units of study (see Table 1.1 on page 13)

The small-group interventions can be taught by classroom teachers (tier 1), supplemental teachers (tiers 2 and 3), and special education teachers (tier 4). The intensity of each intervention is determined by group size, which ranges from two to five students. Following diagnostic assessment, an intervention team meeting is convened and teachers collaborate on the most appropriate intervention to meet the unique needs of the students.

Each intervention can be implemented within or outside the classroom, with the exception of Reading Recovery, which is always taught as a pull-out intervention, and writing process group, which is always taught within the classroom writing workshop. The comprehension focus group interventions are designed for intermediate and middle school students; and although we will describe them in this section, the subsequent chapters are focused on the K–3 interventions (for more information on the comprehension focus groups, see Dorn & Soffos, 2009b).

Guided Reading Plus Intervention

Guided Reading Plus (GRP) is a small-group intervention for students who are not reading on grade level. The intervention is designed for struggling readers in the primary grades (emergent to transitional levels) and for upper-grade students who are reading below grade level (approximately third- or fourth-grade levels).

The addition of writing and word study to the traditional guided reading group is especially important for struggling readers. Writing plays a special role in lifting reading achievement, as writing slows down the reading process and increases the reader's orthographic and phonological knowledge through motor production. The GRP intervention enables struggling readers to read for understanding, practice efficient decoding strategies, and use what they know about reading to assist with their writing, and vice versa (see Dorn & Soffos, 2009a; 2009c).

Assisted Writing Intervention

The assisted writing (AW) intervention is for students in first to fourth grades who are struggling with literacy processing. *Assisted writing* is an umbrella term for classifying two types of writing interventions: interactive writing and writing aloud. At the emergent to early levels, the interactive writing intervention enables students to:

- Acquire foundational concepts about print
- Understand that writing is about communicating a message
- Apply rereading strategies to predict and monitor reading
- Articulate words slowly and hear and record letters in words
- Use simple resources as self-help tools (e.g., ABC chart, personal dictionary)
- Become fluent with correct letter formation
- Build a core of high-frequency words
- Cross-check multiple sources of information

The writing-aloud intervention is designed for students who are reading at higher levels, but experiencing difficulty with the writing process. The goal is to assist students in understanding that writing includes a process of generating ideas, drafting a message, revising, editing, and preparing a piece for a particular audience. The writing-aloud intervention includes five elements:

- Explicit teaching through minilessons
- Group compositions
- Individual writing
- Teacher conferences
- Student self-assessments

 ## Writing Process Group Intervention

The writing process (WG) group is delivered within the writing workshop block of the classroom. It is a supplemental intervention taught by a specialty teacher (CIM Interventionist, Title I, Reading Recovery, special education). The interventionist comes into the classroom during the writing workshop block and gathers a small group of struggling writers to a table where she assists them with their writing, including composing a meaningful message, applying problem-solving strategies for working on words, revising and editing the message, and maintaining a focus for completing the writing task. The interventionist observes the writing behaviors of individual students within the group and provides tailored support that enables each student to accomplish the classroom writing goals.

 ## Comprehension Focus Group Interventions

Comprehension focus group (CFG) interventions are designed for intermediate and middle school students who are struggling with reading comprehension (see Dorn & Soffos, 2009b). *Comprehension focus group* is an umbrella term that includes two types of comprehension units: genre unit and content unit. Each intervention consists of a series of reading and writing lessons with a specific focus that occurs over a period of weeks. The intervention is organized around units of study that require readers to apply higher-level comprehension strategies to analyze relationships within and across texts. Reading and writing are viewed as reciprocal processes; therefore, students are taught to use their knowledge from reading to support their writing and vice versa. The CFG intervention consists of four phases (also see Table 1.1):

- Preparing
- Reading
- Discussing the book
- Writing

TABLE 1.1 CIM Portfolio of Small-Group Interventions

Intervention	Role of Reading	Role of Writing	Entry and Exit Assessments	Progress Monitoring	Informal Assessments	Materials
Guided Reading Plus (GRP)	Reading strategies, fluency, vocabulary, comprehension, word-solving strategies	Writing about reading, word solving/spelling strategies, composing and planning strategies, linking reading and writing	Text Reading Level, Comprehension Rubric, Fluency Measure, Word Test, Phonological Assessment	Text Reading Level, Writing About Reading Prompt and Rubric	Running records, anecdotal notes, record of high-frequency words, writing journals/logs	Leveled texts, magnetic letters, word/pattern charts, writing journals/logs, graphic organizers (upper levels), dry erase boards
Assisted Writing Group • Interactive Writing (IW) Group	Concepts of print, reading and writing connections, letter and word knowledge, early reading strategies	Concepts of print, composing meaningful messages for reading, phonological awareness, word-solving strategies	Text Reading Level, Word Test, Writing Prompt and Rubric, Phonological Measure	Text Reading Level, Writing About Reading Prompt and Rubric	Writing journal/draft, record of high-frequency words, anecdotal notes	Student word dictionaries, ABC charts, writing journals or logs, magnetic letters, dry erase boards, writing checklists, sound/letter books
• Writing Aloud (WA) Group	Reading and writing connections, vocabulary, word-solving strategies	Organizing writing, composing message, editing and revising process	Text Reading Level, Writing Prompt and Rubric			Writing journals or logs, published dictionary, published thesaurus, writing checklists, dry erase boards
Writing Process (WP) Group	Reading and writing links	Writing process, writing strategies	Text Reading Level, Writing Prompt and Rubric	Text Reading Level, Writing Prompt and Rubric	Writing journal/draft or portfolio, anecdotal notes	Writing journals, portfolios, or logs, writing checklists
Comprehension Focus Group (CFG) • Genre/Text unit • Content strategy unit	Reading strategies, text structures, deep comprehension, vocabulary, reading and writing connections	Writing strategies, text structures, writing process, reading and writing connections	Text Reading Level (oral and silent reading), Comprehension Rubric, Writing Prompt and Scoring Rubric	Text Reading Level, Comprehension Rubric, Writing Prompt and Rubric	Running Records, Reading Response log with comprehension rubric, writing samples with rubrics for assessing writing development; anecdotal notes	Book units, response logs, writing checklists, strategy checklists, text maps, writing guides, writing resources

Matching Interventions to Students

The portfolio approach is grounded in the belief that children possess unique strengths and needs; therefore, an intervention should be carefully selected to match the particular student. The identification of students with reading difficulties is a complex process that requires a comprehensive literacy diagnosis (see Dorn & Henderson, 2010b). The diagnosis consists of a battery of literacy assessments, including classroom observations. Following the literacy diagnostic, the intervention team (e.g., classroom teachers, specialists, administrators) meets to discuss the student's progress and select the most appropriate intervention for the student.

Once the student is selected to receive an intervention, the team completes an Intervention Planner (see Figure 1.4). The Intervention Planner is a collaborative tool for aligning and layering services across classroom and supplemental programs. For example, if a student's diagnostic indicates a weakness in phonics, the student's classroom intervention (tier 1) might include a 10-minute word study lesson prior to the guided reading lesson for three days a week; and the supplemental intervention (tier 2 or 3) might be GRP with careful attention to the development of word knowledge in both reading and writing. The Intervention Planner serves as a chronological history for any intervention that a student receives (classroom, small group, or one-to-one) and outlines the plan for instruction, how the plan will be monitored, and the intensity and duration of the intervention (see Meyer & Reindl, 2010).

Closing Thoughts

In this chapter, we proposed that students with reading difficulties have developed inefficient systems for regulating their reading, and that intervention can prevent or reverse the reading problems. The goal of intervention is create a learning context that enables students to acquire metacognitive strategies for planning, monitoring, and self-correcting their reading. These strategies are grounded in higher-level psychological processes of consciousness, attention, and voluntary memory. An intervention should focus on the development of self-regulation and transfer, in contrast to the acquisition of simple items of knowledge.

The CIM is a theoretical framework for layering interventions across classroom and intervention settings, ensuring consistency for the most fragile learners. The portfolio of interventions is based on the theory that struggling readers have unique needs, and a range of interventions provide options for matching the intervention to the learner. The portfolio is based on four principles:

- Teachers select the most appropriate intervention to meet student needs.
- Intervention aligns with high-quality classroom instruction.
- Student progress is closely monitored across interventions and classroom instruction.
- Intervention teams collaborate on student learning and make data-based decisions for continued improvement.

FIGURE 1.4 RtI Plan for Aligning and Layering Literacy Interventions

Student Goal: Developing a Self-Regulated Learner

Student _____ Grade _____ Classroom Teacher _____ Date _____

DEGREES OF INTENSITY →

LAYERS OF SUPPORT/EXPERTISE →

Layer	Tier	Individual	Small Group	Whole Class	Independent Work
Classroom: Tier 1	**Universal**	**Individual** ☐ Reading Conference ☐ Writing Conference	**Small Group (4–5)** ☐ Guided Reading Group ☐ Literature Discussion Group ☐ Reading and Writing Conferences ☐ Language Investigations ☐ Genre, Text, and Author Studies ☐ Tailored Minilessons	**Whole Class** ☐ Read Aloud ☐ Shared Reading ☐ Minilessons ☐ Spelling/Phonics ☐ Share Time	**Independent Work** ☐ Familiar/Easy Reading ☐ Writing Process ☐ Phonics or Vocabulary Tasks ☐ Literature Extensions ☐ Research Projects ☐ Internet Projects
	Intervention	**1:1 or Small Group (2–3)** ☐ Reading Conference ☐ Writing Conference	**Small Group (4–5)** ☐ Word Study (prior to Guided Reading) ☐ Writing about Reading (following Guided Reading) ☐ Assisted Writing Group	Plan/Monitoring/Duration	
Intervention Specialist	**Tier 2**	**Small Group (2–3)** ☐ Guided Reading Plus Group ☐ Comprehension Focus Group ☐ Assisted Writing Group ☐ Writing Process Group (push-in)	**Small Group (4–5)** ☐ Guided Reading Plus Group ☐ Comprehension Focus Group ☐ Assisted Writing Group ☐ Writing Process Group (push-in)	Plan/Monitoring/Duration	
	Tier 3	**1:1** ☐ Reading Recovery ☐ Targeted Intervention (beyond first grade)	Plan/Monitoring/Duration		
Special Education	**Tier 4**	**1:1** ☐ Targeted Intervention	**Small Group (2–5)** ☐ Guided Reading Plus Group ☐ Comprehension Focus Group ☐ Assisted Writing Group ☐ Writing Process Group (push-in)	Plan/Monitoring/Duration	

Team Members Present _____ Next Meeting: _____

Adapted and used with permission from *The Journal of Reading Recovery*.

The heartbeat of the CIM is the responsive teacher who understands that if is a child is not responding to intervention, the problem is with the intervention, not the child. In the following chapters, we present details for implementing the CIM as a process for preventing the reading failure of kindergarten to third-grade students.

NOTES

1. Paris, Lipson, and Wixson (1994) claimed that less skilled readers have little knowledge of how text features, task goals, and strategies influence their reading. As a result, they engage in inefficient reading behaviors. In contrast, skilled readers understand how to use strategies for managing and controlling their cognitive activities in a reflective and purposeful way. Paris and colleagues relate these cognitive processes to metacognition, task persistence, motivation, and instructional goals. Harris and Pressley (1991) emphasized involving students in instructional planning, having students practice strategies in a wide array of materials and settings, monitoring long-term strategy use, and involving special education and regular education teachers in collaboration with each other.

2. James Zull (2002) provided an insightful look at the functions of the two integrative cortices in learning. He described how the back integrative cortex deals predominately with the past and the front integrative cortex is about the future. According to Zull, we store our facts and memories in the back integrative cortex; and the front integrative cortex is where we develop our ideas, make plans, organize our thoughts into bigger pictures, and generalize knowledge.

3. Vygotksy's theory of "positive differentiation" has particular relevance for RtI. According to Gindis (2003), Vygtosky's main premise was "that a child with a disability must be accommodated with experiences and opportunities that are as close as possible to the mainstreamed situation, but not at the expense of 'positive differentiation.' This should be based on a child's potential rather than on his or her current limitations" (p. 213).

4. Spear-Swerling and Sternberg (1996) cautioned that poor readers diagnosed as having LD or RD [reading disability] may actually be harmed rather than helped. In particular, the diagnosis of reading disability may exacerbate certain phenomena [e.g., lowered expectations, motivation, levels of practice] commonly experienced by youngsters who are poor readers" (p. 9).

5. Marie Clay (1987) was an early advocate of systematic observations and responsive teaching for preventing reading failure; she claimed that there is no evidence to suggest that children with learning disabilities should be taught any differently than children with reading difficulties. She maintained that many of the challenges faced by struggling readers could be traced back to the quality differences among teachers and the programs they deliver to their students.

A Comprehensive Assessment System

Within the Comprehensive Intervention Model (CIM) portfolio, assessment and instruction are viewed as reciprocal and recursive processes. The teacher uses assessment to design the best intervention for each student, while assessing the effectiveness of the intervention according to how well the student is responding. Response to Intervention (RtI) serves two purposes:

- To provide intervention for students who are at risk of school failure.

- To develop more valid procedures for identifying students with reading disabilities.

Students at risk of reading failure may exhibit haphazard behaviors when responding to problems; therefore, the assessment process should involve multiple perspectives and sources of data. In order to make valid decisions, teachers must be sensitive observers of literacy behaviors, specifically how students are responding to instruction and be able to adjust their teaching to accommodate their students' learning. Therefore, teachers must understand that:

- Learning occurs along a psychological continuum, from simple to complex processing.

- The student's capacity to learn is shaped by instructional opportunities with a knowledgeable and responsive teacher.

All interventions in the CIM are designed to take place in the student's zone of proximal development (Vygotsky, 1978). Vygotsky described how intellectual development occurs as children work in two complementary learning zones:

- *Zone of actual development (ZAD).* The child can accomplish a learning task independently.

- *Zone of proximal development (ZPD).* The child is able to accomplish a task but requires the assistance and guidance of a more knowledgeable person. The ZPD is the area of the child's potential development, but success depends on the teacher's ability to structure appropriate tasks and use language that lifts the child's understanding to a higher level.

According to Vygotsky, the child's cognitive, language, and social functioning in educational settings are not innate abilities or disabilities; rather, these processes are formed during instructional interactions with a more knowledgeable person. Vygotsky insisted that the assessment of the child's ability to learn through collaborative activity is a better predictor of future cognitive functioning than measures of independent performance through traditional assessments (Kozulin, 2003).

In this chapter, we discuss the role of assessments in the CIM. We describe how schools can create a comprehensive literacy diagnostic (CLD) as an RtI assessment and intervention process. We then take a close look at various assessments that are part of the CLD.

A Comprehensive Literacy Diagnostic

A comprehensive literacy diagnostic (CLD) is a portfolio of literacy assessments that serves three purposes as an RtI method: (1) to identify students who are at risk of reading failure; (2) to match students to the appropriate intervention; and (3) to monitor students' responsiveness to the intervention (Dorn & Henderson, 2010b). This comprehensive process greatly reduces the problem of misidentification: providing intervention to students who do not need it (false positives) or denying intervention to students who do need it (false negatives) (see Pedhazur & Schmelkin, 1991).

The CLD includes three types of assessments that are administered at designated periods: (1) pre- and postassessments to determine the student's actual level of development prior to and after the intervention; (2) dynamic ongoing assessments to determine the student's potential to learn from the intervention; and (3) progress-

TABLE 2.1   Assessments in a Comprehensive Literacy Diagnostic

Pre- and Postintervention	During the Intervention
Diagnostic assessments for identifying the student's strengths and needs on systematic measures	Ongoing dynamic assessments for measuring how the student is responding to intervention
Comprehensive portfolio of assessments that includes both formative and summative measures for triangulating the diagnostic process	Progress-monitoring assessments at designated intervals for monitoring the student's growth in comparison to average performing peers

monitoring assessments to measure the student's rate of learning on independent tasks administered at frequent intervals (see Table 2.1).

Pre- and Postintervention: Diagnostic Assessments

The assessment process begins with the classroom teacher who recommends a student for diagnostic assessment based on the student's difficulty in the classroom literacy program. The school's reading specialist administers the appropriate assessments to determine the student's strengths and needs. For example, a kindergarten student with at-risk behaviors in the classroom might be identified for further testing on several diagnostic measures such as the Observation Survey, Emergent Writing Assessment, Record of Oral Language, and a phonological assessment. Other examples of diagnostic assessments for struggling readers include: text reading assessment, comprehension measure, fluency measure, word test, and writing assessments.

The diagnostic assessments are administered at pre- and postintervention periods; therefore, alternative versions of each assessment must be available. Diagnostic assessment requires an in-depth analysis of a student's literacy behaviors in order to identify strengths and needs in specific areas. Prior to intervention, the teacher compiles the information into a diagnostic summary with specific recommendations for intervention. After the intervention, the posttest version is administered and results are documented, including specific recommendations for monitoring the student's progress over a designated period.

A Comprehensive Assessment Portfolio

Following diagnostic testing and prior to intervention, the RtI team collects other assessments to create a comprehensive portfolio of the student's learning. These supplemental assessments may include both formative and summative measures. *Formative assessments* provide evidence of the student's ability to learn from classroom instruction and include measures such as observation checklists, selected work samples, running records, and informal rubrics. *Summative assessments* provide evidence of the student's ability to accomplish particular tasks with proficiency and without assistance.

The RtI team examines the full range of assessments to determine if the student needs an intervention. If the student does need an intervention, the team discusses and selects the most appropriate intervention(s) for the student. The team uses an Intervention Planner to align interventions across classroom and supplemental layers (see Chapter 1, Figure 1.4 on page 15; also Meyer & Reindl, 2010). The Intervention Planner provides a record of the student's interventions (classroom, small group, or one-to-one) over time and outlines the plan for instruction, how the plan will be monitored, and the intensity and duration of the intervention.

During the Intervention: Dynamic Assessments

Dynamic assessment (DA) occurs during the intervention. DA is intertwined with teaching, thus the student's ability to respond to instruction is observed carefully during the process of learning. The goal is to discover whether and how much the learner will change under the influence of scaffolding activities (Lidz & Gindis, 2003). Essentially, DA is interactive, open ended, and generates information about the responsiveness of the learner to intervention. From an RtI perspective, dynamic assessment is especially relevant, because it embeds intervention within the assessment procedure.

Dynamic assessment occurs in the student's zone of proximal development; therefore, the teacher must understand how to scaffold the student's learning in order to accomplish new tasks. In DA, assessment and intervention are reciprocal and generative processes. The following example of a word study lesson during the Guided Reading Plus (GRP) intervention illustrates this process.

1. The teacher assesses a student's knowledge of spelling patterns.

2. The teacher designs a word study lesson that is based on what the student knows about words, as well as what the student needs to know.

3. The teacher creates conditions for the student to use existing knowledge, while scaffolding the student to accomplish the new task.

4. The teacher assesses the student's ability to learn from instruction.

Running records and writing samples are two DAs that provide authentic data for planning instruction on a day-by-day, student-by-student basis. During the GRP intervention, the teacher uses running records to analyze how a student is responding to the intervention as well as inform the teacher's decisions about book selections and teaching prompts. If a student is not progressing, the problem is with the instruction, not with the student.

Progress-Monitoring Assessments

Progress-monitoring (PM) assessments are administered at designated intervals to determine the student's responsiveness to the particular intervention. A well-designed PM assessment includes three features:

1. It occurs on new material.

2. It uses a standardized administration (e.g., book introduction, purpose for reading, or writing prompt).

3. It aligns with grade-level benchmarks.

Teachers can use text reading levels (TRL) as a valid measure for progress monitoring (see Dorn & Henderson, 2010b). The first step is to determine benchmarks for beginning, quarterly, and end-of-year text reading levels. The student's beginning text reading level is then plotted, and an "aim line" is drawn from the beginning-of-year benchmark to end-of-year, grade-level expectation for text reading level. This line marks the path a teacher will need to take in order to move a student from his current level of performance to grade-level norms. By drawing a line from a student's current benchmark to end-of-year expectations, the teacher can determine whether the student is progressing (accelerating) enough to reach grade-level norms by the end of the school year. As long as the student's performance is at or above the aim line the teacher can be reasonably assured that the intervention is instructionally appropriate.

The student's growth along the aim line is assessed through progress monitoring at frequent intervals (see Appendix B1 on pages 130–132 for reproducible forms). Figure 2.1 is an example of a student's responsiveness to intervention over a one-year period. At the beginning of second grade, the student scored significantly below the average reading level and was recommended for Guided Reading Plus intervention. The GRP intervention included six TRL assessment points for progress monitoring throughout the year. The aim line revealed a significant dip in reading acceleration at week 18; therefore, the RtI team met to discuss any adjustments to the student's intervention plan. Upon further examination of the student's writing journal, the team concluded that writing was a weak area for the student and recommended that the Writing Aloud (WA) intervention be alternated with the GRP intervention (i.e., one week for GRP followed by one week for WA). In this example, the teacher's decision to combine a more targeted writing intervention with the reading intervention increased the student's acceleration on text reading levels.

If the intervention fails to alter the trajectory of the student's progress, the intervention team reconvenes to engage in continued and collaborative problem solving. This problem-solving process includes:

■ Identifying additional information that may need to be collected

■ Determining how to best obtain that information

■ Interpreting and evaluating the new information against previous information

■ Adapting or designing instruction within the portfolio of interventions to ensure the student's literacy growth

FIGURE 2.1 Monitoring the Impact of Interventions on Reading Progression

Progress Monitoring Grade 2

Student: _____   Teacher: _____

Record Instructional Level

Book Level					
N					
M					
L					
K					
J					
I					
H					
G					
F					
E					
D					
C					
Book Title, Accuracy Rate, Self-Correction Rate	My New Pet, 98, 1:3	The Storm, 95, 1:3	Little Mouse, 96, 1...:2	Termites, 96, 1:3	Forecasting the Weather, 95, 1:4	Sea Lights, 98, 1:2
Date of Progress Monitoring Interval	9/1–3	10/18–22	12/13–12/17	2/14–18	4/18–21	End of Year
Week of Intervention	01	08	16	24	32	
Tier 1	CRI	CRI	CRI	CRI	CRI	
Tier 2	GRP	GRP	GRP WA	GRP WA		
Tier 3						
Tier 4						

Layering and Mixing Interventions		
GRP: Guided Reading Plus	IW: Interactive Writing	WP: Writing Process
CFG: Comprehension Focus Group	WA: Writing Aloud	CRI: Classroom Intervention

Note: The eight-week interval was established for data collection across multiple sites. The RtI team should set additional PM intervals (e.g., every two or four weeks) to meet student needs.

Assessments in the Comprehensive Intervention Model

There are a number of assessments in the CIM and details of each follow, including how a range of literacy assessments is aggregated into a CLD for each child. Some of the assessments may be used for multiple purposes; for example, the writing prompt/rubric might be included in the preintervention portfolio, but also used to monitor a student's progress during the intervention. Table 2.2 illustrates the assessment system for each intervention in the CIM.

TABLE 2.2 CIM Assessment and Intervention System

Intervention (Type, Level, and Setting)	Diagnostic Assessments (Pre- and Postintervention)	Comprehensive Literacy Diagnostic (Pre- and Postintervention)	Dynamic Assessment (Ongoing Informal Assessments)	Progress-Monitoring Assessments (Designated Intervals)
Guided Reading Plus (GRP) Emergent–Transitional Grades 1, 2, 3 (pull-out or push-in setting)	Text Reading Level, Comprehension Checklist, Fluency Measure, Word Test, Phonological Assessment	Summary of diagnostic assessments, classroom observation checklist, selected work samples from classroom, test results from district assessment, classroom rubrics/checklists	Running records, known words in personal dictionary, writing journal or response log, anecdotal notes from reading and writing observations	Text Reading Level (running record), Reading Behavior Checklist, Fluency Scale, Comprehension Checklist, Writing About Reading Prompt and Rubric
Writing Process Intervention Early–Transitional Grades 1, 2, 3 (push-in setting only)	Text Reading Level, Writing Prompt with Rubric	Summary of diagnostic assessments, classroom observation checklist, writing samples and scoring guides, test results from district assessment	Writing samples from classroom portfolio	Text Reading Level (running record), Reading Behavior Checklist, Fluency Scale, Comprehension Checklist, Writing Prompt and Rubric
Assisted Writing—Interactive Writing Emergent–Beginning Early (pull-out or push-in setting)	Text Reading Level, Word Test, Writing Prompt with Rubric, Phonological Assessment	Summary of diagnostic assessments, classroom observation checklist, selected work samples from classroom, classroom rubrics/checklists, test results from district assessment	Writing journal, known words in personal dictionary, anecdotal notes from writing observations	Text Reading Level (running record), Reading Behavior Checklist, Writing Prompt and Rubric
Assisted Writing (Writing Aloud Group) Late Early–Transitional (pull-out or push-in setting)	Text Reading Level, Word Test, Writing Prompt with Rubric, Phonological Assessment		Writing log or writing samples in a portfolio, known words in personal dictionary, anecdotal notes from writing observations	Text Reading Level (running record), Reading Behavior Checklist, Fluency Scale; Comprehension Checklist, Writing Prompt and Rubric

Observation Survey of Early Literacy Achievement

The Observation Survey of Early Literacy Achievement was developed by Marie Clay (2002; 2006) to "capture some of the rapid change that occurs in early literacy awareness" (p. 1). The survey includes six subtests: Letter Identification, Word Test, Concepts About Print, Hearing and Recording Sounds in Words, and Writing Vocabulary Test. The measures should not be used in isolation. Instead, teachers should examine the child's progress across all measures and identify his or her strengths and areas of needs. The teacher writes a diagnostic summary that includes recommendations for intervention.

Emergent Writing Assessment

The emergent writing sample is designed to assess a child's ability to draw a picture, compose an oral message based on the picture, and use written symbols to represent the message (see an example in Figure 2.2). The assessment should be administered in a standardized format, according to the following procedures:

1. The teacher prompts the child to draw a picture. Some sample prompts may ask the student to draw a picture of himself or someone in his family, a picture of a favorite animal, a friend, or a picture of a favorite food. Let the child know that there will be a time limit and encourage him to work quickly. If a child says he cannot draw, encourage him by saying something like, "just do your best." Tell the child that you also want him to tell the story of the picture by writing it.

2. After the child completes the drawing, ask the child to write about his picture. Tell the child that you will not help him and that whatever he does will be just fine. If necessary, provide a separate sheet of paper for writing. If the child claims he cannot write, tell him to pretend to write. Try not to distract the child from writing by talking to him; however, if a child appears to need encouragement or further prompting, you should provide this extra support. Do not make comments about the child's writing (not even, "You're doing a good job"). If you do not understand something that you observe, ask the child a quick question about it.

3. When the child finishes, ask him to read the piece to you. Record what the child reads or pretends to read.

4. Respond to the content of the writing in a specific and positive way, for example, "It sounds like you and Betsy had a wonderful time playing together."

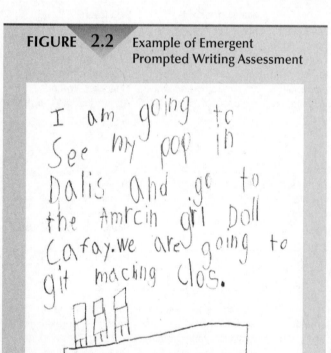

FIGURE 2.2   Example of Emergent Prompted Writing Assessment

5. Use Clay's (1975) Writing Sample Assessment Rubric to score the writing.

6. During the next two days, collect two additional pieces of writing from the child using this same method. Use the three assessments to diagnose the child's strengths and needs in writing.

Record of Oral Language

The Record of Oral Language (ROL; Clay, 2007) is used to assess a student's knowledge and control over oral language structures. The ROL provides teachers with a tool for observing and recording a child's level of language performance, measuring progress over time, and isolating areas of difficulty. The ROL, as part of a literacy diagnostic, can be used to identify students for an emergent language and literacy intervention with an emphasis on oracy instruction.

Oral Language Acquisition Inventory

The Oral Language Acquisition Inventory (OLAI; Gentile, 2003) is an assessment and intervention method for children with low language proficiency. The OLAI serves two purposes in an RtI method: (1) it provides teachers with information about the most common language structures children use expressively, and (2) it provides intervention techniques for English language learners (ELLs) and children who could benefit from language instruction. The OLAI contains four assessments: (1) repeated sentences and sentence transformations; (2) story reconstruction and narrative comprehension; (3) picture drawing, narration, and dictation; and (4) information processing and critical dialogue.

Timed Word Writing Prompt

A quick assessment for determining a student's word knowledge is a 10-minute timed word writing measure. The assessment is structured to provide insights into the student's knowledge about print: (1) types of words the student writes, such as words from the environment (e.g., McDonald's), interesting words (e.g., dinosaur), or important words (e.g., names of friends or family); (2) words the student is able to write correctly (e.g., high-frequency words); and (3) words the student attempts to write, including strategies used to spell the words.

As the student writes, the teacher records evidence of risk-taking behaviors, writing fluency, letter formation, and pattern knowledge. The assessment begins with general writing prompts: "Can you write your name?" "Can you write anyone else's name?" "Do you know any other words?" This interval is followed by more specific prompts for assessing a student's knowledge of commonly occurring words (e.g., *I, am, is, can, me, go, my, he, come, it*) from easy texts. (See Figure 2.3 on the following page for an example.)

Phonological Awareness Assessment

Phonological awareness refers to a child's understanding of the sounds of speech as distinct from their meanings. This understanding follows a developmental continuum

FIGURE 2.3 Example of Timed Word Writing Assessment

Kensley   Cats   Up
Klayton   Go   you
Katy   Going   me
Cabe   to   my
Kennedy   a   no
Ellie   at   See
Jet   and   She
the   Can   So
Thursday   am   to
That   do   We
This   he   What
Cat   like   where
hat   in   green
Bat   it   red
             I   Black
                        yellow

that moves from less complex to more complex. Instruction along the continuum begins with rhyming activities, then progresses to blending and segmenting of words into onset and rime, ultimately advancing to blending, segmenting, and deleting phonemes.

A student must also have an awareness of phonemes in order to grasp the alphabetic principle that underlies the system of written language. If children understand that words can be divided into individual phonemes and that phonemes can be blended into words, they are able to use letter-sound knowledge to read and build words. Researchers have shown that this strong relationship between phonological awareness and reading success persists throughout school (Adams, 1990).

Assessment in phonological awareness serves two purposes: (1) to initially identify students who appear to be at risk for difficulty in acquiring beginning reading skills, and (2) to monitor the progress of students who are receiving an intervention. Typically, kindergarten students are screened for risk factors in acquiring beginning reading skills in the second semester of kindergarten. Schools should select a good phonological measure as a component of the CLD.

Writing Prompt with Rubric

Many schools and states have included writing assessments as a routine measure of literacy achievement. The assessments are administered to all students in the classroom and include: (1) a writing prompt, (2) standard procedures, and (3) a timed period. If this classroom measure is available, it is included in the literacy diagnostic. For schools that do not have a preestablished writing assessment, we recommend they locate a good writing assessment for first- to third-grade students.

Running Record on Keystone Text

The ultimate goal of intervention is to ensure that the struggling reader develops efficient problem-solving strategies while reading for meaning. This process can only occur during the reading of connected texts. Therefore, all interventions in the CIM include an assessment of text reading for progress monitoring. The running record is analyzed for evidence of the student's processing behaviors.

A *keystone book* is a text that has been leveled (generally by a publisher), and it represents an exemplar level that most students can read successfully. It is important for teachers to have a collection of high-quality, leveled texts that can be used for progress monitoring. We encourage teachers to pull an unseen text from their classroom collections, rather than rely on published kits.

Keystone books are a collection of books that was compiled by teacher leaders and literacy coaches for purposes of progress monitoring. On the back of each book is a label that includes the guided reading level, word count, error count (to determine instructional level), genre, item number, publisher, and a short book introduction (see Figure 2.4 for an example).

There are three important reasons why the keystone books can be useful for progress monitoring. They

1. represent a wide variety of text types, genres, formats, and writing styles;

2. are not aligned with any particular publisher; and

3. can be used interchangeably for guided reading group and for progress monitoring.

Text Reading Level Assessment

A text reading level (TRL) assessment is administered to determine an instructional reading level for placement in an intervention. Teachers can select from several published assessments, which include leveled texts,

FIGURE 2.4 Samples of Keystone Books with Book Introduction and Assessment Procedure

Title: I Meowed by Janice Boland
Publisher: Richard C. Owen Publishers, Inc.

Level GRL: D DRA: 6 Word Count: 58 Errors 7
Genre: Realistic Fiction

Introduction: This cat wanted in the house so she meowed at different places around the house until the door opened. What did she want?

Oral Reading: Take a running record on entire text. Use comprehension checklist and reading behavior checklist.

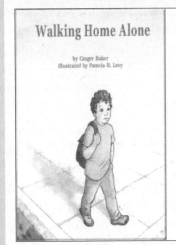

Title: Walking Home Alone by Ginger Baker.

Publisher: Richard C. Owen Publishers, Inc.
Level GRL: J DRA 18 Word Count: 327 Errors 16
Genre: Realistic Fiction

Introduction: When Roberto's brother couldn't go to school, Roberto had to walk home alone for the first time. He wasn't sure if he could do that. What happens when he meets Brent?

Oral and Silent Reading:
Oral Reading: Take a running record on pp. 2-6. Do a comprehension check to ensure understanding.

Silent Reading: Ask the student to finish reading silently to find out what happens next. Do a comprehension check to ensure understanding.

Source: Used with permission from Richard C. Owen Publishers, Inc.

standardized procedures for administration, and scoring rubrics for interpreting results. During text reading, the teacher records how the student applies strategies to solve problems within texts at three levels of difficulty: easy, instructional, and hard. The assessment also includes measures for assessing reading comprehension and fluency.

There are several reasons why teachers should include reading levels in an RtI assessment method (Dunn, 2007). First, the reading level of a child in first grade is a predictor of future reading success. Second, a student's reading level can be charted over time and compared with grade-level peers (based on benchmark levels). Third, text reading levels have preestablished cut scores, which can be used for measuring individual reading growth from entry to exit, and also for comparing the individual scores with school and district scores. A well-designed text reading measure can be a valuable tool for studying how an intervention is closing the literacy gap between low- and high-performing readers.

Instructional Reading Levels

In an RtI process, the student's instructional reading level is especially important to determine because: (1) it indicates the point at which a student is most receptive to instruction, and (2) it focuses on the student's potential level of development (i.e., what the student can do with teacher assistance). The teacher determines the student's instructional level by triangulating four sources of reading data: percentage of words read correctly (accuracy rate), strategies used at points of difficulty (monitoring, searching, self-correcting behaviors), comprehension (purposeful reading), and fluency (rate and prosody). Accuracy rates for instructional texts are adjusted as students read materials that increase in complexity (an accuracy rate of 90% to 94% would be appropriate for beginning readers, and 95% to 98% would be expected for text level 28 and above).

Teachers can use a standard protocol for measuring a student's instructional reading level, including procedures for assessing a student's ability to read for a particular purpose. This comprehension assessment is in contrast to methods that require students to answer a long list of comprehension questions. The reading protocol follows a set of standardized procedures:

1. The teacher reads a scripted introduction that includes a purpose for comprehending a particular passage (e.g., to discover a relationship between multiple events or to locate content-specific information). The passage length is approximately 100 words.

2. The teacher takes a running record of the student's oral reading behaviors, including evidence of how the student initiates problem-solving strategies on unknown words.

3. After the reading, the teacher assesses the student's ability to read for a specific purpose, while prompting the student to provide evidence from the text to support his or her thinking.

For students at higher reading levels (generally transitional and above), the teacher adds a silent reading measure. The goal is to determine if a discrepancy exists between the student's oral and silent reading comprehension. As an RtI method, this is important data, because it could indicate that an instructional gap has occurred from lack of opportunities to develop silent reading competencies. Following the oral reading assessment, the teacher provides a scripted introduction to a new passage, gives the student a specific purpose for reading this section, and instructs the student to read silently approximately 100 words. After the silent reading, the teacher assesses the student's ability to read for a particular purpose, while prompting the student to locate evidence from the text to support the comprehension goal.

Reading Behavior Checklist

The reading behavior checklist identifies critical reading behaviors that indicate print-solving strategies at the emergent, early, transitional, and fluent levels. At the emergent level, the reading behaviors include: uses meaning and language to read simple texts, points to words with one-to-one matching on one and two lines of print, notices (self-monitors) unknown words in text, uses knowledge of some letter-sound relationships to initiate an action at point of difficulty, articulates first letter in unknown words, notices unknown words and searches for cues in picture and print, and rereads to cross-check first letter with meaning and structure cues. As students progress to higher levels, the reading behavior checklist focuses on more sophisticated problem-solving strategies, such as solving multisyllabic words by noticing parts within words and using word meaning (e.g., prefixes, suffixes, roots, compound words) to solve unknown words.

Table 2.3 (page 30) presents a reading continuum from emergent to fluent levels, and in Figure 2.5, you can see how a reading checklist and running record are used to analyze student progress at the late early level (see Appendixes B1–B5 on pages 130–147 for reproducible forms of emergent to fluent reading checklists). As the student reads a new text, the teacher takes a running record of the student's independent reading behaviors. After the reading, the teacher selects one or two teaching points and prompts the student to solve the reading problems. The reading checklist is used to document the student's processing at two levels: (1) what the student can

FIGURE 2.5 Running Record and Reading Behaviors Checklist for Late Early Reader (Caleb)

TABLE **2.3**   Emergent to Fluent Reading Processing Behaviors

Emergent Guided Reading Levels: A–C	Beginning Early Guided Reading Levels: D–E	Late Early Guided Reading Levels: F–G	Transitional Guided Reading Levels: H–M	Fluent Guided Reading Levels: (N–T)
■ Uses meaning and language to read simple text ■ Points to words in a one-to-one match throughout two to three lines of text ■ Notices (self-monitors) unknown words; searches for cues in picture and print ■ Rereads to cross-check first letter with meaning and structure cues ■ Uses knowledge of letter-sound relationships to initiate an action at point of difficulty; articulates first letter and attends to some endings ■ Reads known high-frequency words with fluency ■ Self-corrects using known high-frequency words and other print cues	■ Reads without using finger to track print ■ Notices errors (self-monitors); cross-checks multiple sources of information to make self-correction (checks to be sure the reading makes sense, sounds right and looks right) ■ Uses knowledge of letter-sound relationships to initiate an action at point of difficulty ■ Searches through unknown words in a left-to-right sequence; blends letters into sounds; repeats words to confirm ■ Takes apart simple unknown words using simple word parts/patterns ■ Reads high-frequency words with fluency ■ Uses simple punctuation to regulate phrasing and fluency (prosody)	■ Notices errors (self-monitors); initiates multiple attempts to self-correct; *integrates* multiple sources of information (checks to be sure the reading makes sense, sounds right and looks right) ■ Self-monitors with greater ease; uses known words, word parts/patterns and inflectional endings to check on reading and self-correct ■ Takes unknown words apart at the larger unit of analysis including onset and rime or at meaningful and logical units ■ Reads high-frequency words with fluency ■ Uses simple punctuation to regulate phrasing and fluency (prosody)	■ *Orchestrates* multiple sources of information (meaning, structure, and visual cues); reads texts with greater accuracy and more efficient self-correction ■ Takes apart multisyllabic words; uses knowledge of word parts/patterns to solve words quickly ■ Uses word meanings to solve problems (prefixes, suffixes, compound parts) ■ Expands reading vocabulary; shows interest in unknown words ■ Reads complex high-frequency words with fluency and ease ■ Uses more complex punctuation to regulate phrasing and fluency (prosody)	■ *Orchestrates* multiple sources of information (meaning, structure, and visual cues); reads texts with greater accuracy and more efficient self-correction ■ Reads longer text with specialized content and unusual words; learns new words daily ■ Applies knowledge about word meanings across different texts; makes predictions about word meanings and checks within texts; refines word knowledge ■ Takes apart multisyllabic words on the run and with flexibility; uses knowledge of complex word parts/patterns to solve words quickly; makes excellent attempts at solving multisyllabic words ■ Reads complex high-frequency words with fluency and ease ■ Uses complex punctuation to regulate phrasing and fluency (prosody)

do *without* assistance (actual level), and (2) what the student can do *with* assistance (potential level). It is important for teachers to identify the student's potential level of development, as this is the zone where responsive teaching is aimed. The reading behavior checklist and the comprehension guide (discussed next) are analyzed together to determine how the student is responding to the intervention.

Comprehension Guides

Comprehension guides can be valid measures for assessing a student's literal comprehension after reading a new text (see Appendix B3 on pages 138–139). The student's deeper level of comprehension is assessed through discussion groups and reading response logs (see Dorn & Soffos, 2005c). The comprehension guide (Figure 2.6) is triangulated with the fluency scale (discussed later) and the running record and reading behavior checklist (Figure 2.5) to assess the student's reading competency on an instructional level text.

Following the reading of a fiction text, the teacher prompts the student to discuss the purpose for reading. If the student needs further assistance, the teacher increases the level of support by asking specific prompts on the comprehension guide. The measure includes an assessment of the student's comprehension behaviors:

- Understands the purpose for reading
- Identifies and describes main character
- Discusses plot
- Asks questions (e.g., word meanings, character's actions, and/or events)

The teacher uses a comprehension guide for expository text to measure a student's ability to recall important details from the text. Following the reading, the teacher prompts the student to discuss the purpose for reading. If a student experiences difficulty, the teacher asks specific prompts to probe for understanding. This measure is used to assess the student's literal understanding of an expository text:

- States the main idea from text
- Includes key points from text to support main idea
- Uses some content-specific vocabulary from text
- Uses text features/aids to support understanding
- Identifies new learning; compares previous understandings to new learning
- Asks questions (e.g., content, vocabulary, etc.)

FIGURE 2.6 Comprehension Guide for Fiction Text for Late Early Reader (Caleb)

Comprehension Guide for Fiction Text
(Assessing *Literal Level* Comprehension on an Instruction Level Text)

Student: Caleb   Date: 3-10-09   Text Level: _____

Directions: After the teacher locates the student's **instructional level**, then the teacher checks on comprehension by prompting the student to discuss the set purpose for reading. The teacher can use some sample prompts below to stimulate the student's thinking as needed.

Comprehension Behaviors	Unprompted	Prompted	Sample Prompts to Probe for Further Understanding	Student's Response
Understands the purpose for reading	✓		What happened when...? What happened to... when...?	
Identifies main character	✓		Who was the main character in the story?	
Describes main character		✓	Can you think of some words to describe....?	excited, nice, kind, scared
Describes how... changed over time			Describe how...changed over time. What was he/she like at the beginning, middle and end of the story?	
Discusses the plot		✓	What event/s caused the character/s to think and act a certain way? Did the event/s have an effect on the setting?	The wolf tricked her and caused her to get eaten up!
Asks questions e.g., word meanings, characters actions or an event		✓	Was there any vocabulary that the author used that you didn't understand? Do you have any questions about a specific character/s in the story? Do you have any questions about what happened in the story?	Woodcutter (discussed meaning)

The results recorded on the comprehension guide, running record, and reading behavior checklist are analyzed for evidence of the student's reading strategies for problem solving and comprehending an instructional level text. The student's progress is constantly monitored and instruction is adjusted as needed.

Oral Reading Fluency Scale

The fluency scale from the National Assessment of Educational Progress (NAEP) is a useful measure for assessing change over time in fluent reading (see Pinnell et al., 1995). The NAEP scale measures fluency at three language levels: (1) grouping or phrasing of words as revealed through intonation, stressing, and pausing; (2) using author's syntax for representing the message; and (3) expressiveness.[1] A student's fluency is measured on a four-level scale.

Level 1: Reads primarily word-by-word. Occasional two-word or three-word phrases may occur, but these are infrequent and/or they do not preserve meaningful syntax.

Level 2: Reads primarily in two-word phrases with some three- or four-word phrases with some three- or four-word groupings. Some word-by-word reading may be present. Word groupings may seem awkward and unrelated to larger context of sentence or passage.

Level 3: Reads primarily in three- or four-word phrases. Some smaller groupings may be present. Some larger groupings may be present. The majority of the phrasing seems appropriate and preserves the syntax of the author. Little or no expressive interpretation is present.

Level 4: Reads primarily in large, meaningful phrase groups. Although some regressions, repetitions, and deviations from text may be present, they do not detract from the overall structure of the story. Preservation of the story is read with expressive interpretation.

Writing about Reading Checklist

This written measure is used to provide evidence of a student's understanding of a text through a special prompt. This assessment, which aligns with the Phase II component of the Guided Reading Plus intervention (see Chapter 4), includes rubrics at the emergent, early, and transitional reading levels (see Figure 2.7 and Appendix B4 on pages 140–143). Each rubric is designed to measure how well the student is integrating multiples sources of information through writing about reading. The charts are based on a continuum of literacy behaviors in five areas:

■ Writing behaviors that document the student's knowledge of spelling strategies for problem solving on unknown words and the ability to transcribe known words with accuracy and fluency

■ Composing strategies that indicate the student's knowledge of rehearsal techniques for holding ideas in memory, use of a practice page for planning and organizing the message, and rereading strategies for monitoring the production of a meaningful message

---

FIGURE 2.7 Writing Samples and Writing about Reading Checklists at Emergent, Late Early, and Transitional Levels

EMERGENT WRITER

Student: Anastashia

Writing in Response to Reading for Emergent Intervention
(Levels 1-3/A-C)
Check all behaviors observed without support.

Behavior								
Writes letters fluently and with correct formation.	X	X	X	X				
Writes easy high-frequency words fluently. (is, me, the, at)				X				
Says words slowly; hears and records beginning and ending consonants; at times, vowels may appear although they may not be correct.			X	X				
Uses simple VC phonogram patterns to help spell words. (c-up, c-at)								
Uses resources to help with writing letters and spelling words. (ABC Chart)	X	X	X	X				
Uses a practice page to think strategically about writing letters and spelling unknown words.				X				
Demonstrates movement from semi-phonetic to phonetic stage of spelling.								
Rehearses response; holds language in memory while transcribing message.	X	X	X					
Uses the rereading strategy (returns to beginning of sentence) to remember the next word and to monitor meaning and language.	X	X	X	X				
Demonstrates understanding of text and prompt.	X	X	X	X				
Incorporates some vocabulary that reflects attention to reading.	X	X	X	X				
Uses written language structures that reflect a shift from informal oral language structures to more conventional written language structures. • composes simple sentences (noun + verb)	X	X	X	X				
• uses prepositional phrases (on the floor, in the bag)	–	–	X	X				
• uses conjunctions (and)	–	–	–	–				
Controls left to right and top to bottom representation; leaves spaces between words.			X	X				
Demonstrates some awareness of ending punctuation (periods) but over-generalizes. i.e., uses a period as a marker to separate words or designate the end of each line or page.	X	X	X	X				
Progress Monitoring Date	1/19	2/13	2/16	3/1				
Total Number of Observed Behaviors	8	9	11	13				

LATE EARLY WRITER

Student: Cindy

Writing in Response to Reading for Late Early Intervention
(Levels 9-12/F-G)
Check all behaviors observed without support.

Behavior								
Writes more complex high-frequency words fluently. (there, where, when)	–	–	–					
Uses a practice page to think strategically about spelling unknown words.	X	X	X					
Says words slowly; hears and records beginning, ending, and middle consonants including blends, clusters, and digraphs; spells most words using visual analysis (bike, stripe).	X	X	X					
Uses familiar words and word parts to spell unknown words; spells word endings (s, ing, ed, es) correctly; uses complex rime patterns (phonogram patterns) to spell unknown words (down-crown).	–	X	X					
Demonstrates movement from phonetic to transitional stage of spelling development.	–	X	X					
Uses the rereading strategy (phrases, words, word) as needed to help with writing a meaningful response.	X	X	X					
Response is longer and more complex; reflects fluency of thinking, fluency of encoding, and an increase in language control.	X	X	–					
Response reflects understanding of the text and prompt.	X	X	X					
Incorporates a writing vocabulary that reflects attention to reading; uses vocabulary appropriate for topic.	X	X	X					
Demonstrates use of language structures that reflects increasing complexity in conventional language patterns, i.e., • composes simple sentences (noun + verb) • uses prepositional phrases (on the floor, in the bag) • uses conjunctions (and, but) • uses modifiers (red dress)	–	X	–					
Rereads writing and thinks about punctuation and capitalization, i.e., • uses ending punctuation appropriately (periods, exclamation marks, question marks) • capitalizes sentence beginnings and proper names	X	X	–					
Progress Monitoring Date	4/19	4/29	5/12					
Total Number of Observed Behaviors	7	10	7					

Writing Sample, February 19

DKS. DKVV!
Ducks can swim. Ducks can't waddle!

Writing Sample, March 1

my fesh LSX
My fish is playing with me!

Writing Sample, April 29

Is your pail Full? littar Ber trid to feed the berds bt thet Floow away.

Little bear tried to feed the birds but they flew away.

Writing Sample, May 12

the Huhg ry Giant wo Fhe giant wos meah he tod the pepol to get hem food.

The giant was mean he told the people to get him food.

FIGURE 2.7 Writing Samples and Writing about Reading Checklists at Emergent, Late Early, and Transitional Levels (continued)

TRANSITIONAL WRITER

Student: John

Writing in Response to Reading for Transitional Intervention (Level H-M)
Check all behaviors observed without support.

Writing Behavior (Spelling strategies and writing fluency)	Writes more complex high-frequency words fluently. (**because, once, knew**)	—	—	—	—	X	X	
	Uses complex rime patterns (phonogram patterns) to spell unknown words (**down-crown**).	—	—	—	—	—	X	
	Breaks multi-syllabic words into parts and records new words in parts.	—	—	—	X	X	X	
	Uses **transitional** and/or **conventional** spelling for most words.	—	—	—	—	X	X	
Composing	Plans response (**notes, outline, chart, web**) on the planning page to organize thinking.	—	—	—	—	X	X	
	Uses the rereading strategy (**phrases, words, word**) as needed to help with writing a meaningful response.	X	X	X	X	X	X	
Comprehension	Response reflects understanding of the text and prompt.	X	X	X	—	X	X	
	Incorporates a writing vocabulary that reflects attention to reading; uses vocabulary appropriate for topic.	—	X	X	X	X	X	
Language Structure	Demonstrates use of language structures that reflects increasing complexity in conventional language patterns. • Uses modifiers (**red dress**) • Uses two phrases linked by a relative pronoun (who, that, what, which) • Uses two phrases linked by an adverb (when, where, how, however, whenever, wherever)	X	—	—	X	X	X	
Conventions	Rereads writing and thinks about punctuation. • Uses ending punctuation appropriately (**periods, exclamation marks, question marks**) • Uses additional forms of punctuation appropriately (**quotation marks, apostrophes in contractions or possessives, commas to identify a series, ellipses to show pause**) • Capitalizes sentence beginnings and proper names.	—	—	—	X	—	—	
	Progress Monitoring Date	10/1	10/23	11/24	12/14	3/1	5/18	
	Total Number of Observed Behaviors	4	4	4	6	8	9	

Writing Sample, May 18

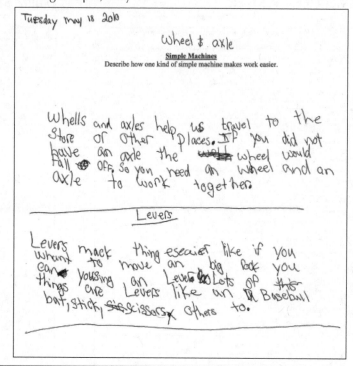

- Comprehension strategies that indicate the student's ability to read for specific information, including utilizing the vocabulary and ideas from the text while responding in writing to an oral prompt

- Language behaviors that document the student's increasing control of written language as shown by the use of more complex sentence structures and language patterns

- Knowledge of print conventions, including punctuation, capitalization, and grammar functions

Writing Behavior Checklist

The Writing Behavior Checklist identifies critical writing behaviors that indicate encoding strategies and writing fluency at the emergent and early levels. At the emergent level, the writing behaviors include: writes known words with correct formation, uses spaces between words, recognizes the link between sounds and letters, uses ABC chart as a resource, and writes a few high-frequency words. As students progress to the transitional level, the writing behaviors focus on understanding how to write narrative and expository texts (see Appendix B5 on pages 144–147 for checklists for kindergarten through third grade).

District Assessments

This assessment includes the district or state assessment, for example, the Stanford Achievement Test or the State Benchmark Examination. The student's performance on these measures is aggregated with other assessments in the literacy diagnostic.

Selected Work Samples

A student's performance on authentic curriculum-based tasks is measured through selected work samples. The teacher selects three or four work samples to include in the literacy diagnostic. These samples are assessed with classroom writing rubrics and scoring guides.

Classroom Rubrics, Checklists, and Writing Scoring Guides

These assessments are curriculum-based measures that directly reflect how well students are performing on specific literacy tasks. These assessments can be teacher-made or published rubrics.

Writing Portfolio District Checklist

Most districts have expectations for types of writing that students should control in kindergarten to third grades. These expectations generally align with state writing standards. The writing portfolio checklist is a record that documents student's writing in the expected genre and modes.

Anecdotal Notes

An assessment system would not be complete without a teacher's anecdotal notes, including observation notes of children's literacy behaviors during guided reading, independent reading, writing conferences, word study activities, and other authentic events.

 **Record-Keeping Forms**

Record-keeping forms provide an accounting of a student's progress over time. One helpful form is the Recording Sheet for Guided Reading Plus Word Study intervention at the early level (see Appendix B6 on page 148). This form provides teachers with a record of words and patterns that have been taught during the word study component. The first column includes high-frequency words that are processed fluently and have been added to the student's word dictionary, and the second column includes rime patterns that have been taught and have been recorded on spelling charts. This record of word learning is a useful tool for planning effective word study that is based on students' strengths and needs (see Figure 2.8 on the following page).

FIGURE 2.8 Recording Sheet for Guided Reading Plus Word Study

Group Members:

High-Frequency Words			Rime Patterns		
✓ Can read and write fluently			✓ Taught and have been recorded on students' independent chart		
a*	at*		an	at	
am*	an*		am	ap	
and *	all		and	ash	
are	ask		ack	ank	
asked	after		all	ake	
away	be		ale	ame	
big	but		ain	ate	
by	back		ar	ay	
can*	car		aw		
come	did				
do*	day		et	ed	
for	from		est	ell	
go*	going		eat		
get	gets				
he*	had		in	ip	
has	have		ill	ick	
him	his		ink	ing	
here	her		ine	ice	
how	I*		ide	ight	
I'm	if		ir		
in*	into				
is*	it*		op	ock	
just	like*		oke	or	
look	little		ore		
me*	man				
my*	make		ug	uck	
mom	no*		ump	unk	
not*	now				
on	or				
of	one				
out	our				
over	put				
play	so*				
see*	she*				
saw	said				
to*	too				
the*	them				
than	that				
then	this				
their	there				
up*	us				
very	we*				
will	with				
went	was				
were	when				
what	where				
who	you				
your	zoo				

* Words that students should know at the end of kindergarten.

Closing Thoughts

Assessments should never be viewed in isolation, because this could lead to a narrow or deficit interpretation. Instead, multiple assessments should be analyzed for evidence of the student's knowledge, thinking, and problem solving, including observations of student's learning during routine classroom instruction, as well as consultation with educators who have worked with the student (see IRA and NCTE Assessment Standards, 2009).

The Comprehensive Intervention Model is a diagnostic model that uses assessment and intervention as reciprocal and generative processes. Therefore, assessment must include a balance of measures that reflect the student's learning at two developmental levels. The actual level of development is determined through summative assessments that indicate the student's independent level of performance. This level is identified through pre- and postassessments and progress-monitoring materials that are administrated in formalized contexts. The teacher must know the student's independent level as well as the student's proximal (or potential) level of development in order to determine the best intervention. As an RtI method, intervention can only be effective if it promotes acceleration; and acceleration occurs when the student is able to access new information through instruction.

The Comprehensive Literacy Diagnostic represents a balanced and multifaceted method that ensures a more accurate identification of students who are at risk of reading failure. During the intervention, the teacher uses dynamic assessment to monitor the student's responsiveness to instruction. This interactive process provides the teacher with ongoing data for planning and evaluating how well the intervention is meeting the needs of the particular student. At designated intervals during the intervention, the teacher monitors the student's reading development on unseen texts and compares his actual growth with where he needs to be in order to catch up with average-performing peers.

In Chapter 3, we describe how differentiated instruction in the classroom is the first line of defense in preventing reading failure. In subsequent chapters, we present three interventions in the K–3 CIM: Writing Process Group, Assisted Writing Intervention, and Guided Reading Plus.

NOTE

1. Fluency is much more than fast reading; it is an indication of the reader's ability to transfer knowledge of spoken language to written language in order to construct meaning. This language process is defined as *prosody*, which can be observed in the reader's voice as he or she strives to understand the text. Prosodic behaviors include pitch variations, stress or emphasis, intonation, meaningful phrasing and syntax, and pausing at appropriate places: a compilation of spoken language features that result in expressive reading. The teacher's ability to assess students' oral reading fluency is essential for developing their prosodic or expressive reading skills. Many researchers have examined the importance of prosody in reading comprehension, for example, Allington (1983), Kuhn, Schwanenflugel, and Meisinger (2010), Kuhn and Stahl (2003), and Farstrup and Samuels (2006).

Chapter 3

Differentiated Classroom Instruction

The classroom literacy program is the first line of defense against illiteracy. In Chapter 1, we claimed that if more than 15 to 20 percent of students in a school are struggling in literacy, the classroom program might be the problem. Interventions are designed to supplement (not replace) high-quality classroom instruction; therefore, any discussion about interventions must begin with a discussion about the classroom curriculum. Is the curriculum differentiated to meet the needs of all students? Does it include evidence-based practices? How much time is devoted to reading and writing? How is assessment used to monitor student learning? Do interventions align with the curriculum?

Creating a literate environment conducive to reading is a necessary step in developing motivated learners who read for pleasure and purpose. The environment should be designed to guarantee every child's success in reading. To achieve this goal, teachers need to differentiate their instruction in order to meet the diverse needs of all students. The reading curriculum should include a blend of whole-group, small-group, and individual instruction, as well as opportunities for students to read independently. Differentiated teaching also applies to the degree of assistance provided to the learner for accomplishing a particular task. A workshop approach allows for differentiation, because it provides a supportive context that enables teachers to meet the literacy needs of all students (Dorn & Soffos, 2005b). Therefore, if a student is not responding to high-quality differentiated classroom instruction, the student should be assessed for intervention.

The Comprehensive Intervention Model (CIM) provides a portfolio of small-group interventions to meet the needs of individual learners. The portfolio is built on four principles:

1. Teachers select the most appropriate intervention to meet student needs.

2. The intervention aligns with high-quality classroom instruction.

3. Student progress is closely monitored across interventions and classroom instruction.

4. Intervention teams collaborate on student learning and make data-based decisions for continued improvement.

Within this theory, classroom instruction and interventions are viewed as reciprocal and recursive processes. A collaboration among teachers will ensure that students have opportunities to transfer their knowledge across multiple settings.

In this chapter, we discuss how classroom instruction and interventions are intentionally aligned within a layered design (see Chapter 1). We illustrate how the workshop framework provides a structure for differentiating instruction, and how interventions (both pull-out and push-in) are positioned within this structure. Then we focus on writing workshop and describe how the writing process (WP) intervention is delivered to struggling writers who need more targeted instruction in specific areas of the writing process. Finally, we discuss the role of assessment in the writing process, with an explanation of how writing develops along a writing continuum.

A Workshop Framework

The ultimate goal of a workshop approach is to enable learners to acquire strategies for self-regulating their learning. Once teachers understand the framework, they can implement workshops in all areas of the literacy curriculum: reading, writing, language, and content. In each workshop, clear demonstrations, guided participation, active engagement, scaffolding, assessment, and targeted interventions are dynamically linked to facilitate student learning. Within each block of the sample workshop schedule shown in Figure 3.1, you can see how targeted interventions are delivered.

Workshop blocks are designed to promote an integrated curriculum. For instance, during reading workshop, teachers can introduce nonfiction texts that relate to the

FIGURE 3.1 Example of Reading, Writing, Language, and Content Workshops and Targeted Interventions within Each Workshop

Elementary Workshop Schedule with Tier 1 and Tier 2 interventions

Classroom Literacy Program and Intervention	Supplemental Interventions
Reading Workshop (90 minutes)	
❑ Reading Minilesson	
○ Targeted Minilesson	
❑ Guided Reading Group	Guided Reading Plus
○ Word Study Intervention	
○ Writing in Response to Reading Intervention	
○ Assisted Writing Intervention	Assisted Writing Intervention
❑ Teacher/Student Conferences	
○ Intervention Conference	
❑ Sharing/Closure	
○ Assessment of Learning	
Language Workshop (30 minutes)	
❑ Language Minilesson	Intervention Group or Individual Conferences
○ Targeted Minilesson	
❑ Small-Group Language Investigations/Author Studies	
○ Intervention Group	
❑ Teacher/Student Conferences	
○ Intervention Conference	
❑ Sharing/Closure	
○ Assessment of Learning	
Writing Workshop (45 minutes)	
❑ Writing Minilesson	Writing Process Intervention
❑ Independent Writing	Assisted Writing Intervention
❑ Teacher/Student Conferences	
❑ Sharing/Closure	
○ Assessment of Learning	
Content Workshop (45 minutes)	
❑ Content Minilesson	
❑ Small-Group Investigations, Experiments, Content Reading Groups	
○ Content Reading Intervention	
❑ Sharing/Closure	Content Reading Intervention or Individual Conferences
○ Assessment of Learning	

content workshop; and during writing workshop, teachers can provide minilessons that focus on the reading/writing connection, including an analysis of how writers craft text to support readers' comprehension (see Dorn & Soffos, 2005b). The purpose of an integrated curriculum is for students to notice relationships among common concepts and apply flexible strategies for learning new information.

The workshop framework is based on a continuous cycle that begins with a minilesson and ends with a sharing component (see Figure 3.2). The framework provides a differentiated structure with varying degrees of support for meeting students' needs. Students who require additional assistance are provided with targeted interventions that align with the literacy curriculum. The five components of a workshop follow.

Minilessons. The minilesson is aimed toward the majority of students in the class. It is an explicit teaching demonstration that focuses on strategies, skills, and procedures for learning a process. For students who are not responding to the whole-group lesson, the teacher might provide an additional minilesson (intervention) in a targeted area.

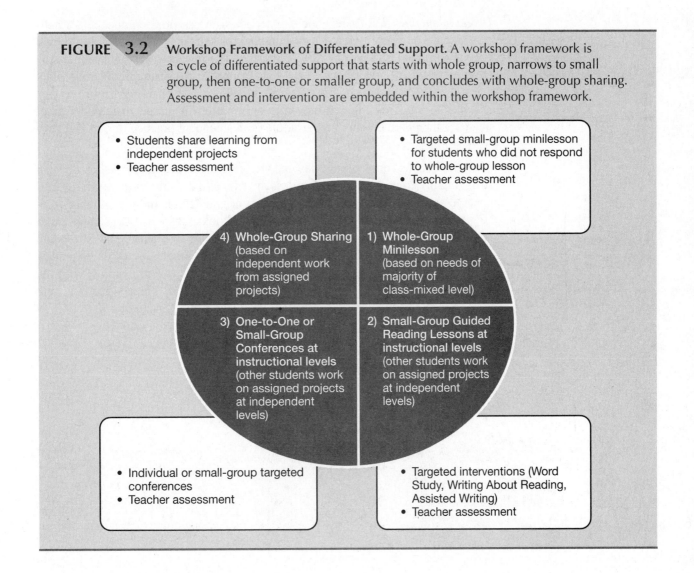

FIGURE 3.2 Workshop Framework of Differentiated Support. A workshop framework is a cycle of differentiated support that starts with whole group, narrows to small group, then one-to-one or smaller group, and concludes with whole-group sharing. Assessment and intervention are embedded within the workshop framework.

- Students share learning from independent projects
- Teacher assessment

- Targeted small-group minilesson for students who did not respond to whole-group lesson
- Teacher assessment

4) Whole-Group Sharing (based on independent work from assigned projects)

1) Whole-Group Minilesson (based on needs of majority of class-mixed level)

3) One-to-One or Small-Group Conferences at instructional levels (other students work on assigned projects at independent levels)

2) Small-Group Guided Reading Lessons at instructional levels (other students work on assigned projects at independent levels)

- Individual or small-group targeted conferences
- Teacher assessment

- Targeted interventions (Word Study, Writing About Reading, Assisted Writing)
- Teacher assessment

Small-group instruction. During small groups, the teacher provides focused instruction to students with similar needs. The teacher selects instructional-level materials and prompts students to use what they already know to accomplish new learning goals. During reading workshop, the teacher serves small groups on an alternating basis (generally two to three groups daily) and meets with the lowest achieving students daily, providing targeted interventions to meet their literacy needs (e.g., word study and/or Writing About Reading interventions).

One-to-one or small-group conferences. The literacy conference serves two essential goals for differentiating instruction: (1) allows the teacher to collect sensitive data on how well the student is responding to instruction, and (2) provides the student with personalized support for achieving the learning goal. The teacher provides regularly scheduled conferences (generally 2 to 3 minutes in duration) with approximately three students daily. For the struggling learner, the teacher conducts an intervention conference, providing more intensity in three areas: duration (5 to 7 minutes), frequency (2 to 3 days a week), and precision (highly tailored instruction).

Independent practice. Independent practice is an essential component of self-regulation. The teacher creates opportunities for students to transfer their knowledge and strategies to an unassisted situation. For instance, during a minilesson, the teacher might model how to use text features to aid reading comprehension; and during independent practice, students would locate examples from text and describe in their reading log how this information increased their understanding. (See the photo below of an example of independent practice during language workshop.)

Share time. This component is designed to bring closure to the workshop through revisiting the content from the minilesson. The teacher calls on three or four students to share their learning from independent practice, including evidence from books, response logs, and other literacy artifacts. The workshop cycle enables students to understand the relationship between the minilesson, guided practice, and their independent work.

During language workshop, a student searches a nonfiction text for text features that were discussed during the minilesson.

Writing Workshop

In the previous section, we presented the general framework for a workshop approach. In this section, we shift our attention to writing workshop, and we illustrate how the writing process (WP) intervention is embedded into the writing workshop.

Writing workshop is a differentiated framework within which students learn the processes of how to write. The teacher structures the time to ensure that students have an opportunity to plan, organize, and carry out writing projects. During writing workshop, students learn how to select their own topics, write in response to class topics, and develop these topics through revising and editing processes (see Dorn & Soffos, 2001b).

The act of writing is associated with four interrelated phases: planning, drafting, revising, and editing. These phases are not static, for writing is much too complex to place in a sequence. Instead, good writers engage in simultaneous processes; for example, during drafting, the writer might revise on the spot or edit a spelling error when it is noticed. Good writers understand that the goal of writing is the creation of the message; therefore, any mechanical diversions during the drafting phase are carried out with minimal interruption.

The four phases provide the writer (and the teacher) with a flexible framework for developing a piece of writing.

Planning. The first step in writing begins with planning. Talking about a topic is one of the best ways to develop an idea for writing. During writing workshop, the teacher encourages students to share ideas for writing with one another. Additionally, the teacher uses minilessons to demonstrate how students can use planning tools (e.g., writing guides, text maps, notes) to organize their thoughts for writing.

Drafting. Once the topic is determined, the writer begins drafting the message on paper. For beginning writers, the greatest challenge occurs with transcribing the print while holding the ideas in working memory. At this level, the stories are short enough to be held in memory as students deal with the mechanical issues of getting their message on paper. As students acquire more skill with print, their transcribing process becomes smoother and more automatic. As a result, they write longer and more coherent texts; and they might have multiple drafts in process at one time. In the photo on page 44, a student reviews several drafts in his writing portfolio, and selects a piece to work on today.

Revising. The revising process is regulated by the desire to express a clear and comprehensible message. Good writers revise at two developmental levels. The first level occurs during the composing process: the writer self-monitors the message for clarity and revises it when the meaning is threatened. This behavior is a natural part of the meaning-making process. The next level occurs after the writing is completed: the writer applies revising and crafting techniques to improve the clarity of the message. This behavior is the result of specialized knowledge that the writer has acquired through reading and writing experiences.

Editing. The editing process involves monitoring the writing for mechanical errors: punctuation, grammar, and spelling. As with the revision process, good

A third-grade student keeps multiple drafts of his writing in a writing portfolio. He selects a draft of an expository text that he started in content workshop to work on today.

writers apply editing processes at two developmental levels. During the composing process, the writer notices an error when it occurs and makes a quick correction at that point. After the piece is completed, the writer searches for mechanical errors and uses editing tools to self-correct.

Writing Conferences

The writing conference provides the student with the highest degree of differentiation. The tailored nature of the writing conference enables the teacher to respond at the student's instructional level. This occurs within the student's zone of proximal development (i.e., the point at which a student is able to acquire new understandings with teacher assistance) (Vygotsky, 1978). The teacher's prompting is central to the student's performance; therefore, the teacher should ask three important questions: (1) How might my prompting help the writer? (2) How might my prompting hinder the writer? (3) Am I promoting dependency or independency behaviors within the writer?

The instructional goal is to engage the students in the problem-solving process, while keeping the focus on constructing a clear and meaningful message. Some prompts for encouraging students to expand and elaborate on their message include:

- What do you mean by that?
- Can you say more?
- Can you explain this to me?
- Can you help me understand this part?
- Can you say this another way to help your reader understand it better?

Writing Process Intervention

If a student is not responding to differentiated instruction during writing workshop, the student might be assessed for a writing process (WP) intervention. The assessment begins with the systematic observation of the student's unassisted activity during the independent writing block. The intervention teacher records the number of minutes the student is able to work without help. If a student is unable to sustain his attention during the independent writing block, the student might be assessed for a WP intervention. The goal of the writing intervention is to provide tailored support within the classroom for a small group of students who are at risk of failure in writing.

For the intervention to be most effective, the classroom teacher and intervention teacher must collaborate. The WP intervention is aligned with the classroom writing workshop, beginning with the classroom minilesson. If students are not responding to the minilesson, the intervention teacher provides a small-group minilesson (approximately 5 to 7 minutes) to support their needs, followed by independent writing and conferences. During independent writing, the students use their writing journals or portfolios from the classroom workshop. They might develop a new piece or continue to work on a piece that was started during writing workshop. The writing intervention is typically 20 minutes, and is designed to provide struggling writers with "just right" support, while also ensuring they will have time to work independently within the classroom writing program.

In assessing students for a writing intervention, teachers follow a five-step process (see Figure 3.3 on the following page):

1. Provide a high-quality differentiated writing program to all students. Analyze student performance according to benchmark writing behaviors.

2. Use data to determine if students will need a writing intervention.

3. For students who are nearing proficiency, the classroom teacher provides some additional support, for example, tailored small-group minilesson or tailored writing conference.

4. For students who need significant help, the intervention teacher comes into the classroom and provides a 15- to 20-minute process writing intervention.

5. Students' progress is monitored at designated intervals using benchmark writing guides.

Assessing Writing Development

During writing instruction, teachers must understand the complexity of the process and strive to create a balance between the composing and transcribing processes. If teaching becomes unbalanced, the student's view of the writing process will reflect this bias. When teachers analyze students' writing, they can design their writing program based on what students already know and what they need to know to move their writing forward (Dorn & Soffos, 2001b).

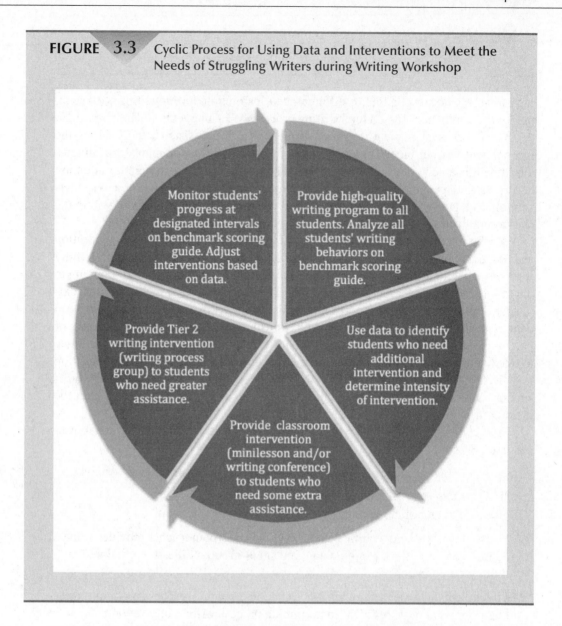

FIGURE 3.3 Cyclic Process for Using Data and Interventions to Meet the Needs of Struggling Writers during Writing Workshop

The success of a writing intervention is based on two types of knowledge: the teacher's knowledge of the writer and the teacher's knowledge of the writing process. This means that the teacher will respond differently to an early writer than to a fluent writer. The teacher's level of scaffolding will be gauged by the writer's ability to accomplish the task.

Using a Writing Continuum

A writing continuum can be a valuable tool for assessing the link between instruction and learning. A continuum serves three purposes in a writing program: (1) it describes writing behaviors in clear and positive language; (2) it aligns with national and state standards; and (3) it provides teachers with a practical and manageable system for assessing the link among curriculum, teaching, and student learning. However, in order for writing continuums to be effective, teachers must be able to:

- Recognize and understand the behavioral changes that occur as writing moves along a developmental continuum of simple to complex

- Understand the role of responsive instruction for accelerating writing growth

Table 3.1 (pages 48–50) includes the typical student behaviors as they move along a writing continuum, beginning with emergent (kindergarten) and ending with transitional (third grade). The behaviors are classified under the phases of the writing process (planning, drafting, revising, and editing). For example, in the planning phase, the typical kindergarten writer is able to plan ideas by drawing a picture; at the transitional level, the typical third-grade writer uses a writing guide related to text structure for planning ideas. In the drafting phase, the typical kindergarten writer uses a practice page to experiment with spellings; at the transitional level, the third-grade writer uses a planning page for word choices. As students progress along the revising and editing continuum, they acquire more skills, strategies, and knowledge for improving their writing. Scoring guides for assessing change over time in writing behaviors along a writing continuum for grades K–3 are provided in Appendix C (see pages 149–156).

Closing Thoughts

All students must be provided with high-quality, differentiated classroom instruction. If a student is not responding to this instruction, the classroom teacher initiates steps for intervention. The intervention teacher begins the assessment process, and meets with the school team to select the most appropriate intervention. In Chapter 1, we presented the portfolio of interventions in the CIM, and in this chapter, we discussed how the writing process intervention is implemented during writing workshop. In the next chapter, we describe how the Interactive Writing and Writing Aloud interventions are used as RtI approaches.

TABLE 3.1	Change Over Time in Planning, Drafting, Revising and Editing Behaviors, Emergent to Transitional Writers

	Emergent Behaviors	Beginning Early Behaviors	Late Early Behaviors	Transitional Behaviors
Planning	■ Generates topics or ideas for writing across genres with teacher assistance ■ Organizes ideas prior to drafting; uses planning ideas to compose message ● Plans writing by drawing a picture(s) or symbols in journal or on writing paper that represents an event or several loosely linked events ● Plans informational/explanatory writing by drawing a picture(s) or symbols to represent some information ● Plans persuasive piece by drawing a picture(s) that represents their opinion about a book or topic ■ Rehearses message orally (expresses ideas) with teacher	■ Generates topics or ideas across genres with or without teacher assistance; begins to demonstrate some understanding of author's purpose and its relationship to text structure ■ Organizes ideas prior to drafting; draws picture(s) of key ideas on writing paper organized to support structure ● Plans simple recount by drawing picture(s) to represent events or key ideas ● Plans informational/explanatory writing by drawing picture(s) to represent information about topic and topic details ● Plans persuasive piece by drawing and discussing their opinion on an idea or topic; uses language to support opinion and reasons ■ Rehearses message orally (expresses ideas) with teacher or peers	■ Generates topics or ideas for writing across genres; demonstrates an understanding of author's purpose and its relationship to text structure ■ Organizes ideas prior to drafting; narrows focus on a topic ■ Uses writing guide related to text structure ● Plans recount by using words or phrases to support event sequence and details ● Plans informational/explanatory writing by gathering information pertinent to a specific topic or to answer a question(s) using a variety of provided text sources; sorts information into major categories ● Plans persuasive piece by taking a stance on an idea or topic; uses words and/or phrases to provide opinions and reasons ■ Rehearses message orally (expresses ideas) with teacher or peers as needed	■ Generates topics or ideas for writing across genres; demonstrates an understanding of author's purpose and its relationship to text structure ■ Organizes ideas prior to drafting; narrows focus on a topic ■ Uses writing guide related to text structure ● Plans story by recording words and/or phrases to develop event sequence and actions of characters ● Plans informational/explanatory writing by researching and gathering information pertinent to a specific topic or to answer questions using a variety of text sources; sorts information into major categories ● Plans persuasive piece by taking a stance on an idea or topic; uses words and/or phrases to provide opinion and reasons ■ Rehearses message orally (expresses ideas) with teacher or peers as needed

TABLE 3.1 Change Over Time in Planning, Drafting, Revising and Editing Behaviors, Emergent to Transitional Writers (continued)

	Emergent Behaviors	Beginning Early Behaviors	Late Early Behaviors	Transitional Behaviors
Drafting	■ Establishes a relationship between print and pictures ■ Writes left to right across several lines of text; uses spaces between words with greater accuracy ■ Holds simple sentences in memory while encoding message; rereads to remember next word ■ Writes some alphabet letters fluently and with correct formation ■ Analyzes unknown words using slow articulation; records letters in word sequence ■ Uses parts of known words to help spell parts of unknown words (analogy) ■ Spells most unknown words phonetically drawing on phonemic awareness and sound-letter relationships ■ Uses a practice page to try out letters or word spellings ■ Uses resources for sound-letter link (e.g., ABC chart, name chart and/or letter books) ■ Writes easy high-frequency words fluently and accurately ■ Uses syntax of oral language; may include some book language and content-specific vocabulary ■ Experiments with simple punctuation (e.g., uses punctuation as markers between words or to designate the end of each line or page)	■ Holds simple ideas in memory while encoding message ■ Rereads to remember next word or phrase; begins to reflect on meaning, sentence structures, and word choice ■ Writes alphabet letters fluently and with correct formation ■ Analyzes unknown words using slow articulation; records letters in word sequence; spells grade-level words conventionally (e.g., words comprised of short vowel patterns) ■ Breaks unknown words into onset and rime or at meaningful and logical units; uses common spelling patterns to spell words conventionally ■ Uses known words and spelling patterns to spell unknown words ■ Uses known words as a base for adding simple inflectional endings (e.g., s, ing, ed) ■ Writes grade-level high-frequency words fluently and accurately ■ Uses a practice page to try out letters or word spellings ■ Uses resources less often for sound-letter link (e.g., ABC chart, name chart and/or letter books) ■ Includes some words that reflect attention to vocabulary and word meanings from reading ■ Applies appropriate standard English grammar ■ Applies appropriate conventions of standard English e.g., capitalization and punctuation)	■ Holds ideas in memory while encoding message ■ Rereads to remember next idea; reflects on meaning, sentence structures, and word choice ■ Analyzes unknown words on the run; thinks visually about how words look; spells grade level words conventionally (e.g., words comprised of long vowel patterns) ■ Breaks unknown words into syllables, onset and rime, or at meaningful and logical units; uses common spelling patterns to spell words conventionally ■ Uses known words as a base for adding inflectional endings (e.g., s, es, ing, ed) ■ Writes grade-level, high-frequency words fluently and accurately ■ Uses practice page to try out word spellings less often; analyzes unknown words on the run ■ Begins to use practice page for trying out word choice; begins to consider words and phrases from reading to support craft ■ Includes words that reflect attention to vocabulary and word meanings from reading ■ AApplies appropriate standard English grammar ■ Applies appropriate conventions of standard English (e.g., capitalization and punctuation)	■ Holds more complex ideas in memory while encoding message ■ Rereads to remember next idea; reflects on meaning, sentence structures, and word choice ■ Analyzes unknown words on the run ■ Breaks words into syllables, syllables into onset and rime, or at meaningful and logical units; uses common and irregular spelling pattern knowledge to spell words conventionally ■ Uses known words as a base for adding inflectional endings (e.g., prefixes, suffixes, and homophones) ■ Uses word meanings to spell words conventionally (e.g., prefixes, suffixes, and homophones) ■ Writes grade-level high-frequency words with fluency and accurately ■ Writing includes words that reflect attention to vocabulary and word meanings from reading ■ Uses planning page to try out crafting techniques (word choice, leads, endings, etc.) ■ Applies appropriate standard English grammar ■ Applies appropriate conventions of standard English (e.g., capitalization and punctuation)

TABLE 3.1 Change Over Time in Planning, Drafting, Revising and Editing Behaviors, Emergent to Transitional Writers (continued)

	Emergent Behaviors	Beginning Early Behaviors	Late Early Behaviors	Transitional Behaviors
Revising and Editing	■ Rereads message and reflects on meaning when prompted	■ Uses a simple writing checklist to check on writing process ■ Rereads message and reflects on meaning and sentence structures when prompted ■ Crosses out unwanted words; revises language for more appropriate word choice to stimulate imagery when prompted ■ Eliminates some redundant and unnecessary information when prompted ■ Circles a few words that do not look right; uses a simple dictionary to look up words and to self-correct spelling ■ Revises for appropriate standard English grammar ■ Revises for appropriate conventions of standard English (e.g., capitalization and punctuation)	■ Uses a simple writing checklist to check on writing process ■ Rereads message and reflects on meaning and sentence structures more independently ■ Crosses out unwanted words; revises language for more appropriate word choice to stimulate imagery when prompted more independently ■ Eliminates redundant and unnecessary information when prompted ■ Circles words that do not look right; uses a dictionary to look up words and to self-correct spelling ■ Revises for appropriate standard English grammar ■ Revises for appropriate conventions of standard English (e.g., capitalization and punctuation)	■ Uses a writing check-lists to check on writing process ■ Rereads message and reflects on meaning and sentence structures ■ Eliminates redundant and unnecessary information ■ Revises and groups ideas by rearranging words, sentences, or phrases; uses cut-and-paste, circles, and lines to group ideas ■ Revises language to stimulate imagery; uses a thesaurus to support craft as needed ■ Circles words that do not look right; uses a dictionary to self-correct spelling and to check on word meanings ■ Revises for appropriate standard English grammar ■ Revises for appropriate conventions of standard English (e.g., capitalization and punctuation)

Chapter

4

Assisted Writing Intervention

Reading and writing are language processes that use many of the same strategies to communicate meaning. Writing is a powerful intervention for increasing reading achievement, but only if reading and writing are taught as reciprocal processes. The physical act of writing slows down the reading process, which allows the learner to focus on word-solving strategies and concepts of print while composing a message. If the writing is meaningful, it promotes the integration of four language systems: (1) comprehension of ideas (semantic system), (2) expression of ideas (syntactic system), and (3, 4) facility with mechanics (orthographic and phonological systems). The links between reading and writing are established as students use their written messages as reading materials.

Learning to write is both a cognitive and social process. Young children are apprenticed into writing through meaningful interactions with a more knowledgeable person. As an intervention, the physical action of transcribing language, while keeping the message up front, is a complex neurological activity. It engages higher-level psychological functions, such as conscious awareness (i.e., I need to pay attention to this), working memory (holding important information in place while acting upon it), integration (pulling related sources together), and problem solving (using strategies to deal with barriers). When children write, they acquire cognitive strategies for attending, monitoring, searching, evaluating, and self-correcting their actions. These invisible processes are made more visible through the overt actions of transcribing a message.

Healy (2004), a child psychologist, presents a strong case for the power of writing in orchestrating brain activity (also see Levine, 2002). A young writer must be able to utilize information (background knowledge) from the semantic, syntactic, phonological, and orthographic systems—along with a set of useful strategies (intentional actions)—in order to achieve a purposeful goal. In constructing a writing system, the writer must:

- Assemble background information for expressing ideas (semantic system);

- Formulate an original statement that represents the message to be communicated (semantic and syntactic systems);

- Find the right words to express the ideas in a clear and precise way (semantic and syntactic systems);

- Place the words in the correct order to communicate meaning (semantic and syntactic systems); and

- Hold the ideas in working memory long enough to transcribe the message on paper (semantic, syntactic, phonological, and orthographic systems).

In this chapter, we describe how a writing intervention is used to increase the achievement of struggling readers at the emergent, early, and transitional levels. We describe two types of assisted writing (AW) and the specialized procedures for implementing each intervention (see Dorn, French, & Jones, 1998; Dorn & Soffos, in process).

Assisted Writing Intervention

Assisted writing is an umbrella term for classifying two types of writing: interactive writing (IW) and writing aloud (WA). At the emergent to early levels, the interactive writing intervention provides a language context for enabling students to:

- Compose simple messages
- Acquire foundational concepts about print
- Understand that writing is about communicating a message
- Apply rereading strategies to predict and monitor the reading
- Articulate words slowly and hear and record letters in words

- Use simple resources as self-help tools (ABC chart, personal dictionary, writing checklist)

- Write letters fluently and with correct letter formation

- Build a core of high-frequency words

The writing-aloud intervention is used with writers who have knowledge of foundational writing concepts, but who are struggling with the writing process. The goals of writing aloud are to assist students to:

- Develop an understanding of the writing process and to apply problem-solving strategies for organizing, composing, editing, and revising a meaningful message

- Understand how to use resources for planning, monitoring, and regulating the writing process

In Table 4.1 (on the following page), we describe the differences and similarities of the interactive and writing-aloud interventions. In selecting the best intervention, the teacher must understand three learning theories:

- *Theory of the student*—what the student knows about writing and how this knowledge can be used to acquire new information

- *Theory of the intervention procedure*—why and when a specific procedure is implemented

- *Theory of contingent scaffolding*—how to adjust scaffolding based on what the student needs to accomplish the learning goal

---

FIGURE 4.1 Interactive Writing before Guided Reading

For kindergarten and first-grade students with low concepts about print, the teacher might place these students in the interactive writing (IW) intervention for a minimum of two weeks prior to the Guided Reading Plus (GRP) intervention. Also, the teacher might choose to layer the two interventions (e.g., GRP on Monday to Thursday and IW on Friday). Teachers can use the following questions to determine the most appropriate intervention based on a student's knowledge about print:

- Can the student distinguish between text and illustration?
- Does the student have some understanding of directionality?
- Does the student have some knowledge of one-to-one matching?
- Does the student know the difference between letters and words?
- Does the student know the letters of the alphabet and a few frequently encountered words (e.g., *I, the, a*)?
- Does the student actively participate in shared reading by predicting events and language structures that show an awareness of comprehension, rhythm, and rhyme?

(See Dorn, French, & Jones, 1998.)

TABLE 4.1 Comparison of Interactive Writing and Writing-Aloud Interventions

Interactive Writing	Writing Aloud
A short read-aloud, a story told by the teacher, or a personal experience may be the basis of the group composition.	A short story read-aloud, a story told by the teacher, or a concrete experience may be the basis of the group composition.
The text is negotiated. The final text is decided upon by the group and rehearsed before writing.	The text is negotiated, and the teacher thinks aloud about the process.
The children and the teacher share the role of scribe. The children actively contribute by writing known letters and/or words from the text on individual dry erase boards. The teacher transcribes the text on the class chart, while inviting individual children to record a few known words on the class chart.	The teacher is the primary scribe who guides the children in composing a meaningful and interesting message. The teacher selects two or three examples from the text and invites the children to apply problem-solving strategies to the words.
The teacher models early reading and writing strategies as she engages the children in creating the text.	The teacher thinks aloud as she writes and involves the children in constructive dialogue about the text and the writing process.
The goal of writing is to develop an awareness of print concepts within the context of a meaningful language composition. Students learn how to use resources for planning and monitoring their thinking. The writing is used as a text for teaching important reading and writing concepts.	The goal of writing is to develop an understanding of the writing process and to apply problem-solving strategies for organizing, composing, editing, and revising a meaningful message. Students learn how to use resources for planning and monitoring their thinking.
The finished text ranges from one to five sentences in length and is read as a shared experience with the teacher.	The finished text is well developed and may be organized according to text conventions. The teacher and children read the text together several times during the writing process.
The finished text is accurate.	The finished text may include many revisions and editing techniques.
The writing of a single text is completed in one sitting.	The writing of the text may occur over several days.
The writing is displayed in the room and might be used for shared or familiar reading.	A published version is not produced since the focus is on the process. The revised version may be displayed in the room, but it is not generally used for rereading.

 **Intervention Framework for Interactive Writing**

The lesson framework for interactive writing occurs in two phases (reading phase and writing phase) with 30 minutes of instruction each day. Each phase includes specialized procedures for building students' knowledge of the reading and writing connection. It is essential for students to have daily instruction as they strive to build connections between past and future learning. With struggling readers, familiarity and recency are the cornerstones of accelerated learning.

Phase One: The Reading Phase

The reading phase begins with the shared reading of a familiar text. During this component, the teacher reads with the students, and the students actively contribute to the reading with the teacher's guidance. As the students become more familiar with the text, the teacher's support fluctuates in response to observations of the students' developing control. The teacher uses the familiar context of the shared text as a tool for directing the students' attention to a new problem-solving activity.

The next component uses activities to develop the students' knowledge of sounds, letters, and words (see Chapter 6). One procedure focuses on the shared reading of an enlarged alphabet chart. The purpose is to help the students acquire letter-sound cues they can use when they are reading and writing. Each child has a reduced version of the chart, which is also used during independent writing. During the shared reading, the teacher leads the students in saying the name of each upper- and lowercase letter and pointing to a drawing of an item beginning with that letter. The letters are read fluently, and the teacher pauses occasionally to allow the students to say the letters or the name of the picture symbol. Another activity relates to the students' personal word dictionary: (1) the students record their known words in alphabetical order under a special picture cue; (2) the students read the words to promote fast visual recognition; and (3) the teacher uses the students' word knowledge as a resource for learning new words.

The final component in the reading phase is the interactive read-aloud. During this component, the students acquire knowledge about book concepts, text structures, literary language, and specialized vocabulary and begin to anticipate that particular language structures will occur within written language. This knowledge gives them a personal foundation for making meaningful predictions as they read stories on their own. The purposes of the interactive read-aloud component are to: (1) provide a good model of fluent and expressive reading; (2) provide opportunities for writing; (3) provide opportunities for retelling; (4) increase children's concept and vocabulary knowledge; and (5) promote an enjoyable and engaging experience with books.

A student reads from her small alphabet chart as the teacher reads from the large alphabet chart during the shared reading component.

Phase Two: The Writing Phase

In the writing phase, the teacher designs instruction with specialized procedures for linking the reading and writing processes. The writing phase begins with interactive writing—a collaborative experience during which the teacher and students co-construct a meaningful message. Language development is embedded in all aspects of the interactive writing intervention. Therefore, teachers need to consider two language-based principles: (1) students must have adequate time to engage in a meaningful discussion around a common event, and (2) students must be fully invested in the words and ideas they will work within their message. These principles imply that the teacher cannot decide in advance exactly what the message will say; however, the teacher can plan for a shared experience that will engage the students in a meaningful and interesting discussion.

The interactive writing component provides a context for helping students acquire early reading and writing behaviors. The teacher uses specialized language to activate the students' problem-solving strategies (planning, monitoring, searching, confirming, self-correcting actions). Some examples of instructional prompts are:

- Reread and make sure your message makes sense and sounds right.
- Say the word slowly to help you spell the word.
- What do you hear first? Next? Last?
- Can you think of another word that could help you write this word?
- Use your ABC chart to help you start that word.
- What two letters would you need to make the word look right?

Following interactive writing, the students are ready to write on their own, and the teacher conducts individual writing conferences. Each writing conference includes specialized procedures for validating and activating the student's knowledge. The teacher:

- Prompts the student to read the message. If the student struggles with a word, she joins the reading, keeping the focus on fluency and comprehension. At the end of the reading, the teacher validates the student's writing by responding to the message as the goal of reading.
- Validates the student's phonological and orthographic knowledge by going through each letter in a left-to-right sequence, and placing a light checkmark above the correct letter-to-sound match, including whole words that are spelled correctly (see Figure 4.2).
- Writes the student's message at the bottom of the page. She explains, "I'll write it the way it looks in a book." Then she prompts the student to point to the words and read his message. The goal of the interaction is to validate the student's work while simultaneously modeling how written language looks in a book.

 ## Materials

Interactive writing is designed to increase students' reading development through a writing intervention. The intervention includes a predictable framework, established

FIGURE 4.2 Validating the Student's Phonological and Orthographic Knowledge

Validating & Activating Knowledge

Teacher praises child for correct responses as he/she places a light check over the correct responses.

√   √√   √√   √ √   √√   √   √ √

I   lk   mi   dge   he   s   ns.

Teacher writes story at the bottom of page. The teacher models saying words slowly as he/she writes the child's story.

I like my dog.   He is nice.

routines, and clear procedures. It is critical that the teacher is well organized with all materials easily accessible. The teacher's materials include: large poetry charts, big books, books for read-aloud, large chart tablet, black marker and eraser, large alphabet chart and name chart, language and strategy charts, and large writing checklist. The students' materials include: small ABC chart, small dry erase board, black marker and eraser, magnetic letters and small bowl for holding letters, letter/sound books, personal word dictionary, and unlined writing journal with practice page at top.

Planning for Instruction

Planning is a critical component of a successful interactive writing intervention. Prior to instruction, the teacher selects the appropriate materials and plans specific activities to meet the instructional goals. We have included two resources to assist teachers with effective planning. First, the guidesheet provides procedural steps for implementing the IW group with consistency (see Figure 4.3 and Appendix D1 on pages 157–159 for reproducible copy). Within this framework, teachers should base their instructional decisions on systematic observations of students' learning and ongoing assessments (see Chapter 2). The second document is the IW lesson planner, which provides teachers with a framework for planning data based instruction that is responsive to students' needs (see Table 4.2 and Appendix D3 on pages 161–162 for reproducible copy).

FIGURE 4.3 Guidesheet for Interactive Writing

Phase One: Reading

1. **Reread Familiar Text (Big Books, Songs, Nursery Rhymes or Poetry):** The goal is for the students to develop knowledge of written and oral language.

   - The teacher uses a familiar text to demonstrate how the four language systems—meaning (semantic), structure (syntactic), auditory (phonological), and visual (orthographic)—work. The teacher:
     - Rereads the text with prosody with the students.
     - Discusses with the students specific literary aspects of text and responds personally to the text (e.g., story structure, concepts about print, letter and word knowledge).
     - Uses the text experience to develop phonological and phonemic awareness.
     - Directs the student's attention to various aspects of the text, including the awareness of sounds in connection with the visual features of words.
     - Engages the students in explicit word analysis (e.g., high-frequency words, saying words slowly, connecting letters to sounds).

2. **Phonological and Phonemic Awareness:** The goal is for students to develop awareness of sound patterns that can be used to learn about words. The teacher:

   - Provides an opportunity for the students to develop phonological and phonemic awareness (e.g., manipulate individual sounds and sound patterns).
   - Gives explicit instruction in hearing syllables, recognizing rhyming words, generating rhyming words, and segmenting and blending onset and rime to say new words (phonological).
   - Shows students how to hear and manipulate individual phonemes in different ways (phonemic).

3. **Shared Reading of ABC Chart**
   ABC Chart: The goal is for the students to acquire letter-sound alphabet cues to be used during reading and writing. (see Figure 4.4). The teacher:
   - Says the name of each upper and lowercase letter fluently, with the students, and points to the adjacent picture that begins with that letter.

   - Provides an opportunity for the students to fluently read the ABC chart in a variety of ways to develop print knowledge.

4. **Phonics: Letter/Word Work:**

   Letter Work: The goal is for students to develop letter knowledge (i.e., become familiar with letters, features of letters, and relate letters to sounds). The teacher:

   - Provides explicit instruction in letter learning by helping students learn how to look at letters, for example directing the students' attention to the features of letters by providing them with an opportunity to trace over letters (sandpaper, magnetic letters, salt, shaving cream) and describing the path of movement.
   - Engages students in kinesthetic experiences (salt, sandpaper, shaving cream) to help the students learn the directionality principle, features of letters and letter names.
   - Gives the students the opportunity to feel the features of the letters as they trace over the letters.
   - Explains letter learning explicitly so that students can learn to make links between letters and sounds.
   - Provides an opportunity for students to make links between letters and sounds by reading letter books.
   - Encourages students to link letter learning to a key word by using their ABC chart and name chart.
   - Provides an opportunity for the students to become fluent and flexible with letter knowledge.
   - Helps students with identifying letters (e.g., pull down letters and say letter names quickly) so that students will become fluent with letter indentification.
   - Provides an opportunity for students to become fluent with writing letters (e.g., write the letter "h" on your board quickly).

   AND/OR

FIGURE 4.3   Guidesheet for Interactive Writing (continued)

5. **Word Work:** The goal is for the students to develop knowledge of how words work and to use their phonological and orthographic knowledge to develop systems for learning words. The teacher:

- Provides explicit and systematic instruction to help students learn how words work (e.g., helping the students learn that letters in words occur in a left-to-right order; showing students the directionality principle by building their name, new words or known words; encouraging students to recognize the link between known sounds and letters by building simple one-syllable (CVC) words; building, writing, and locating high-frequency words in print, and promoting fluent word knowledge by prompting the students to write known or partially known words for fluency).

- Provides explicit and systematic instruction in breaking known words into larger parts (onset and rime) (e.g., prompting students to build a known word; encouraging students to apply their orthographic knowledge to break the word into onset and rime; supporting students as they generate other words that sound the same; helping the students to change the onset to make new words; allowing students to read the new words; recording the word pattern and generated words that contain that pattern on a chart and the students read the words fluently).

6. **Personal Dictionary:** The goal is for the students to acquire a core of high frequency words to be used in reading and writing. The teacher:

- Provides an opportunity for the students to record known high-frequency words in their personal dictionary.

- Supports the students as they read their recorded words from several pages in their dictionary for word fluency practice.

Pattern Chart: The goal is for the students to acquire knowledge of spelling patterns to be used in reading and writing. The teacher:

- Provides the students with a resource that helps them make connections across words (e.g., providing an opportunity for students to notice simple word patterns; prompting the students to use a known word from a prior word work experience to notice patterns in words.

7. **Introduce a New Text (Poem, Song, Nursery Rhyme, Shared Text or Interactive Read-Aloud):** The goal is for the student to develop ways of thinking about texts, extend their linguistic structures, and build vocabulary through a supportive and engaging contexts.

Orientation New Text
The teacher:

- Introduces the text by reading the title and author; discusses genre.

- Activates background knowledge through a discussion about the title and pictures and allows for predictions to be made based on the summary statement or the major theme of the book, story, or poem.

- Sets the purpose for reading and/or listening comprehension.

During Reading
The teacher:

- Reads the text with prosody and at times encourages the students to make predictions, ask questions, or make inferences.

- Allows for ongoing discussions at strategic places as the meaning unfolds.

- Encourages students to join in on repetitive parts if applicable.

- Rereads the text with prosody with the students if applicable.

After Reading
The teacher:

- Provides an opportunity for the students to deepen their level of understanding of the text by engaging in a lively and meaningful discussion.

- Encourages the students to go deeper with their understanding of the text by facilitating and scaffolding a discussion about the text (e.g., the author's message or theme and relate text message or theme to the world, respond personally to text and form opinions, make further predictions and inferences, discuss characters' actions and outcomes, retell or summarize the text, or discuss new learning gained from nonfiction reading)

(continued)

FIGURE 4.3 Guidesheet for Interactive Writing (continued)

Phase Two: Writing

1. **Types of Writing:** The goal is for the students to apply strategies for writing across different genres. The teacher:
   - Thinks critically about the type of writing the students need to learn more about (e.g., informational/explanatory, opinion, narrative or respond to piece of previously read literature).
   - Records the type of writing for the lesson.

2. **Resources to Support Group Writing:** The goal is for the students to use resources to assist them in writing. The teacher:
   - Provides each student with a small copy of the ABC chart and their personal dictionary that houses previously learned high-frequency words.
   - Makes available a large group co-constructed word pattern chart to be referred to during the writing lesson.
   - Prompts the students to use their phonological and word pattern knowledge to write words fluently.

3. **Interactive Writing Lesson:** The goal is for the students to acquire strategies for writing across different genres.

   Negotiate and Generate Group Message
   The teacher:
   - Prompts the students to engage in a conversation around a common experience (e.g., a text that has been previously read and discussed or some new learning).
   - Listens carefully to the students' ideas and converses with them about their ideas.
   - Captures an idea/s from the conversation and gently shifts the conversation to "Could we write that?"

   Record Generated Message
   The teacher:
   - Records the partial or entire message on lesson planner while the students rehearse the message or part of the message.

   Co-Construction of Message
   The teacher:
   - Makes a quick decision based on students' knowledge of encoding which letters and/or words to take to fluency, which words to use as a tool for helping the students learn how to create links between sounds, letters, and words (sound analysis), which processes to demonstrate, and which letters, or words to be written by teacher.
   - Shares the responsibility of transcribing the message with the students.
   - Prompts the students to apply writing strategies while encoding message (e.g., reread to

   think about what word to write next, say words slowly and record letters, use ABC chart, pattern chart and dictionary as resources and reflect on message; that is, does our writing make sense, sound right and look right so far?).
   - Models and encourages the students to use their practice page to think more metacognitively about word solving.

   Reflect on Group Message
   The teacher:
   - Guides the students to use a simple writing checklist to reflect on their problem-solving processes while transcribing the message.

4. **Independent Writing:** The goal is is for the students to apply writing strategies. The teacher:
   - Holds a genuine but short conversation with each student about a picture they have drawn in relationship to the previously read text (e.g., a personal experience, an opinion about a specific aspect of story or poem, or some new learning from a nonfiction text).
   - Supports the students as they rehearse their message and provides language scaffolds as needed.
   - Makes sure the language comes from the students.
   - Provides an opportunity for the students to write their message in a journal that includes a blank practice page at the top for applying problem-solving strategies as needed.

5. **Individual Conferences:** The goal is for the students to learn from teacher assistance. The teacher:
   - Prompts the students to apply rereading strategies to prepare for the next move.
   - Encourages the students to apply visual processing strategies within their zone of proximal development.
   - Assists individual students to initiate problem-solving actions needed to complete a specific task.
   - Celebrates each student's completed message by inviting the student to reread his or her message.
   - Provides explicit praise by placing a light checkmark over the student's contributions and writes the message at the bottom of the page.
   - Gives the students an opportunity to read their message that has been written conventionally.
   - Records anecdotal notes of each student's problem-solving strategies.

Dorn, L., & Soffos, C. (2013, in process). *Interventions that Work: Assisted Writing.* Boston, MA: Pearson.

FIGURE 4.4 Interactive Writing Checklist

Writing Checklist

- ❑ Did you start in the right place?

- ❑ Did you leave spaces between words to make it easier to read?

- ❑ Did you say the words slowly and write the letters that make those sounds?

- ❑ Did you use the alphabet chart to help you with letters and sounds?

- ❑ Did you reread to help you know the next word to write?

- ❑ Did you use your practice page to help you work on the hard parts?

- ❑ Did your story make sense?

- ❑ Did you use a ? or ! or . at the end of each sentence?

The student writes a known word in a personal word dictionary. The picture icon matches the picture on the ABC chart.

TABLE 4.2 ▶ Planner for Assisted Writing: Interactive Writing

Phase One: Reading

Group Members: _____   Date: _____   Week: _____   Lesson: _____

Shared Reading of Familiar Text, Phonological Awareness, *and* Word Study	Introduce and Read New Poem, Shared Text, or Interactive Read-Aloud Text
Familiar Text (Poem, Song, Nursery Rhyme or Shared Text): Title of Text: **Phonological/Phonemic Awareness:** **Shared Reading of ABC Chart (consider an option below):** ☐ Read entire ABC chart with fluency ☐ Read every other letter ☐ Read consonants or vowels **Phonics: Letter Work and/or Word Work:** ☐ Letter Learning: ☐ Word Work: **Personal Dictionary and/or Pattern Chart:** (consider an option below): ☐ Add _____ word to dictionary ☐ Read words from _____ page(s) ☐ Create pattern chart ☐ Read pattern chart	**New Text:** (consider an option below): ☐ Read Poem, Song, Nursery Rhyme ☐ Read Big Book ☐ Read-Aloud Text (Narrative or Nonfiction) **Orientation to New Text:** ☐ Title: ☐ Author: ☐ Genre: **Before Reading:** (Activate background knowledge and set a purpose for reading and/or listening comprehension) **During Reading:** (Identify critical stopping places to support comprehension) ☐ Page numbers and language prompts: **Discussion after Reading:** (Language prompts to promote deeper comprehension)

Dorn, L., & Soffos, C. (2013, in process). *Interventions that Work: Assisted Writing*. Boston, MA: Pearson.

TABLE 4.2 Planner for Assisted Writing: Interactive Writing (continued)

Phase Two: Writing

Group Members: _____ Date: _____ Week: _____ Lesson: _____

Planning for Writing: Before Co-Construction of Message	During Co-Construction of Group Message and after the Co-Construction of Group Message
Planning for Writing: **Type of Writing:** ❏ Informational/Explanatory ❏ Opinion ❏ Narrative ❏ Response to Literature **Resources to Support Group Writing:** ❏ ABC chart ❏ Personal dictionary ❏ Pattern chart **Before Co-construction of Message:** **Negotiate and Generate Group Message:** ❏ Engage in a genuine and rich conversation around a particular element of a previously read text or topic to be described or explained. **Generated Group Message:**	**During Co-Construction of Message:** **Early Concepts of Print:** ❏ CAP: **Fluent Writing:** ❏ Letter(s): ❏ Word(s): **Letters and/or Words to Teach a Process:** ❏ Letters: ❏ Word(s): **Writing Strategies:** ❏ Reread to think about next word ❏ Reread to check on meaning, structure, and language ❏ Say words slowly ❏ Hear individual sounds and record corresponding letters ❏ Use resources to assist with sound-letter match **After Writing Group Message:** ❏ Use writing checklist to check on strategies used during writing **Independent Writing:** ❏ Rehearse individual message ❏ Write a meaningful message **Individual Conferences:** (Record notes on labels) ❏ Conduct one-to-one conferences; validate message and problem-solving processes and prompt student to apply writing strategies

Dorn, L., & Soffos, C. (2013, in process). *Interventions that Work: Assisted Writing*. Boston, MA: Pearson.

Moving into Writing Aloud

The writing-aloud intervention is designed for students who are reading at higher levels, but who are experiencing difficulty with the writing process. Teachers can determine if a student is ready for writing aloud by observing behaviors that indicate knowledge of early writing. The following questions can guide the teacher's observations and decision-making process.

1. Does the student understand concepts of letter, word, and punctuation?

2. Does the student reread to predict the next word and/or to confirm the text thus far?

3. Does the student recognize basic high-frequency words during reading?

4. Does the student spell correctly some basic high-frequency words (e.g., *I, a, like, am, come, can, he, me, my*)?

5. Does the student say words slowly when writing?

6. Does the student hear and record dominant consonant sounds and some vowels?

7. Does the student apply simple analogies to problem solve on unknown words?

8. Does the student compose simple messages of three to five sentences?

If the teacher answers "yes" to most of these questions, yet the student is having difficulty with the writing process, the writing-aloud intervention might be a good choice for the struggling writer. The goal of the writing-aloud intervention is to assist students in understanding that writing is a process of generating ideas, drafting a message, revising, editing, and preparing a piece for a particular audience. The writing-

The teacher models how to use a large writing guide during writing aloud, and students use a small writing guide to plan and organize their writing during independent writing.

aloud intervention uses clear demonstrations, explicit teaching, guided practice, and scaffolding techniques to enable young writers to acquire knowledge of the writing process. The intervention includes four essential components: (1) minilesson on a writing skill, strategy, or craft; (2) group composition around a common event; (3) independent writing; and (4) teacher/student conferences.

Intervention Framework for Writing Aloud

The writing-aloud intervention focuses on assisting students to learn how to compose longer messages, problem solve on more complex words (including vocabulary), and apply revising, editing, and crafting strategies. An additional focus is to assist students to learn how to use literacy resources for planning their writing, monitoring their thinking, correcting their spellings, and selecting good word choices. The intervention is organized into two phases: reading phase and writing phase. Each 30-minute phase includes authentic experiences, predictable routines, explicit teaching, and scaffolding techniques.

The reading phase (phase one) consists of four procedural steps: (1) teacher introduces and reads a new or familiar poem; (2) teacher demonstrates a word-solving strategy and the students apply knowledge to solving new words; (3) teacher reads aloud a book and engages the students in discussion; and (4) teacher and students create a language chart that will be used as a resource in future lessons.

The writing phase (phase two) consists of the following steps: (1) teacher models the thinking process for composing a text; (2) teacher writes the message on a large chart tablet and engages the students in contributing to the message; (3) teacher stops at strategic points to problem solve on particular aspects of the writing process; and (4) teacher uses clear demonstrations, explicit teaching, and guided participation to keep the students actively involved in the learning.

Materials for Writing Aloud

The efficiency of any intervention is largely dependent on the teacher's ability to engage the students' attention, promote their concentration, and facilitate good responses. The teacher assembles the following materials for the writing-aloud intervention: large chart tablet for writing the group text, dry erase board for demonstrating problem-solving strategies, large laminated writing checklist, variety of large laminated writing guides (see Appendix D2 on page 160), and beginner's published dictionary and thesaurus. During the intervention, the teacher and students create word pattern charts based on the word study lessons. Most of the students' materials are smaller versions of the teacher's tools, including writing guides and writing checklist, which are used during independent writing. Early writers use a writing journal with a practice page at the top (as in interactive writing), but as the students acquire more knowledge of the writing process, they write on lined paper and file their writing pieces in a writing portfolio.

Planning for Instruction

The focal point of writing aloud is the shared message: a co-constructed event that enables the teacher to demonstrate important writing concepts while engaging the students in the process. This component requires careful planning on the teacher's part. First, the teacher must create a common message that will involve the students. Then she must select an appropriate writing guide (see Appendix D4 on pages 163–168 for reproducible copies of writing guides) for planning the message. The message can be related to a shared book, a mentor text, a particular type of writing, or a field experience; and the writing guide is used to organize the content into a conventional language structure. Prior to the demonstration, the teacher creates the message, selects the appropriate writing guide, and identifies critical places where she can involve the students in specific learning (e.g., applying word-solving strategies, revising the message for better word choices, and using a writing checklist to reflect on the quality of the message). The teacher uses two resources for planning instruction in the writing-aloud intervention. The guidesheet (see Figure 4.5 and Appendix D5 on pages 169–170) provides specialized procedures for implementing the intervention, and the planner presents a tool for planning lessons within the WA framework (see Table 4.3 and Appendix D6 on pages 171–172).

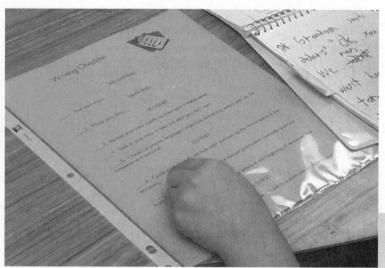

The student uses a small writing checklist during independent writing.

FIGURE 4.5 Guidesheet for Writing Aloud

Phase One: Reading

1. **Reread Shared Poetry:** The goal is for the students to experience the rhythm, rhyme, and cadence of language by rereading poetry over and over again. Reading poetry leads to increased participation and discovery. The teacher:

   - Provides an opportunity for the students to experience language by reading aloud a poem with fluency and prosody.
   - Discusses the poem and encourages the students to respond personally to the text.
   - Uses poetry to direct students' attention to the awareness of sounds in connection with the visual features of words.
   - Engages the students in explicit word analysis

2. **Phonics (Word Work):** The goal is for students to develop knowledge of how words work and to use their phonological and orthographic knowledge to develop a system for learning about words. The teacher:

   - Provides explicit and systematic instruction to help students learn how words work (i.e., helping the students to develop a larger core of more complex site words—contains more complex word patterns using their knowledge of how words work; providing an opportunity for the students to develop a core of more complex high-frequency words; and assisting students as they recognize the link between sound and word patterns).
   - Provides explicit and systematic instruction to help students break known words at meaningful and logical units. The following represent some *possibilities* for expanding their orthographic system. The teacher:
     - Teaches the students a new and important word that would expand their repertoire of known words and support efficient processing during reading and writing.
     - Directs the students' attention to a word pattern and the teacher and students highlight or underline the pattern.
     - Prompts the students to build a known word; prompts the students to break the word at meaningful and logical units; draws the students' attention to the word pattern within the word.
     - Prompts the students to generate other words that have the same sound and visual pattern; prompts the students to categorize the words according to sound and visual patterns.
     - Prompts the students to build two known words; after the teacher asks the student to build two known words, prompts the students to take the onset of one word and the rime from another word and read the new word.
     - Provides the students with an unknown word (written on a card) and prompts them to take the word apart and read the new word; asks the students to draw lines to represent how they took the word apart.

3. **Orientation to New Text (Poem or Interactive Read Aloud):** The goal is for the students to develop ways of thinking about texts, extend their linguistic structures, and to build vocabulary through a supportive and engaging context.

   Orientation to New Text
   The teacher:

   - Introduces the text by reading the title and author.
   - Encourages the students to identify the genre.
   - Activates and builds background through a discussion.
   - Invites students to ask questions and make predictions.
   - Draws the students' attention to the illustrations including charts, graphs, maps, etc.
   - Sets the purpose for reading.

   During Reading
   The teacher:

   - Reads the text with fluency and prosody.
   - Allows for ongoing discussions at strategic places as the meaning unfolds.
   - Stops at strategic places and prompts the students to think about a word meaning, make connections, summarize information thus far, and check on their understanding.

   After Reading
   The teacher:

   - Provides an opportunity for the students to go deeper with their understanding of the text by facilitating and scaffolding a discussion about the text (e.g., the author's message or theme in relation to the world, respond personally to text or form opinions, make further predictions and inferences, discuss characters actions and outcomes, retell or summarize the text, or discuss new learning gained from nonfiction reading).

(continued)

FIGURE 4.5   Guidesheet for Writing Aloud (continued)

Phase Two: Writing (across subsequent days)

1. **Writing-Aloud Lesson (teacher's message may be modeled over several days):** The goal is for students to acquire knowledge of the writing process through a supportive and engaging context.

Prior Planning for the Writing-Aloud Lesson
The teacher:

■ Considers genre and plans accordingly.

■ Composes entire message on paper prior to the writing-aloud lesson.

■ Records composing, revising, word-solving, and editing strategies to be demonstrated or modeled at strategic times over the next few days.

Day One: Planning the Message
The teacher:

■ Tells the students that the purpose for the writing is to create a message that others will enjoy and/or learn from.

■ Orally shares his or her message with students.

■ Organizes his or her thinking on a writing guide related to author's purpose and genre.

Subsequent Days
The teacher:

■ Orally reviews writing guide.

■ Considers the part of the pre-planned message to be modeled for this lesson (e.g., introduction, paragraph [events or section] or conclusion).

■ Considers all writing strategies needed to be modeled in today's lesson.

■ Invites the students to assist her as she composes her message, adds details, and applies spelling strategies.

■ Focuses on composing a meaningful message as she models the conventions of writing and spelling strategies.

■ Transcribes the message and invites the students to engage in the problem-solving processes throughout the composition of the message.

■ Composes her message over several days.

■ Completes message and teacher and the students engage in the revision and editing processes.

■ Uses a thesaurus or dictionary to reflect on word spellings.

■ Guides students to use a writing checklist to reflect on the writing process.

2. **Independent Writing (student's message is written on over several days):** The goal is for the students to apply knowledge of the writing process across genre. The teacher:

■ Supports students in choosing a topic to write about (related to the genre and structure the teacher used as a model).

■ Provides an opportunity for the students to orally rehearse their message.

■ Supports the students if needed as they rehearse their message.

■ Gives the students an opportunity to plan their writing using an appropriate writing guide or outline.

■ Has students write their message using lined paper and also provides a blank practice/planning page for applying problem-solving strategies while composing.

■ Makes available a dictionary for the students to use to look up word spellings during the editing process.

■ Supplies each student with a writing checklist daily to check on where they are in the writing process.

3. **Individual Conferences:** The goal is for the students to learn from teacher assistance. The teacher:

■ Supports students with selecting a topic, completing a writing guide or outline for composing their message.

■ Prompts students to apply rereading strategies to prepare for next move and to think about meaning and language.

■ Encourages students to use resources to support craft.

■ Prompts students to apply visual processing strategies within their zone of proximal development.

■ Suggests that individual students initiate problem-solving actions needed to complete a specific task.

■ Celebrates each student's completed message by allowing the student to reread his or her message.

■ Records anecdotal notes on each student's understanding of the planning, crafting, and problem-solving processes used during the writing of the message.

Dorn, L., & Soffos, C. (2013, in process). *Interventions that Work: Assisted Writing.* Boston, MA: Pearson.

TABLE 4.3 Lesson Planner for Assisted Writing: Writing Aloud

Phase One: Reading

Group Focus: _____　Date: _____　Week: _____　Lesson: _____

Shared Reading of Poetry and Word Work	Introduce New Poem or Read-Aloud Text
Reread a Familiar Poem: Title of Poem: **Word Work:**	**New Text** (consider an option below): ❏ Read poem ❏ Read Aloud Text (Fiction or Nonfiction) **Orientation to New Text:** Title: Author: Genre: ❏ Narrative ❏ Expository (nonfiction) ❏ Poetry **Before Reading:** (Build and/or activate background knowledge and set a purpose for listening comprehension) **During Reading:** (Identify critical stopping places to support comprehension) ❏ Page numbers and language prompts: **Discussion after Reading:** (Language prompts to promote deeper comprehension beyond the text, e.g., revisit purpose for listening and comprehending) **Build or Add to Language Chart Using Examples from Text:** ❏ Text Structure ❏ Author's Craft Including Text Features ❏ Vocabulary Charts (words instead of . . . , examples used to describe being sad and etc.) ❏ Language Use and Conventions (Grammar, Spelling, Punctuation)

(continued)

Dorn, L., & Soffos, C. (2013, in process) *Interventions that Work: Assisted Writing.* Boston, MA: Pearson.

TABLE 4.3 Lesson Planner for Assisted Writing: Writing Aloud (continued)

Phase Two: Writing
(Phase two may extend across two to four days)

Group Focus: Date: Week: Lesson:

Planning and Introducing Writing	During the Co-Construction of Message
Planning:	**Draw Students' Attention to Writing Strategies During the Composition:**
Type of Writing:	❏ Composing Strategies:
❏ Informational/Explanatory	
❏ Opinion	
❏ Narrative	
❏ Response to Literature	❏ Word-Solving Strategies:
Resources to Support Writing:	
❏ Mentor text(s)	
❏ Co-constructed language charts	❏ Revising and/or Editing Strategies:
❏ Writing checklist	
Before Writing Aloud Lesson:	
Introduce Lesson:	**After Writing Group Message:**
❏ Explain author's purpose:	❏ Use writing checklist to check on strategies used during writing
❏ Genre: (narrative, informational/explanatory or persuasive)	
❏ Complete writing guide to support organization	**Independent Writing:**
OR	❏ Rehearse individual message
❏ Revisit previous day's writing	❏ Write a meaningful message
❏ Review, as a writer, where you are in the writing process and set purpose for today's composition	**Individual Conferences**
Message for This Lesson:	❏ Conduct one-to-one conferences; validate message and prompt student to apply writing strategies

Dorn, L., & Soffos, C. (2013, in process) *Interventions that Work: Assisted Writing*. Boston, MA: Pearson.

Closing Thoughts

As an intervention, writing is a powerful way to lift reading achievement. When reading and writing are taught as reciprocal processes, students are able to build pathways between multiple systems (visual, auditory, motor, language) and use strategies to monitor and regulate a meaningful production. The assisted writing interventions reflect a continuum of writing development, and can be implemented by intervention teachers or classroom teachers. One of the advantages of the Comprehensive Intervention Model is that different interventions can be mixed or layered to address the students' strengths and needs. The RTI team should look at student data and determine the best interventions to meet the unique needs of struggling learners.

Chapter

5

Guided Reading Plus Intervention

Reading is a complex thinking process that requires the use of efficient strategies for dealing with problems as they arise within texts. The reader must keep the focus on meaning at all times, while simultaneously developing a toolbox of visual searching strategies for solving words with speed and efficiency. Through the act of reading, the reader learns to integrate multiple sources of information, access background knowledge, apply monitoring strategies, use content skills, and regulate attention and pacing in order to gain the deepest understanding from the reading act. Certainly, reading is more than visual information; however, without visual information, reading cannot occur.

Can a reading intervention promote the use of effective visual strategies, while also keeping the focus on comprehension? Can writing be used as an intervention to accelerate reading achievement? We know that writing can work wonders for helping readers develop fast and efficient visual processing strategies. Also, a well-designed word study can help readers acquire orthographic and phonological knowledge for decoding and spelling words. If these two components were added to a guided reading lesson, what would the intervention look like? More importantly, would it affect the reading achievement of struggling readers?

In this chapter, we will discuss Guided Reading Plus (GRP) as a diagnostic intervention for struggling readers at the emergent, early, and transitional levels. We will present the intervention framework and the specialized procedures for implementing GRP as a component of a Comprehensive Intervention Model (CIM).

Guided Reading Plus Intervention

The GRP intervention is designed for students who are reading at the emergent to transitional levels of reading and writing, but are lagging behind their classmates in reading abilities. The goal is to enable the struggling reader to acquire flexible strategies for solving problems in reading and writing, while maintaining a focus on comprehension. Writing plays a special role in lifting reading achievement, as writing slows down the reading process and increases the reader's orthographic and phonological knowledge through motor production. The addition of writing and word study to the traditional guided reading group is especially important for struggling readers.

The lesson format spans 2 days with 30 minutes of instruction per day. Day 1 includes four components: preplanned word study activity, orientation to the new book, independent reading with teacher observations and tailored support, and follow-up teaching points, including discussion of the message. On day 2, the teacher takes a running record on two students while the other students read easy or familiar texts. Then the focus shifts to the writing component, which includes four distinct parts: teacher provides a prompt that requires students to think more analytically about the previous day's guided reading text; students verbally respond to the prompt and teacher scaffolds their responses; students write messages independently; and students participate in one-to-one writing conferences with the teacher. The GRP intervention enables struggling readers to read for understanding, think critically about their reading, practice efficient decoding strategies, and use what they know about reading to assist with their writing, and vice versa.

Guided Reading Plus is based on three principles for increasing reading achievement.

1. *Leveled Texts Provide Scaffolds for Promoting Monitoring Strategies.* Struggling readers need text scaffolds that enable them to integrate information and develop self-monitoring strategies. Leveled texts are important because they include gradients of difficulty that increase in complexity as readers move up the levels.

2. *Writing about Reading Develops Literate Language.* When students write about the books they are reading, they are more likely to use the structures and vocabulary associated with these texts. This experience shapes their knowledge of how

written text is organized. In the process, they learn to consolidate their spontaneous (everyday) language with literate (academic) language, which forms the basics of good writing. Additionally, when students write about their reading, this literary response affects their reading comprehension. (Graham & Hebert, 2010). In Figure 5.1 we have analyzed the writing sample of a typical student from a

FIGURE 5.1 Writing Sample and Analysis of Responding to Reading (Late Early Level)

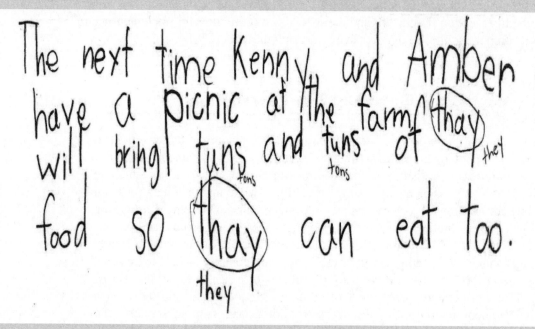

Knowledge of Meaning Making (Comprehension)

Responds to the reading prompt. Makes a logical inference for characters' future action (they will bring tons of food) and establishes a cause/effect relationship (so they can eat too). Uses characters' names and other details (farm, picnic) to express a clear message. Uses descriptive language (tons and tons) to enhance meaning.

Knowledge of Syntax (Language)

Uses complex sentence structures to communicate the message. Uses 'next time' to indicate when the event will occur, and adds the word 'too' at the end to indicate other people will be at the picnic. Uses correct subject/verb match. Integrates meaning and structure to communicate a clear and precise message.

Knowledge of Orthographic Information (Spelling)

Spells 21 out of 24 words correctly.

Knowledge of the Writing Process (Revising and Editing)

Composes and records the message with fluency, as evidenced by the focus on meaning. Monitors by circling misspelled word 'they'. During writing conference, teacher wrote correct spellings under word, also 'tons'.

The teacher prompts the student to use a word pattern chart to assist with spelling an unknown word during writing.

Guided Reading Plus intervention. The sample indicates that reading, writing, and spelling are language processes that work together to communicate clear and precise messages.

3. *Visual Resources Promote Automaticity with Known Words and Build Pattern Knowledge.* It is important for struggling readers to have a record of what they know and how to use this knowledge for learning new information. Two resources are used to accomplish this instructional goal: the personal word dictionary and word pattern charts. The personal word dictionary provides students with a resource for storing known words. The teacher provides lessons that focus on building high-frequency words with magnetic letters, writing the words quickly, recording the words in the word dictionary, and using the words as tools to learn new words (see Dorn, French, & Jones, 1997). The word pattern charts provide students with a visual tool for organizing and classifying word knowledge according to conventional patterns. Both resources provide a record of the students' knowledge; this is useful information for both the teacher and the students.

Assessments

The Guided Reading Plus intervention is formatted to provide opportunities for teachers to collect ongoing assessments throughout the intervention. This assessment component is an important feature of a Response to Intervention approach (see Chapter 2).

During one-to-one reading conferences, the teacher takes a running record of the student's ability to read the previous day's guided reading book. This ongoing assessment occurs at least once a week and is used by the teacher to study how well the student is responding to the reading intervention. At designated intervals (generally 4–6 weeks), the teacher takes a running record of the student's ability to read an unseen text with a standard introduction. This measure allows the teacher to determine the student's independent reading level in comparison to average performing peers (see Chapter 2).

During one-to-one writing conferences, the teacher observes the student's ability to respond to a writing prompt based on the previous day's guided reading book. During ongoing assessment, the teacher notes the student's writing behaviors and uses this information to plan instruction. At progress monitoring intervals, the teacher asks the student to respond in writing to the book, and scores this sample with the Writing About Reading checklist (see Chapter 2 and Appendix B3 on pages 138–139). This writing measure provides additional documentation of the student's reading development.

Intervention Framework

The Guided Reading Plus intervention consists of two phases that are implemented over a two-day period (see Appendix E1 on pages 175–176). Each phase includes specialized procedures that are formatted within a predictable, 30-minute structure. Daily instruction is critical, because the struggling reader is attempting to build connections across events; and lapses in time can present extra challenges.

Procedural Steps for Phase One

1. Teacher provides a word study lesson for the group, while providing tailored support for students within the group who need extra assistance. Students record known words in their personal word dictionary and/or the teacher creates a word pattern chart as a visual resource.

2. Teacher provides a group orientation to the guided reading text, and students engage in constructing meaning for the text.

3. Students read the text independently while the teacher conducts one-to-one reading conferences with each student.

4. Teacher convenes the group for a follow-up discussion that includes one or two teaching points.

Procedural Steps for Phase Two

1. Teacher takes a running record on two students while the other students read independently.

2. Teacher provides a group prompt for responding to the reading of yesterday's guided reading text.

3. Each student composes orally a personal response to the teacher's prompt.

4. Each student writes a response in a writing journal, and the teacher conducts one-to-one writing conferences with each student.

FIGURE 5.2 Guidesheet for Guided Reading Plus Groups

Phase One

1. **Fluent Writing:** The goal is for the students to write fluently a large core of high-frequency words. The teacher:

   ■ Selects one or two partially known high-frequency words for the students to write fluently.

2. **Phonological Awareness:** The goal is for the students to hear and manipulate larger units of sound (e.g., word boundaries); hear, say and generate rhyming words; hear and manipulate smaller phonemes within words, (e.g., phoneme segmentation, deletion, addition, and blending [Phonemic Awareness]). The teacher:

   ■ Provides explicit instruction in hearing and manipulating the sounds of language.

   ■ Provides explicit instruction in identifying word boundaries, hearing, and generating rhyming words, segmenting onset and rhyme, and syllables.

   ■ Provides explicit instruction in hearing and manipulating individual phonemes.

AND/OR

3. **Phonics (Letter/Word Work):** The goal is for the students to become familiar with letters and features of letters and to connect letters and sounds; build a core of high-frequency words to be read quickly; use word-solving strategies fast, fluently, and flexibly while processing in continuous text. The teacher:

   ■ Provides explicit instruction in letter learning.

   ■ Provides explicit and systematic phonics instruction to help students learn how words work.

   ■ Provides explicit and systematic instruction in breaking words into parts (e.g., onset and rime or at meaningful and logical units).

   ■ Provides explicit and systematic instruction in how to use known words and known word parts to build, read and write unknown words.

   ■ Provides an opportunity for the students to use known words and word patterns to read and write new words.

4. **Personal Dictionary:** The goal is for the students to acquire a core of high-frequency words that can be used in reading and writing. The teacher:

   ■ Provides an opportunity for the students to record known high-frequency words in their personal dictionary.

   ■ Provides the students with an opportunity to read their recorded words from a few pages in their dictionary for word fluency practice.

OR

5. **Pattern Chart:** The goal is for the students to acquire knowledge of spelling patterns to be used in reading and writing. The teacher:

   ■ Provides the students with a resource that helps them make connections across words (e.g., provides an opportunity to notice simple word patterns, prompts to use known words from a prior word work experience to notice patterns in words).

6. **Guided Reading**

   Orientation to New Book: The goal is for the students to apply their knowledge of content, language, and reading strategies to prepare for the text reading. During the discussion, the teacher:

   ■ Provides an overview of the text and the teacher and the students co-construct meaning by discussing the pictures.

   ■ Uses specific language structures that will enable the students to predict the language during reading.

   ■ Discusses relevant or new vocabulary that will help the students read the text with understanding.

   ■ Guides the students to locate known and/or unknown words using their knowledge of letters and sounds.

   ■ Points out important features within text (e.g., illustrations, text structure [organization] and/or text features to support comprehension).

   During Reading of New Book: The goal is for the students to use meaning, structure and visual information in an orchestrated way to read fluently and with comprehension. The teacher:

   ■ Holds one-to-one conferences, listens to the student read orally and notes his/her reading fluency, word solving strategies, and checks on comprehension through a brief discussion.

   ■ Prompts the student to think about the text meaning, structure, and/or initiate problem-solving strategies.

   After Reading New Book: The goal is for the students to engage in a meaningful discussion and to reflect on their problem-solving and comprehending strategies. The teacher:

   ■ Discusses the book at the meaning level with the students (e.g., theme, new learning, and personal responses to the text).

   ■ Validates processing strategies used during reading.

   ■ Explicitly teaches for strategy development if processing strategies were neglected.

(continued)

FIGURE 5.2 Guidesheet for Guided Reading Plus Groups (continued)

Phase Two

1. **Reading Assessment:** The goal is for the teacher to code, score and analyze the students's reading behaviors and to use the data to plan for instruction. The teacher:
   - Takes a running record on two or more students using the guided reading text from the previous day's lesson.
   - Analyzes the behaviors used and/or neglected during reading.
   - Uses language to validate and/or activate processing during reading.

2. **Independent Reading:** The goal is for students to read texts with high levels of efficient processing and with comprehension. The teacher:
   - Provides an opportunity for students to read easy or familiar texts from their independent reading boxes.

3. **Writing about Reading**

   Writing about Reading Lesson: The goal is for the students to extend their understanding of text and apply fluent transcription processes to encode their thinking about the text. The teacher:
   - Provides the students with an oral prompt to promote deeper thinking about the text.
   - Supports the students in thinking about the text (e.g., supports the planning, encoding and problem-solving processes).
   - Models and/or prompts for word-solving strategy use.
   - Engages students in problem-solving processes on their individual wipe-off boards, if applicable.
   - Prompts the students to use known letters, sounds and words to write unknown words.

   OR

   Writing Prompt: The goal is for students to extend their understanding of text by thinking about the text at higher levels and by using efficient problem-solving writing strategies to transcribe their message fluently. The teacher:
   - Provides students with a comprehension prompt that stimulates deeper thinking.
   - Supports the students in composing messages in response to prompt.
   - Prompts students to rehearse their response before writing and provides support if needed.
   - Invites the students to use their practice page to problem-solve on unknown letters or words.
   - Encourages the students to use a planning page to organize their thinking before responding and to experiment with word choice, language phrases and creating techniques during composing.

   Individual Conferences: The goal is for students to initiate writing strategies (composing and transcription) independently. The teacher:
   - Prompts students to apply rereading strategies to prepare for next move and to initiate visual processing strategies while encoding their thinking.

4. **Reading and Writing Analysis:** The goal is for the teacher to use data across reading and writing to check on reading and writing and plan next lessons. The teacher:
   - Reflects on focus for lessons.
   - Uses reading and writing data to validate progress.
   - Uses reading and writing data to prepare a new focus and writes predictions of progress.

Dorn, L., & Soffos, C. (2009). *Interventions that Work: Guided Reading Plus.* Boston, MA: Pearson.

Guided Reading Plus Lesson Planners

The teacher must spend time planning for the Guided Reading Plus intervention, including reading the guided reading book, planning the book orientation, designing the writing prompt, selecting the word study activities, and analyzing the students' running records and writing journals. The lesson planner provides teachers with a tool for making these decisions. In Figure 5.3, we have included a sample planner for a group of early readers. In Appendix E2 (see pages 177–178), we have included a blank lesson planner for duplication.

FIGURE 5.3 Planner for Guided Reading: Phase One

Group Focus: At the point of difficulty, use meaning, structure and efficient visual searching strategies to problem-solve and self-correct.

Date: 3-20   Week: #15   Lesson: #74

Group Members:

Fluent Writing, Phonological Awareness, and/or Phonics	Orientation to New Book	Orientation to New Book	After Reading New Book
Word/s for Fluent Writing: Where, This	**Title:** Cookies Week	**Unfamiliar Language Structures:** There was . . . There were . . .	**Discussion Prompts:**
Phonics (Letter/Word Work): Let's build a word you know. Line up the letters across the top of your board.	**Level:** F	Use these specific language structures conversationally throughout the book orientation.	■ Let's discuss the character, Cookie. What do you think about Cookie?
j u p m	**Orientation to New Book:** The name of our new book is Cookie's Week. Cookie is a mischievous cat. Mischievous means you cause trouble or you are irresponsibly playful. Every day of the week, Cookie causes trouble. But, at the end of the week, something happens. What do you think might happen at the end of the week? Let's look inside the book and see what happens to Cookie at the end of the week.	**Relevant Vocabulary:** Windowsill: Have children repeat the word and point to the picture of the windowsill in the book to make sure the children understand the vocabulary.	■ What was the problem in the story?
■ Make the word jump.			■ Was the problem solved (inference)?
■ Break jump. Blend the parts back together.		**New and Important Word/s:** If you were going to read the word, dishes . . . what would you expect to see first? What part would you expect to see next? What ending would you expect to see at the end of dish to make dishes? Find the word dishes. So, looking all the way through words and using word parts can help you read words quickly.	■ How would you handle a mischievous cat like Cookie?
■ Can you think of another word that rhymes with jump? Provide letters to make new word. Break the word. Blend the parts.			■ What did you learn about mischievous cats?
So in reading, if you get to a tricky word, you will need to look all the way through the word and use word parts to help you read the word quickly.			Encourage discussion and provide opportunities for the children to engage in discourse and encourage them to build discourse chains as they discuss the text.
Personal Dictionary or Word Pattern Chart: Let's add some words to our chart that rhymes with jump.			
Have the students generate other words that sound the same and look the same.			

(continued)

FIGURE 5.3 Planner for Guided Reading (continued): Phase Two

Date: 3-21   Week: #15   Lesson: #75

Assessment: Running Record	Writing about Reading	Reading and Writing Group Analysis
Book Title: Cookie's Week **Book Level:** G **Student's Name:** Kelton **Accuracy Rate:** 94% **SC Ratio:** 1:2 **Student's Name:** Seth **Accuracy Rate:** 96% **SC Ratio:** 1:1	**Writing Strategy Lesson or Writing Prompt:** *Writing Prompt for Independent Writing:* Yesterday we read *Cookie's Week*. Every day of the week, Cookie caused problems. Write about what you would do if you had a cat like Cookie.	**Reading:** ■ The children are monitoring their reading with ease and are reading for meaning. ■ At the point of difficulty, most of the children are rereading and taking words apart on the run. Some still need some support in initiating visual searching strategies. **Writing:** ■ The children are responding to texts in a meaningful way and are encoding their message fluently. ■ They are writing letters and most high-frequency words fluently. ■ At the point of difficulty, they are problem solving using word parts, and patterns to think about the way words look. **Next Steps:** Keep the same focus. ■ Continue to prompt for integration. ■ Continue to build a core of high-frequency words. ■ Continue to teach and prompt for visual searching strategies.

Dorn, L., & Soffos, C. (2009). *Interventions that Work: Guided Reading Plus.* Boston, MA: Pearson.

Emergent and Early Readers

For emergent and early readers, the intervention includes two additional components for promoting the fast and fluent control of visual information. The first component focuses on acquiring a core of high-frequency words (see Appendix E on pages 175–176 for word list), approximately 150 by the end of the early level. The teacher selects one or two partially known words for the children to write fluently. This fast motor production of common words promotes automaticity and leads to the fast retrieval of words during the reading and writing of whole texts. After the words are written, the teacher instructs the children to find the correct page in their personal dictionary and record the new words. The second component focuses on learning about words (see Chapter 6).

Transitional Readers

When students move into transitional levels, the reading component includes a focus on understanding genre types and text features. This implies that teachers must locate appropriate texts that students can read at their instructional levels, such as easy chapter books or informational texts. The students are introduced to text maps, and the teacher guides them to notice how texts are organized according to text conventions.

Anchor charts are created that include genre conventions and structural features of texts, and the teacher and students use this information before, during, and after the text reading (see the figure below for an example of an anchor chart).

Non-fiction	
Special Feature	Purpose
Labels	• Helps us understand the picture or photograph
Pictures/Photographs	• Helps us understand what something looks like
Captions	• Tells us about pictures/photographs
Comparisons	• Helps us understand about the size of something
Cutaways	• Shows us what something looks like on the inside
Maps	• Shows us where things are located.
Bold or Italicized Words	• Calls our attentions to special parts or important words.
Close-ups	• Helps us see details in something small
Table of Contents	• Lets us know the main topics in a book in the order they are presented.
Index	• Helps us find which page something in the book can be found.
Glossary	• Helps us understand what words in the text mean and how to pronounce them.
Key	• Colors show us parts of the picture or diagram.
Title or Heading	• Tells us what will be on the page or section.
Directions	• Tells us how to do something.

Anchor Chart for Study of Informational Texts

At this time, an instructional shift occurs in the writing component, and the students begin to use text maps to help them plan their responses to the text. For instance, after reading a procedural text, the teacher demonstrates how to respond to the reading by organizing the information on a procedural map.

Materials for Guided Reading Plus

The GRP intervention is designed to help struggling readers acquire effective strategies for problem solving in texts while maintaining a focus on comprehension. The materials provide students with opportunities to develop visual processing strategies and to use this knowledge during authentic reading and writing experiences.

- Magnetic letters and individual bowls for storing letters
- Student wipe-off boards
- Small teacher wipe-off board
- Chart paper for constructing anchor charts
- Sliding card for promoting visual searching (see photo)
- Personal word dictionary
- Word pattern charts
- Book boxes for independent reading
- Student writing journals
- Multiple copies of guided reading texts

Changes over Time in Writing Instruction

In the guide sheet, we outlined how the writing component includes two levels of support, with the emergent level designed to promote the students' attention to concepts of print (directionality, spacing, letter formation, letter-sound matching, etc.). When the students are ready for the next level, the teacher introduces the writing prompt. The goal of the writing prompt is to stimulate the reader's attention to think beyond the text and construct a meaningful response to the author's message.

The writing tools are adjusted to reflect changes in writing development. At the emergent and early levels, the students use a writing journal that is bound across the top: the top part of the journal is used as a practice page and the bottom part is used for recording the message. The practice page provides students with a place to try out letters and words and to fluently write high-frequency words. At the late to early transitional levels, the writing journal is replaced with a writing log: the left side of the log is used as a planning page and the right side is used for recording the message. The planning page provides students with a place to organize their thinking, to experiment with word choices and language phrases, and to apply crafting techniques. In this section, we'll discuss the changes that occur over time in writing instruction. (See the photos for samples of writing journal with practice page on the facing page.)

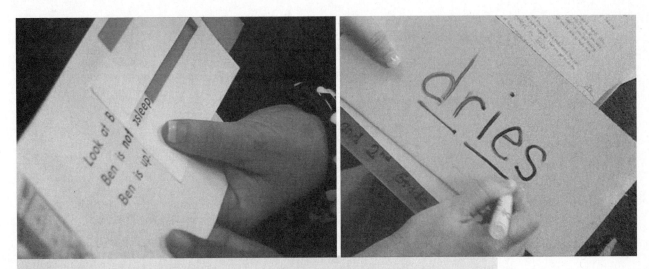

A sliding card is used to direct the student's eyes to search through a word. The teacher slides the card across the word, uncovering parts as she prompts the student to read the word in parts. A small dry erase board can also be used to promote visual searching. The unknown word is written in parts and the student reads the parts as the word is constructed.

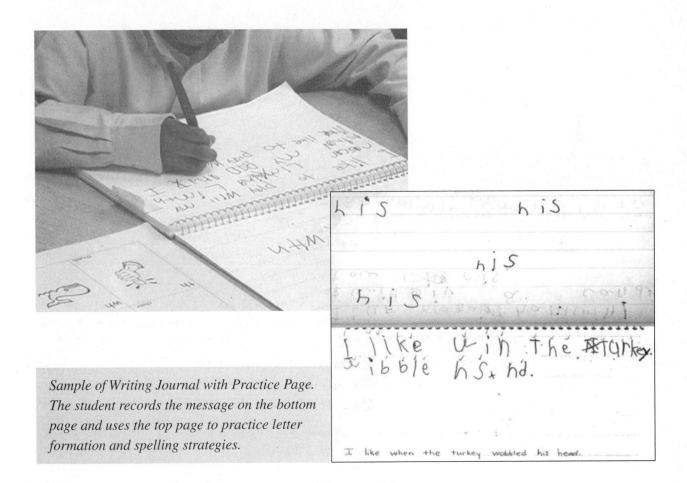

Sample of Writing Journal with Practice Page. The student records the message on the bottom page and uses the top page to practice letter formation and spelling strategies.

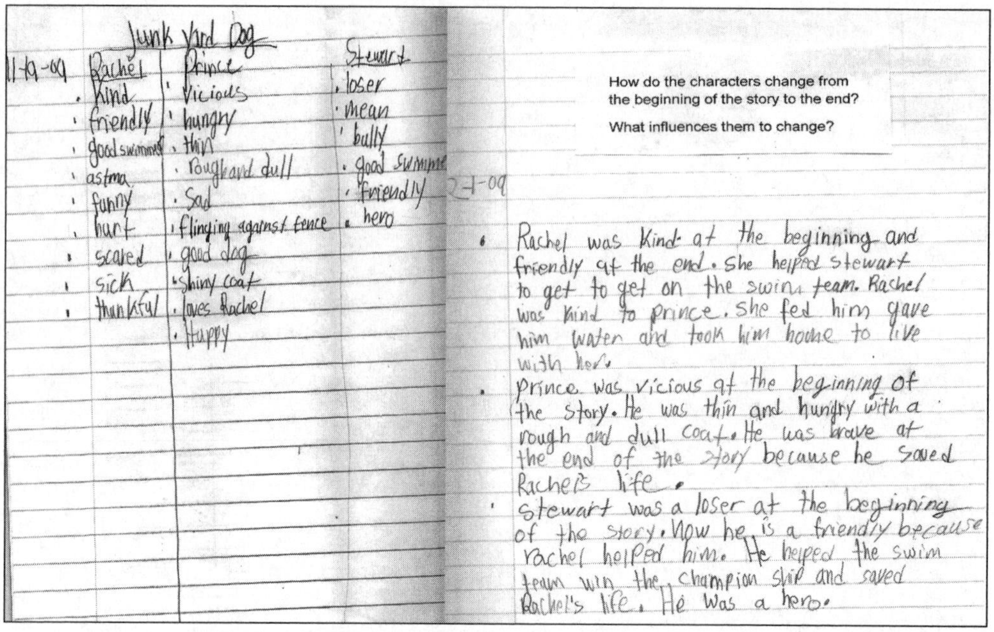

Handwritten writing log samples:

Junk Yard Dog (1-12-09)

Rachel	Prince	Stewart
· Kind	· Vicious	· loser
· friendly	· hungry	· mean
· good swimmer	· thin	· bully
· astma	· rough and dull	· good swimmer
· funny	· Sad	· friendly
· hurt	· flinging against fence	· hero
· scared	· good dog	
· sick	· shiny coat	
· thankful	· loves Rachel	
	· Happy	

How do the characters change from the beginning of the story to the end?

What influences them to change?
_____

2-1-09

· Rachel was Kind at the beginning and friendly at the end. She helped Stewart to get to get on the swim team. Rachel was Kind to prince. She fed him gave him water and took him home to live with her.

· Prince was vicious at the beginning of the story. He was thin and hungry with a rough and dull coat. He was brave at the end of the story because he saved Rachel's life.

· Stewart was a loser at the beginning of the story. Now he is a friendly because Rachel helped him. He helped the swim team win the champion ship and saved Rachel's life. He was a hero.

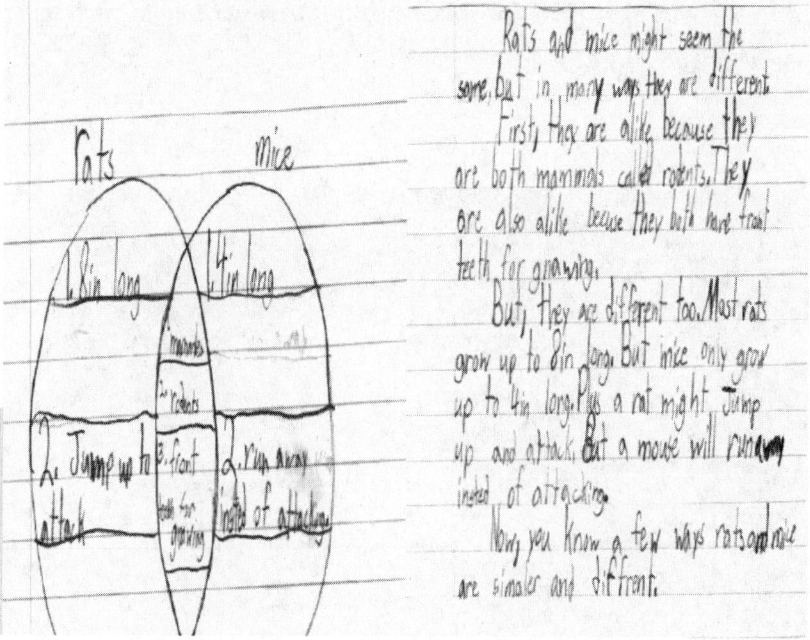

Handwritten Venn diagram: Rats / mice

Rats — 8 in long · Jump up to attack
mice — 4 in long · run away instead of attacking
(center: mammals, rodents, front teeth for gnawing)

Rats and mice might seem the same, but in many ways they are different.

Firstly, they are alike because they are both mammals called rodents. They are also alike because they both have front teeth for gnawing.

But, they are different too. Most rats grow up to 8in long but mice only grow up to 4in long. Plus a rat might jump up and attack, but a mouse will run away instead of attacking.

Now you know a few ways rats and mice are similar and different.

Samples of Writing Log with Planning Page.
The student records the message on the right side and uses the left side to plan the writing.

Writing about Reading at the Emergent Level

Emergent writers are constructing knowledge of the print system, including an understanding of left-to-right order in sentences and words. At this level, the students are reading simple, patterned texts in their guided reading group. In their writing group, they are writing simple sentences (generally one or two). The writing prompt is based on the teacher's knowledge of the students' reading behaviors and how the writing can increase reading knowledge, and vice versa.

During the writing conference, the teacher provides tailored feedback to meet the needs of the individual writer. Each writing conference includes specialized procedures for validating and activating the student's knowledge. At the emergent level, these procedures are:

1. Teacher prompts the student to read the message; and if the student struggles on a word, she joins the reading, keeping the focus on fluency and comprehension. At the end of the reading, the teacher's validates the student's writing by responding to the message as the goal of reading.

2. Teacher validates the student's phonological and orthographic knowledge by going through each letter in a left-to-right sequence, and placing a light check mark above the correct letter-to-sound match, including whole words that are spelled correctly.

3. Teacher writes the student's message at the bottom of the page. She explains, "I'll write it the way it looks in a book." Then she prompts the student to point to the words and read his message. The goal of the interaction is to validate the student's work, while simultaneously modeling how written language looks in a book.

 ## Using Writing Prompts to Respond to Reading

As students become more competent readers, the teacher adjusts the writing instruction to accommodate their strengths and needs. Through the reading of higher-level texts, students increase their problem-solving efficiency as well as their knowledge of new vocabulary, content information, and more complex print conventions (text structures, genre conventions). When students write in response to their reading, they are more likely to borrow the language of the text, therefore, incorporating more complex language structures and academic vocabulary into their compositions.

The success of the writing intervention will be influenced by the teacher's ability to create good writing prompts. The prompts should provide opportunities for students to assemble their knowledge from language experiences and apply their strategies to deal with the goals of the writing task. In order for writing prompts to be effective, the teacher must have three types of knowledge:

Knowledge of the Book

- Author's purpose
- Theme of the book and its underlying meanings
- Important information presented and to be learned
- Genre, text structures, and features of the book

Knowledge of Comprehension Strategies

- Higher-level comprehending strategies for understanding relationships (e.g., inferring, predicting, connecting, analyzing)

Knowledge of Student's Processing Behaviors

- Formative assessments (running records, writing samples) for analyzing reading and writing behaviors.

To illustrate, let's look at an example of a writing prompt for early readers and the students' written responses. The story, *Greedy Cat Is Hungry* by Joy Cowley, is about a persistent, but lovable, cat that is always begging for food. Consequently, he is much too fat. He appeals to members of the family, but they refuse to feed him. He finally achieves success by appealing to Katie, the youngest member. The goal of the writing prompt is to encourage the students to think beyond the text and offer a logical solution to Greedy Cat's problem (i.e., begging for food, which has led to his being overweight). The teacher asks the prompt, "Katie did not help Greedy Cat

FIGURE 5.4   Responding to Different Types of Texts

Informational/Explanatory Writing in Response to Informational Texts
- Responds personally to the text (e.g., gives an opinion of the text and/or responds to the learning from the text)
- Writes some interesting facts learned from text and uses text features to support information (e.g., diagrams, labels)
- Writes a simple report and uses text features to support the information (e.g., uses headings to demonstrate information to follow; list facts from text supported by illustrations)
- Writes a prediction based on information from text
- Writes directions to show a process or a sequence of steps (e.g., lifecycle or how to complete a task such as a recipe or how to make something)
- Writes questions from reading
- Takes notes during reading and summarizes learning after reading
- Writes a letter to someone explaining their learning from text
- Compares and contrasts information from text(s)
- Critiques the text

Narrative Writing in Response to Narrative Texts
- Responds personally to the text (e.g., gives an opinion of the text, character(s), problem, solution, and/or the theme)
- Retells story using a sequence of events
- Writes simple statements to summarize the text
- Writes about favorite part and explains why
- Writes about specific story elements (e.g., setting, problem, solution, or analyzes a character(s))
- Draws inferences (e.g., "What can you infer about . . . from reading this story?")
- Identifies the theme or message gleaned from reading story
- Makes personal connections to text ideas, characters, situations, theme, and/or setting (e.g., I can relate to . . . or I can understand . . . because . . .)
- Makes predictions (e.g., I think . . . because . . .)
- Compares and contrasts different aspects of text
- Writes a book review
- Critiques the text
- Writes questions

learn a lesson. What should Katie do the next time Greedy Cat wants everything for himself?" The writing journals of two students indicate their ability to use the prompt to stimulate logical thinking.

Student One: Katie should teach Greedy Cat to share his food.

Student Two: Katie should give him a little bit of the food and milk.

As the students move into the transitional level, the teacher introduces text maps and incorporates these organizers into the writing component.

 ## Closing Thoughts

In this chapter, we have presented the framework and procedures for implementing the small-group intervention Guided Reading Plus. In our work with schools, this intervention is achieving results with struggling readers at the emergent, early, and transitional levels, as well as upper-grade students who are reading significantly below grade level.

The GRP intervention is based on the following principles:

1. Specialized procedures and predictable routines free the reader's attention to focus on problem solving.

2. Strategy-based prompts during reading and writing promote self-monitoring, searching, and self-correcting behaviors within whole texts.

3. Writing about reading is an effective way to increase reading achievement.

4. Progress monitoring provides systematic data for studying change over time in student's learning and informing teaching decisions.

5. One-to-one conferences during independent reading and writing events enable teachers to tailor instruction to meet the strengths and needs of the learner.

6. Instruction is continually adjusted to accommodate the shifts in student's learning.

Chapter
6

Learning about Letters and Words

The primary purpose of reading and writing is the comprehension of information and ideas expressed through a written message. There is little value in being able to decode words or write letters in a sentence if the meaning of those sentences is not accessed. Acquiring competency in written language is an integrated process that develops along a literacy continuum that moves from simple to more complex processing.

A literacy processing system can be defined as a network of interrelated information that works together to construct meaning for a given event (Clay, 1991; 2001). The system is shaped as children apply their knowledge and problem-solving strategies to tasks that increase in difficulty. When the student's learning is new, the literacy behaviors are more deliberate and intentional; therefore, the teacher is able to observe the changes in the student's learning as the behaviors move from overt to covert. As the student acquires more opportunities to apply flexible strategies in connected texts, the once-observable behaviors become skilled actions. The goal of a word study intervention is to increase students' phonological and orthographic knowledge while simultaneously fostering their word-solving strategies as they read for meaning.

In this chapter, we describe specific behaviors that indicate the changes that occur over time in the development of the phonological and phonemic systems (see Appendix F on pages 179–186 for reproducible copies). We share principles with specific examples for teaching students about letters and words at the emergent, early, and transitional levels. Teachers should use the students' data from reading and writing, along with the resources in this chapter, to plan effective letter and word study activities for the small-group interventions.

Phonological Systems

Learning about Sounds

Understanding the typical development of phonological awareness, including phonemic awareness, is essential for teachers who work with children who are at risk of reading difficulties. Phonological awareness generally emerges in a developmental sequence from awareness of larger units, such as syllables and onset and rimes, to awareness of individual phonemes in words. Phonemic awareness is the ability to hear sounds in words and to be able to identify those sounds. Phonemic awareness continues to develop as children acquire knowledge of sound/letter relationships. Table 6.1 illustrates how the phonological and phonemic systems change over time as the student acquires greater control over these processes. The cognitive tasks described in this chapter grow in complexity from identification to manipulation, from identifying words that begin with the same sound to substituting initial sounds.

Interventions should include opportunities for students to learn about the sounds of language and to apply these processes to their reading and writing. Teachers can use poetry, nursery rhymes, and big books to promote children's phonological and phonemic knowledge in the following ways:

- Draw children's attention to how words have more than one syllable by clapping the parts in some multisyllabic words in the poem.
- Draw children's attention to the rhyming words and how to segment onset from rhyme.
- Draw children's attention to words that begin or end the same.
- Draw children's attention to the sounds within words by saying words slowly and hearing and identifying the individual phonemes in the words.
- Draw children's attention to making new words by substituting sounds or adding onsets to rimes.

TABLE 6.1 Changes over Time in the Development of Phonological and Phonemic Awareness

Becoming Aware—Developing and Extending Control of the System

Emergent	Beginning Early	Late Early
Phonological Awareness	**Phonological Awareness**	**Phonological Awareness**
■ Counts and identifies individual words in spoken phrases or sentences (*I - like - my - dog.*)	■ Hears and identifies syllables in three- to four-syllable words (*ba/nan/a; wa-ter-me-lon*)	■ Develops speed, fluency, and ease in identifying syllables in words
■ Hears and identifies syllables in one- to three-syllable words (1–*dog*, 2–*apple*, 3–*elephant*)	■ Develops fluency and ease in generating rhyming words (*fun, run; sit, split*)	■ Develops speed, fluency, and ease in hearing, saying and generating rhyming words (*play, stray, stay, meat, heat*)
■ Generates rhyming words (*dog, log; cat, mat*)	■ Develops fluency and ease in segmenting and manipulating onset (consonant) and rimes of spoken words (*am, Sam, ham; and, sand, hand*)	■ Develops speed, fluency, and ease in hearing, segmenting and manipulating onset (consonant) and rimes, including consonant blends (*sp-ike, l-ike, str-ike*)
■ Segments and manipulates onset (consonant) and rimes of spoken words (*S-am, h-am; s-and, h-and*)	■ Hears and identifies long and short vowel sounds in words (*make, mad*)	■ Develops speed, fluency, and ease in hearing and identifying long and short vowel sounds in words (*make, mad; heat, hat*)
Phonemic Awareness	**Phonemic Awareness**	**Phonemic Awareness**
■ Segments two- to three-letter words (CVC) into a complete sequence of individual phonemes (*c-a-t*)	■ Segments single-syllable words into a complete sequence of individual phonemes including consonant blends (*c-a-p; f-l-i-p*)	■ Develops speed, fluency, and ease in segmenting words into a sequence of individual phonemes including consonant blends (*s-ea-t, cl-a-m, ch-i-p, t-ar-p*)
■ Blends two to three phonemes in words (*c-a-t, cat; s-u-p, up*)	■ Blends individual phonemes in single-syllable words to form words including words with consonant blends (*c-u-p, cup; p-i-g, pig; b-l-a-ck, s-l-i-p*)	■ Develops fluency and ease in blending single syllable phonemes to form words including words with blends (*c-u-p, cup; p-i-g, pig; b-l-a-ck, s-l-a-p*)
■ Hears and recognizes the same and different sounds in words in beginning, middle, and ending positions (*ball, boat; lip, lit; fat, fit*)	■ Hears and recognizes the same and different sounds in words in beginning, middle, and ending positions (*ball, boat; lip, lit; fat, fit*)	■ Develops fluency and ease in adding or substituting individual phonemes in simple, one syllable words to make new words (*at, sat, mat; mat, map*)
■ Adds or substitutes individual phonemes in simple, one-syllable words to make new words (*at, sat, mat; mat, map*)	■ Adds or substitutes individual phonemes in simple, one-syllable words to make new words (*at, sat, mat; mat, map*)	■ Develops fluency and ease in hearing and recognizing the same and different sounds in words in beginning, middle, and ending positions (*ball, boat; lip, lit; fat, fit*)

Note: Phonemic awareness is reciprocal to learning about letter/sound relationships. This knowledge is best learned when integrated with word study.

Orthographic Systems

Learning about Letters

Letter knowledge has been shown to be a strong predictor of later reading ability. Traditional activities, however, such as copying letters off the board or tracing letters on worksheets, are not productive learning tasks. Instead, learning about letters should be taught as a strategic process, that is, the ability to notice similarities and differences among letters, understand spatial and sequential aspects of letter knowledge, recognize letters within words, and produce well-formed letters with fluency while composing meaningful messages (Dorn, French, & Jones, 1998).

When children learn how to analyze the features of letters, they notice the finer distinctions that occur between the letter shapes. This perceptual process can be accelerated when teachers use language prompts that emphasize spatial orientation and motor sequences (see Figure 6.1 and Appendix F1 on page 179). For instance, in learning the letter a, the teacher would direct the child's attention to the starting point, then describe the path of movement for constructing the letter form in a conventional sequence, "over, around, up, and down." When children learn the appropriate path of movement, they can generalize this knowledge to other letters with the same starting point and initial sequence (s, c, q, d, o, g).

As children attend to letters, they need opportunities to develop automaticity and flexibility. Teachers should draw children's attention to the features of letters through sorting activities, such as sorting by color, letter features, upper- and lowercase letters, or by alphabetical order (see Figure 6.2). Children need opportunities to perceive letters on different planes: on a whiteboard directly in front of them, on a vertical easel, or in a pocket chart. Additional experiences in letter learning include:

- Using magnetic letters or sandpaper letters to draw attention to the directionality and distinctive features of letters

- Using an ABC chart as a reference tool for writing letters and key words that begin with the letters on the chart

- Noticing and locating known letters in big books, pocket chart stories, poems, letter books, and interactive writing texts

- Writing letters in the sand, salt, and on a whiteboard

- Using magnetic letters to construct simple words in left to right order

Learning about Words

As children work with letters and words, they build letter knowledge, letter–sound relationships, spelling patterns, high-frequency words, and word meanings. As they read and write, they apply visual information from known words to solve unknown words within texts. Teachers can help students to understand how words work by focusing on three learning principles:

1. Always work left to right when teaching, building, writing or checking a word. It will enable children to look across the letters in sequence.

FIGURE 6.1 Path of Movement for Describing and Forming Letters

A	slant down, slant down, across	a	over, around and down
B	down, up around, around	b	down. . . n, up and around
C	over, around and open	c	over, around and open
D	down, up, around	d	over, around u . . .p and down
E	down, across, across, across	e	across, over, around and open
F	down, across, across	f	over, dow . . . n, across
G	over, around, across	g	over, around, dow . . .n and curve
H	down, down, across	h	dow . . . n, up and over
I	down, across, across	i	down, dot
J	down, curve	j	down, curve, dot
K	down, slant in, slant out	k	dow . . .n, slant in, slant out
L	down, across	l	dow . . .n
M	down, slant down, slant up, down	m	down, up, over, up, over
N	down, slant down, up	n	down, up, over
O	over, around, close	o	over, around, close
P	down, up, around	p	dow . . .n, up, around
Q	over, around, close, slant out	q	over, around, down
R	down, up, around, slant out	r	down, up, curve
S	over, around, curve	s	over, around and curve
T	down, across	t	down, across
U	down, curve up	u	down, curve up, down
V	slant down, slant up	v	slant down, slant up
W	slant down, slant up, slant down, slant up	w	slant down, slant up, slant down, slant up
X	slant down, slant across	x	slant down, slant across
Y	slant down, slant up, down	y	slant down, slant dow. . . n
Z	across, slant down, across	z	across, slant down, across

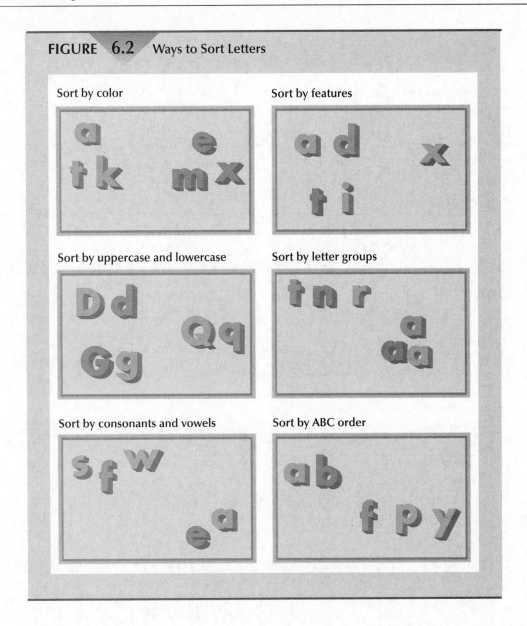

FIGURE 6.2   Ways to Sort Letters

2. Use language so the children understand you are talking about a word and not a letter. For example, run your finger under the word, left to right, as you say the word.

3. Words must be encountered in different contexts (word study, and in reading and in writing) many times before they are known.

The assisted writing (AW) and Guided Reading Plus (GRP) interventions include explicit instruction in word study. For instance, during the AW intervention, the teacher might guide students to sort words that end with *ing* in a pocket chart; or she might teach them to sort words with a particular short-vowel rime pattern (see Figures 6.3 for examples and Appendix F3 on pages 184–186 for spelling patterns that can be used for word study activities). During the word study component of the GRP intervention, the teacher

FIGURE **6.3** Ways to Sort Words

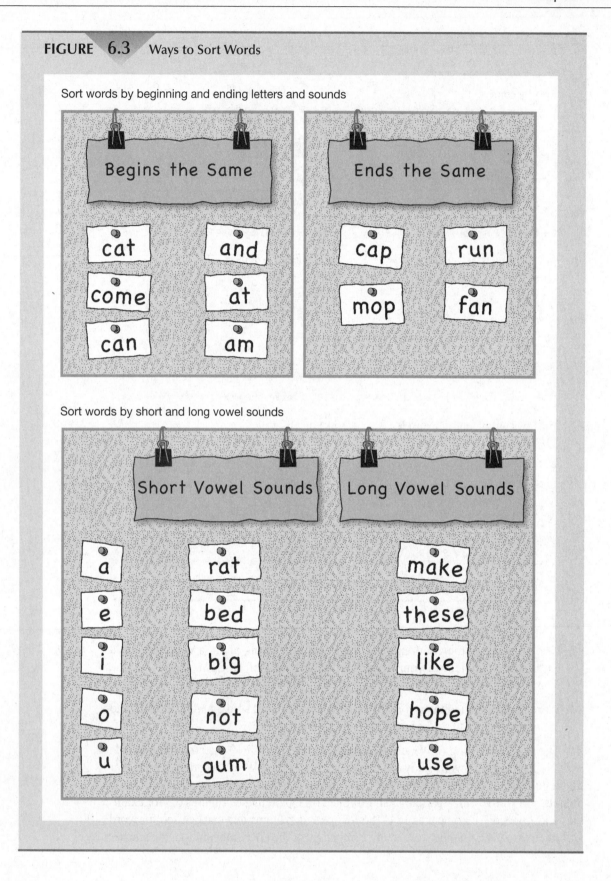

Sort words by beginning and ending letters and sounds

Sort words by short and long vowel sounds

FIGURE   6.3   Ways to Sort Words (continued)

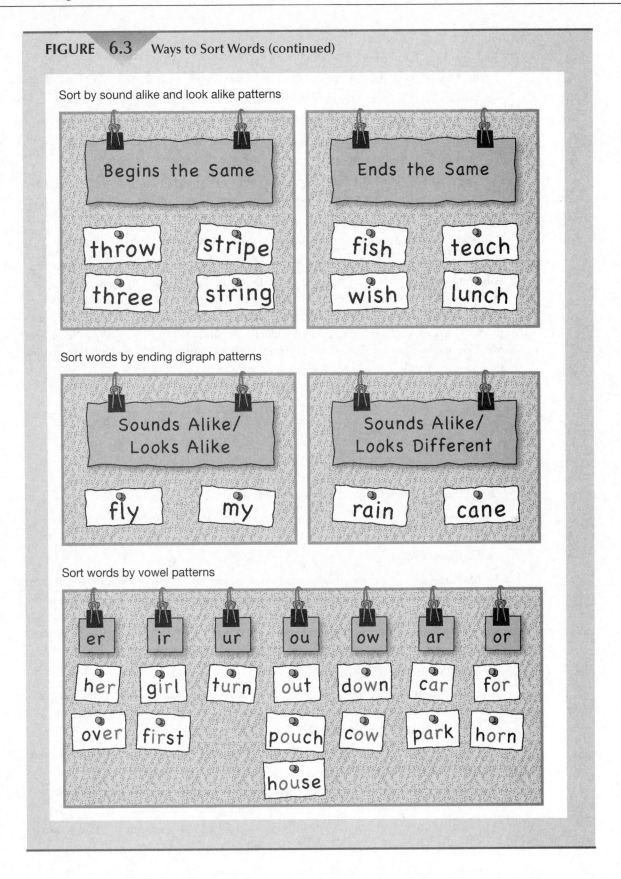

might create a word chart of known patterns; students could use this resource as a spelling tool during the writing component of GRP. Some ways to sort words include:

- Sort by beginning, middle, and ending letters and sounds (*can, come; can, fin*)
- Sort by simple short-vowel rime patterns and sounds (*hat, mat*)
- Sort by beginning and ending letter clusters and sounds (*stop, stump; best, fist*)
- Sort by beginning and ending digraphs and sounds (*the, thin; bath, tooth*)
- Sort by long-vowel rime patterns and sounds (ea—*seat*, ai—*rain*)
- Sort words by *r*-vowel patterns and sounds (*car, shirt*) and other vowel patterns and sounds (*boy, boil; book, cool*)
- Sort words by infrequent vowel patterns (*enough, tough*)
- Sort words by meaningful parts (*do* vs. *undo*; *care* vs. *careless*)

Teachers should examine students' reading and writing for evidence of how they solve unknown words in connected text. Teachers should then use this information along with the word study continuum to plan constructive word study activities (see Figure 6.4 for examples and Appendix F3 on pages 184–186 for word/spelling patterns). A word study intervention would enable students to acquire knowledge for breaking words apart in flexible ways. Here are typical ways that good readers operate on unknown words:

- Letters (*c-a-n*)
- Single consonant onsets and rime (*s-it*)
- Letter cluster onsets and rimes (*str-eet*)
- Inflectional endings (*look-ing*)
- Meaningful and logical units (*str-ee-t*)
- Pronounceable word parts (*an* or *ran* in *ranch*)
- Syllables (*hap-py*)
- Prefixes (*un-do*)
- Suffixes (*week-ly*)

Making connections between words is a powerful way for children to analyze words and to understand how to use known information to assist with unknown words. Children must recognize word parts and understand the concept of substituting, adding, and deleting letters to generalize the process. The following steps provide an example of an instructional framework for learning this process.

1. Have children build a known word.
2. Have children break the word into parts (break word using single consonant or consonant cluster onset and rime or at meaningful and logical units).
3. Have children blend the parts back together to say the word.
4. Have children generate other words that sound the same. Record the words on a large chart or on cards.
5. Have the children sort the words using sound alike/look alike or sound alike categories, and knowledge of word parts and spelling patterns.
6. Draw children's attention to how known words can provide readers and writers with tools for solving unknown words within continuous texts.

FIGURE 6.4 Ways to Break Words

Breaking words letter by letter

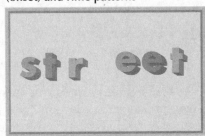

Breaking words using single consonant (onset) and rime patterns

Breaking words using letter clusters (onset) and rime patterns

Breaking words at inflectional endings

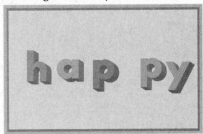

Breaking words at logical units

Breaking words at syllable level

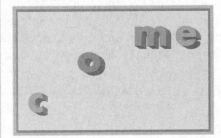

Breaking words at prefix and suffix level

A Word Study Continuum

In order for word study to be effective, teachers must understand that learning about words is a process that is based on a continuum that moves from simple to more complex knowledge about how words work. In Figures 6.5 to 6.8, we present letter and word study activities that develop students' phonological and orthographic knowledge at the emergent, beginning early, late early, and transitional levels (see Appendix F2 on pages 180–183 for guidesheets for word study). In the following chapter, we will refer back to these charts as we discuss the letter- and word-building components of the small-group interventions.

FIGURE 6.5   Becoming Aware of the Phonological and Orthographic Language Systems

Emergent Processing Level
Guided Reading Levels: A–C

Possibilities for Strategic Letter Work

- Reads ABC chart chorally; reads in a variety of ways (reads consonants, reads vowels, every other letter).

- Reads letter books chorally.

- Develops knowledge for how to learn letters (describes path of movement).

- Recognizes and sorts distinguishable features of letters.

- Recognizes and names all upper- and lower-case letters fluently.

- Writes most upper- and lowercase letters fluently.

Possibilities for Strategic Word Work
(Building word knowledge and supporting visual searching processes)

- Builds name letter by letter in left-to-right order using a model and without a model; breaks word (name) letter by letter; rebuilds word (name) letter by letter; reads word (name) with fluency.

- Builds, breaks, and reassembles grade-level, simple high-frequency words letter by letter in a left-to-right order; reads words with fluency.

- Builds simple one-syllable CVC words in left-to-right order; breaks words letter by letter and blends letter sounds back together to say words (*cat, c-a-t, cat, run, r-u-n, run*); reads words with fluency (*is, at, am*).

- Builds simple one-syllable CVC words in a left-to-right order; distinguishes between similarly spelled words by identifying the sounds of the letters that are different (*bat, sat; cat, can; hit, hot*); reads words.

- Records simple high-frequency words or CVC words in personal dictionary using first letter; reads recorded words with fluency.

- Builds known words with CVC pattern; breaks words using onset and rime; blends parts back together; reads words with fluency.

- Builds known words with a CVC pattern; breaks words using onset and rime; rebuilds words; generates other words that sound the same (*h-am, f-an*); manipulates onset to make new words; reads new words with fluency.

FIGURE 6.6 Increasing Awareness of the Phonological and Orthographic Language Systems

Beginning Early Processing Level
Guided Reading Levels: D–E

Possibilities for Strategic Letter Work

- Reads ABC chart chorally.
- Reads letter books chorally.
- Develops knowledge for how to form letter (describe path of movement).
- Recognizes and categorizes distinguishable features of letters.
- Identifies and categorizes letters by vowels and consonants.
- Recognizes and names all upper- and lower-case letters fluently.
- Writes most upper- and lowercase letters fluently.

Possibilities for Strategic Word Work

(Building word knowledge and supporting visual searching processes)

- Builds, breaks, and reassembles simple grade-level high-frequency words letter by letter in a left-to-right order (*w-e-n-t, went*); reads words with fluency.
- Writes simple high-frequency words (grade appropriate) in a personal dictionary using first letter; reads recorded words with fluency.
- Builds simple VC words in left-to-right order; breaks words letter by letter and rebuilds words; reads words with fluency (*is, at, am*).

- Builds simple one-syllable CVC words in left-to-right order; breaks words letter by letter and rebuilds words; reads words with fluency (*cat, c-a-t, cat; run, r-u-n, run*).
- Builds simple one-syllable CVC words in left-to-right order; manipulates consonants or vowels in the beginning, middle, or ending position to make new words (*cat, hat; hot, hit; stop, step*); reads new words with fluency.
- Builds known words with a CVC pattern; breaks words using onset and rime; generates other words that sound the same (*h-am, f-an*); manipulates onset to make new words; reads words with fluency.
- Builds known words with a CVCe pattern in left-to-right order; breaks words letter by letter; rebuilds words letter by letter; reads words with fluency (*have, h-a-v-e*).
- Builds known words in a left-to-right order; adds inflectional endings (*s, ing, ed*) to make new words (*looks, looking, looked*); reads words with fluency.
- Builds words in left-to-right order with consonant clusters and diagraphs in beginning, and ending position; breaks words using onset and rime patterns (*st-ep, f-ish*) or at meaningful and logical units (*sh-i-p, f-i-sh*); builds words; reads words with fluency.

FIGURE   6.7   Gaining Control of the Phonological and Orthographic Language Systems

Late Early Processing Level
Guided Reading Levels: F–G

Possibilities for Strategic Letter Work

- Develops speed, fluency, and ease in identifying and writing all upper- and lowercase letters.

Possibilities for Strategic Word Work

(Building word knowledge and supporting visual searching processes)

- Builds, breaks, and reassembles grade level high-frequency words letter by letter in left-to-right order (*w-h-e-n, when; a-w-a-y, away*); reads words with fluency.

- Reads regularly spelled one-syllable words with fluency using knowledge of word patterns (*much, bake, bring*).

- Reads two-syllable words; breaks words (using basic pattern and syllable knowledge); reads words with fluency (*rab-bit, stop-ping*).

- Reads irregularly spelled words (*said, their, there, none, both*); forms generalizations about words; reads words with fluency.

- Builds base words in a left-to-right order and adds inflectional endings (*-ing, -ed*) (*stop-stopped, stopping*); forms generalizations about word ending; reads words with fluency.

- Builds base words in a left-to-right order; adds (*-s* or *-es*) to base word to form plurals; forms generalizations about word meanings; reads words with fluency (*balls, glasses*).

- Reads regularly spelled, one-syllable short and long vowel words; distinguishes between short (CVC: *cat*) and long vowels (CVCe: *bike*; CVVC: *steep*).

- Builds words with long vowel patterns (vowel teams) in a left-to-right order; breaks words at meaningful and logical units (*sh-e-e-t* or *sh-ee-t* or *sh-eet*; *s-e-a-t* or *s-ea-t* or *s-eat*); attends to vowel word patterns; rebuilds words; reads words with fluency.

- Builds words with long vowel patterns (vowel teams); generates other words that sound the same and look the same; forms generalizations of long vowel word patterns; reads words with fluency.

- Builds words with consonant diagraphs (beginning or ending position) in left-to-right order; breaks words at meaningful and logical units (*sh-ir-t; sh-irt; fish, wash*); attends to diagraphs in beginning or ending position; reads words with fluency.

- Uses known patterns or word parts to build and read new words; reads words with fluency (*stop + day = stay*).

- Builds words with *r* controlled vowels in a left-to-right order; breaks words at meaningful and logical units (*c-a-r* or *c-ar*; *st-a-r-t* or *st-ar-t* or *st-art*); blends parts back together to read words; notices diphthong patterns; generates other words that have the same sound and look the same.

- Builds words with diphthongs in a left-to-right order; breaks words at meaningful and logical units (*h-o-u-s-e* or *h-ou-s-e* or *h-ouse*; *fl-o-w-e-r* or *fl-ow-er*); blends parts back together to read words; attends to diphthong patterns; generates other words that have the same sound and look the same.

- Reads compound words; breaks words at meaningful and logic units (*out-side, sunshine*); forms generalizations about words.

- Builds two known words (*I, am*); removes a letter or letters to form a contraction (*I'm*); forms generalizations about words; reads words with fluency.

- Reads unknown words by breaking words into syllables; uses knowledge that every syllable contains a vowel sound to determine the number of syllables in a printed word; reads words with fluency, (e.g., *can/dy*).

FIGURE 6.8 Developing Control of the Phonological and Orthographic Language Systems

Transitional Processing Level
Guided Reading Levels: H–M

Possibilities for Strategic Word Work

(Building word knowledge and supporting visual searching processes)

- Builds, reads, and writes many high-frequency words with fluency.

- Builds and reads words with long vowel patterns (vowel teams) with fluency.

- Builds words with additional common vowel patterns (vowel teams); breaks words at meaningful and logical units (*l-ou-d, h-oo-p, sn-ow, b-oy, s-oi-l, c-or-n, c-ar-t*); rebuilds words; attends to additional vowel patterns (vowel teams); reads words with fluency.

- Builds and reads words with consonant blends and digraphs in beginning, medial, and ending positions with fluency (*bathtub, spend, splash, chair, whale*).

- Builds regularly spelled two-syllable words with long vowels; uses knowledge of word patterns to make words; breaks words at meaningful and logical units; forms additional generalizations about word patterns; reads words with fluency.

- Builds base words; makes new words by changing letters and adding common prefixes and derivational suffixes; forms generalizations about word meanings (*do* vs. *undo*; *help* vs. *helpful*); reads words with fluency.

- Builds base words; makes new words by adding common prefixes and derivational suffixes (*un, re, mis, ful, less, able*); forms generalizations about base words and changes in meaning when adding or deleting prefixes or suffixes; reads words with fluency.

- Builds base words; makes new words by adding common Latin suffixes (*-tion/sion; -ity, -ment*); forms generalizations about base

words and changes in word meaning when adding Latin suffixes; reads words with fluency.

- Builds base words; makes new words by adding suffixes that form comparatives (*high/ higher/highest*); forms generalization about base words and changes in meaning when adding a comparative suffix; reads words with fluency.

- Builds words with silent consonants; breaks words at meaning and logical units; forms additional generalizations about word patterns; reads words with fluency (*sight, know*).

- Builds and reads a range of contractions (*that's, won't, they're, you've*) with fluency.

- Builds and reads grade-level appropriate irregularly spelled words; forms generalizations about words; reads words with fluency (*through, eyes, busy, people*).

- Builds base words; makes new words by changing and/or adding letter(s) (*s, es*) to form plurals; forms generalizations about word meanings; reads words with fluency (*boys, boxes, stoves*).

- Builds and reads base words; adds inflectional endings (*-ing, -ed*) (*stop-stopped, stopping; lunch, lunches*); forms generalizations about words; reads words with fluency.

- Builds homophones (same pronunciation, but different spelling) or homographs (same spelling, different meanings, and sometimes different pronunciations) using meaning as the basis for building the correct words; forms generalizations about word meanings; reads words with fluency.

- Uses known patterns or word parts to build and read multisyllabic words; reads words with fluency (*whisper, mistake, invention*).

Designing a Word Study Intervention

The goal of word study is to enable the student to understand how words work in order to apply this knowledge for solving unknown words in connected text. In designing word study, teachers must ask three questions:

What does the student understand about words?

What does the student need to understand about words?

How much support will the student need to accomplish the new word-solving task?

A well-designed word study intervention includes four instructional elements: (1) predictable framework with some established routines; (2) clear model using exemplar words that illustrate a learning principle; (3) explicit teaching followed by guided practice; and (4) precise language for scaffolding the student's problem-solving actions. The following is an example of an instructional framework for teaching students a new word.

1. Draw students' attention to the word by pointing to the word while saying it. Use instructional language (e.g., "This word is . . .").

2. Have students observe carefully as you build the word letter by letter in a left-to-right sequence.

3. Do not talk, just model. Make sure the students' eyes are scanning left to right across the word.

4. Read the newly built word as you run your finger under the word in a left-to-right sequence.

5. Provide the students with the correct magnetic letters and ask them to build the word, left to right, paying close attention to the sequence of the letters within the word (provide a model if needed).

6. Have the students run their finger under the word in a left-to-right sequence and check the word.

7. Provide the students with an opportunity to build, check, break, and rebuild the word several times.

8. Provide the students with an opportunity to write the word several times (if fluent, add the word to their personal dictionary or spelling pattern card).

As we discussed earlier, knowledge about words progresses along a continuum of simple to more complex. As students acquire greater competency, teachers adjust their instruction to accommodate students' expanding knowledge. In Figure 6.9, we illustrate how this might look at four points along a processing continuum. In this example, the goal is that students will understand the process of making analogies by using known patterns (onset and rime) to solve unknown words. Each lesson includes three components: (1) the instructional goal for accomplishing the learning task; (2) an assessment prompt that is based on what the students will need to know in order to accomplish the learning task; and (3) an instructional framework for scaffolding the students to acquire the new learning.

FIGURE 6.9 Using an Instructional Framework for Scaffolding Students to Learn about Analogies at Four Points in Time

Instructional Goal 1: Making Analogies across Words—Drawing Students' Attention to the Process of Noticing Word Parts (Onset and Rime)

Assessment Prompt: What do students need to know in order to learn from instruction? Students must be able to break onset from rime and blend the parts back together, and they must know the word in order to learn the process.

Instructional Framework:

1. Have students build a known word.
2. Ask students to break the word into parts using onset and rime.
3. Have the students blend the parts back together to say the word.
4. Instruct students to generate other words that sound the same in the ending position. Record the words on a large chart and underline the ending part. If the students generate a word that sounds the same, but doesn't look the same, tell them that it does sound the same, but it looks different.
5. Draw the students' attention to how using known words and word parts provide readers and writers with tools for solving unknown words fluently within continuous texts.

Instructional Goal 2: Making Analogies across Words—Drawing Students' Attention to the Process of Noticing Word Parts (Onset and Rime or at Meaningful and Logical Units)

Assessment Prompt: What do students need to know in order to learn from instruction? Students must be able to hear and break words into parts, and they must know the word.

Instructional Framework:

1. Have students build the known word _____ (e.g., *start*).
2. Ask students to break the word _____ using onset and rime or at meaningful and logical units (e.g., *start*) into parts (e.g., *st-ar-t* or *st-art*).
3. Instruct the students to blend the parts together and read the word (e.g., *start*).
4. Draw students' attention to how using known parts provides readers and writers with tools for solving unknown words fluently within continuous texts.

Instructional Goal 3: Making Analogies across Words—Drawing Students' Attention to the Process of Using Word Parts to Read New Words

Assessment Prompt: What do students need to know in order to learn from instruction? Students must be able to break onset from rime and blend the parts back together, and they must know the words to learn the process.

Instructional Framework:

1. Have students build the word _____ (e.g., *jump*) and the word _____ (e.g., *stop*).
2. Ask students to break off the first part of the word _____ (e.g., *stop*) and the last part of the word _____ (e.g., *jump*).
3. Tell students to run their finger under the new word and read the word.
4. Draw the students' attention to how using known words and word parts provide readers and writers with tools for solving unknown words fluently within continuous texts.

Instructional Goal 4: Making Analogies across Words—Draw Students' Attention to the Process of Using Known Word Parts to Read Unknown Multisyllabic Words

Assessment Prompt: What do students need to know in order to learn from instruction? Students must be able to break a multisyllabic word into syllables or parts, and they must know the letter patterns or word parts that are needed to take the word apart.

Instructional Framework:

1. Provide the students with an unknown multisyllabic word (write the word on a card for each student or provide the word on a whiteboard).
2. Have the students draw lines to break the word apart or have them write the word in parts to demonstrate how they can look for known parts to read an unknown word.
3. Ask students to blend the parts back together to read the word.
4. Draw the students' attention to how known words and word parts provide readers and writers with tools for solving unknown words fluently within continuous texts.

Closing Thoughts

The ultimate goal of word study is to enable students to decode words rapidly and efficiently in order to keep the focus on message comprehension. If students are unable to transfer their knowledge about words to connected texts, it serves little purpose for the reading act. Therefore, all word study activities must be aligned with the reading and writing processes.

The purpose of this chapter has been to present the rationale for letter and word study in an intervention group. Review Chapters 4 and 5 for more details about how the GRP and AW small-group interventions work together. Each intervention includes a systematic word study component. As you implement these interventions, we encourage you to return to this chapter to assist with the word study component.

Implementing the CIM
as an RtI Method

The Comprehensive Intervention Model (CIM), a systems approach to Response to Intervention (RtI), is grounded in the belief that teachers are the agents of literacy improvement, and that school-embedded professional development creates an authentic context for shaping teacher expertise, thus increasing student achievement. A systems approach to RtI focuses on sustainable improvement by changing the culture of the school. This method places an emphasis on creating structures within the school for promoting teacher collaboration and comprehensive approaches to student learning.

In this final chapter, we provide five case examples[1] of how schools are implementing the CIM as a systemic RtI method. The school examples are framed under five principles:

Principle One: The first wave of literacy defense occurs at the classroom level. An Arkansas district describes how schools use the ESAIL[2] instrument to assess the literacy environment and utilize this information for professional development.

Principle Two: Assessment must be systemic, comprehensive, and multidimensional. A Wisconsin school shares how to implement a comprehensive assessment system that includes an assessment wall[3] to measure systemic changes.

Principle Three: Decision-making teams enable teachers to collaborate on student learning and make informed decisions about interventions. A large school in Wisconsin provides details for organizing and managing collaborative teams for monitoring student progress and aligning interventions across programs.

Principle Four: Alignment between general education and special education creates a seamless intervention model. An Iowa school describes how general education and special education collaborate on a comprehensive intervention plan.

Principle Five: A well-designed RtI plan is an essential component of an effective implementation. A district in Washington State explains how they phased in their CIM, including a plan for training special education teachers in the model.

Case Study Examples

School 1
Assessing the School Environment and Core Instruction

Russellville School District (RSD) consists of six K–4 elementary schools that feed into a fifth-grade upper-elementary school. The RSD enrollment is just over 5,000 students with a total of 53.2 percent eligible for free and reduced lunches. Of the six elementary schools, four are designated as Title I schools. The overall student population is 73 percent Caucasian and 27 percent minorities.

RSD implements the CIM within a layered design as an RtI method. The first layer focuses on high-quality classroom instruction, including a differentiated framework with whole-group, small-group, and individual instruction, as well as an additional classroom layer for students who are lagging behind their peers. The CIM views the classroom as the first line of literacy defense; therefore, the first step in the district's implementation was to examine the school's core literacy program.

Using the ESAIL as a Part of the RtI Method

The Environmental Scale for Assessing Implementation Levels (ESAIL) is an instrument that schools can use to assess their literacy environment. (See Appendix G1 on pages 187–192 for reproducible copy.) The ESAIL identifies specific literacy behaviors that are associated with evidence-based practices. Schools can use the ESAIL for multiple purposes, including: (1) preassessment to determine a school's readiness for implementing a comprehensive literacy model; (2) periodic assessment to study a school's growth over time on one or more literacy criteria; and (3) postassessment to measure a school's improvement over the academic year. Schools can use the ESAIL to guide and monitor schoolwide efforts, including professional development in particular areas.

The RSD used three criteria from the ESAIL to provide baseline data on the school's literacy environment, and to use these data to plan professional development. The literacy coach at each school introduced the ESAIL during the school's literacy team meeting. The coach explained the specific behaviors associated with these criteria: Criterion 1, Creates a Literate Environment; Criterion 2, Organizes the Classroom; and Criterion 4, Uses a Differentiated Approach to Learning (see Figure 7.1 on the following page) for descriptions of each criterion). The staff was invited to ask questions and make comments about the assessment process.

Using the ESAIL at the School Level

The assessment process began by conducting classroom walkthroughs and gathering evidence of specific behaviors under the three criteria. The teachers across classrooms demonstrated a range of competencies, which were based on their experiences with a comprehensive literacy model. Therefore, teachers were not singled out; but rather observations were analyzed for recurring patterns, and the findings were classified as strengths and areas of growth. For instance, in one school, the ESAIL results identified the following strengths across grades:

- Co-constructed anchor charts were used for teaching and learning purposes.

- Tables and desks were arranged to promote collaborative learning.

- Respectful talk and attitudes were promoted and evident among all learners.

- Classroom environment was conducive to inquiry-based learning.

- Instruction was delivered in whole-group, small-group, and individualized settings.

- Routines and procedures were clearly in place.

- The teacher's workspace and instructional materials were well organized.

FIGURE 7.1 Descriptions of Criteria 1, 2, and 4

Criterion 1: Creates a Literate Environment

Teachers create a literate environment by providing a wide variety of reading experiences, including rich and diverse opportunities for students to read, discuss, and write texts across the curriculum. Students' learning at various stages in the reading and writing process is celebrated and displayed on walls within and outside classrooms. Classrooms are arranged to promote whole- and small-group problem-solving discussions. Inquiry-based learning is evident, including relevant and purposeful talk. Respectful talk and attitudes are promoted and used among students, and students' questions are valued by providing additional opportunities for clarifying and seeking information through research.

Criterion 2: Organizes the Classroom

Teachers organize the classroom to meet the needs of diverse learners, including selecting appropriate materials and working with the whole group, small groups, and individual learners. Other features include an emphasis on establishing classroom norms that support the children's ability to self-regulate their literate behaviors for different purposes and across changing contexts, including staying on task, working independently, assuming responsibility for classroom materials, and respecting the rights of others. Teachers' workspace and materials, including assess-

ment notebooks, are organized and used to document learning and plan for instruction. Students' workspace and materials, including students' logs, are organized and easily accessible. Classroom libraries are well organized and contain an abundant amount of reading material across genres, authors, and topics.

Criterion 4: Uses a Differentiated Approach to Learning

Teachers use a workshop approach to learning across the curriculum, including reading, writing, language, and content workshops. Small-group reading and writing instruction is provided to meet the needs of diverse learners; explicit minilessons are tailored to meet the needs of the majority of students across the curriculum. Daily one-to-one conferences are scheduled with students during the workshop framework. Teaching prompts are used to promote problem-solving strategies, higher-order thinking processes, and deeper comprehension. Quality literature is read, enjoyed, and analyzed across the various workshops. A writing continuum is used to meet student needs, plan instruction, and monitor student progress. Writing is taught as a process, including drafting, revising, editing, and publishing processes. Mentor texts and notebooks are used as resources across genres; and inquiry-based learning is promoted and arranged across the content areas.

- Students' materials were organized and easily accessible.
- Explicit minilessons were tailored to meet student needs.
- Quality literature was read, enjoyed, and analyzed across the curriculum.
- Mentor texts were used as resources across genres.

In this example, the ESAIL provided clear evidence of areas where teachers would benefit from professional development. The coaches shared these behaviors, and the teachers selected three areas for professional studies across the year.

- Writing should be taught as a process, and published versions of student work should be on display.

- Writing about reading should be included in the curriculum.

- Students needed more opportunities to engage in elaborated discussions about specific concepts, including an understanding of conversational moves during book discussions.

Additionally, the evidence from the ESAIL documented that most teachers had a good understanding of a comprehensive literacy model, although their practices reflected various levels of knowledge. The teachers used the ESAIL to set professional goals and to self-reflect as they advanced toward these goals. Also, the principal in each school used the ESAIL during classroom observations and teacher conferences. This process promoted a common philosophy within the school, while setting expectations for teacher development and student achievement.

Using the ESAIL at the District Level

At the district level, the ESAIL provided a systematic tool for examining practices across schools; and it created a database for analyzing change over time in instruction and student achievement. The RSD coaches facilitated and coordinated the districtwide process, including identifying the strengths and areas of growth from each school and consolidating these results into a district profile (see Table 7.1 on the following page for example).

The ESAIL provided baseline data for creating a districtwide model for professional growth. In the previous example, the data revealed two specific areas for teacher development.

- Understand the purpose of co-constructed charts for scaffolding student learning.

- Understand the purpose of response logs during reading, writing, and language workshops.

In addition to the district-level goals, the ESAIL provided classroom teachers with data to support their professional goals. In Table 7.1, the grade-level teachers used the ESAIL results to establish learning goals in the following areas:

Kindergarten: Organizing classroom libraries to support students' learning; conducting reading and writing conferences

First grade: Identifying mentor texts for language workshop/read-aloud; creating meaningful and relevant literacy tasks for independent work; organizing literacy assessments

Second grade: Identifying mentor texts for language workshop/read-aloud; organizing classroom library to support students' learning

Third grade: Organizing classroom libraries; conducting one-to-one conferences during reading and writing workshops

TABLE 7.1   Grade Level, Criteria, and Specific Behaviors Indicating Need for Professional Growth

Grade Level	Criterion 1: Creating a Literate Environment
K, 3, 4, 5	Reading responses through writing are displayed on walls and in hallways.
3, 4, 5	Writing is taught as a process and published version is displayed on walls and in hallways.
K, 1, 2	Diverse reading materials are enjoyed, discussed, and analyzed across the curriculum.
1	Tables, clusters of desks, and/or areas are arranged to promote collaborative learning and problem solving.
2	Problem solving is collaborative (pairs or groups) and talk is purposeful.
3	Writing is taught as a process and published version is displayed on walls and in hallways.

Grade Level	Criterion 2: Organizing the Classroom
K, 2, 3, 4, 5	Books in classroom library are organized and labeled according to genre, topic, and/or by author.
K, 2, 3, 4 5	Classroom libraries contain an abundant amount of reading material across genres, authors, and topics.
1	Literature for daily instruction is organized and accessible.
1	Summative and formative assessments are organized for instructional purposes and documentation.

Grade Level	Criterion 3: Using a Differentiated Approach
K, 3	Daily one-to-one reading and writing conferences are scheduled.
K, 1, 2, 3, 4, 5	Mentor texts and notebooks are used as resources across genres.
1, 2, 4, 5	Quality literature is read, enjoyed, and analyzed across the curriculum.

Fourth grade: Identifying mentoring texts for language workshop/read-aloud; organizing classroom library to support students' learning

Fifth grade: Identifying mentor texts for language workshop/read-aloud; organizing classroom library to support students' learning

Closing Thoughts

The Russellville School District is committed to a systemic and comprehensive RtI method for school improvement. The district plan is grounded in four essential elements: (1) provide the highest quality core instruction for all students; (2) increase teacher expertise for differentiating instruction to meet student needs; (3) provide appropriate interventions for students who are responding to classroom instruction; and (4) use varied assessments to monitor improvement at multiple levels, including school, classroom, and individual levels. The ESAIL provides a valuable tool for examining the relationship of instruction to student achievement.

School 2:
Creating a Seamless Assessment
System for Systemic Improvement

Washington School for Comprehensive Literacy is located in Sheboygan, Wisconsin, a city of about 50,000 people positioned on the shores of Lake Michigan. The K–5 school has an enrollment of 325 students. It is one of fifteen elementary schools in the Sheboygan Area School district, which serves almost 10,000 students. Eighty-five percent of the students qualify for free or reduced lunch. English is a second language for 42% of the students. In addition, the school is part of Wisconsin's Student Achievement Guarantee in Education (SAGE) program that ensures a student-to-teacher ratio of 18:1 in kindergarten through third grade.

The school implements the CIM as its RtI method. As described in Chapter 2, this method uses a Comprehensive Assessment System (CAS) for monitoring progress at the individual and the system level. The CAS includes multiple assessments (summative and formative) that provide teachers with varied sources for adjusting instruction and selecting appropriate interventions for students (see Appendix G2 on pages 193–195 for assessment system; also see Meyer & Reindl, 2010). The staff understands that assessment must inform instruction; therefore, assessments are revisited periodically and revised based on curricula changes and student needs.

Once the assessment system is in place, a process for organizing the data is initiated. Teachers use the data collection sheet (see Appendix G3 on page 196) at five data points during the year (three weeks after school begins and again at the end of every quarter). The form uses four proficiency categories—below, approaching, meeting, exceeding—for charting student progress. The form includes a column titled "Conference Notes" in both the reading and writing sections. Each data form includes a place for teachers to mark any special services received by the student. The student's progress is discussed in team meetings that occur around the school's assessment wall.

Using an Assessment Wall

The assessment wall presents a visual display of the school's ability to meet the needs of all students. It provides a tool for assessing the impact of curriculum and intervention(s) on students' learning. As an RtI method, it becomes a focal point for problem-solving discussions around students' progress. Each student has two cards on the wall: one for reading and one for writing (teacher and student names are coded to protect their identities). The wall is divided into four sections (below, approaching, meeting, exceeding) to match the proficiencies from the data sheet. At each data point teachers bring their data forms to grade-level team meetings and move their students' cards on the assessment wall.

If a student is proficient in all assessments, the teacher places the student's card under this category on the wall. However, the decisions about placement

Student cards are moved after grade-level teams review students' assessment forms.

are not always clear-cut. When this occurs, teachers present their questions and concerns to team meetings. For example, a student may be reading at proficiency on the text-level assessment, but the teacher's conference notes and independent reading rubric indicate that the child is at the approaching level. These situations encourage teachers to collaborate on teaching and learning solutions. In the case of this same student, the team might recommend placing the student in the approaching column on the wall, while setting goals for supporting the student during independent reading.

Interventionists also attend grade-level team meetings when teachers update cards on the wall. As classroom teachers and interventionists work together to build and maintain the assessment wall, this partnership creates a shared responsibility for the students' learning.

Screening Process and Intervention Teams

The goal of any intervention is to support struggling students to be successful in the classroom. Therefore, the assessment wall is used to screen students who are not responding to classroom instruction. The screening process begins during grade-level meetings that focus on updating the wall. If a student is not responding to core instruction, the classroom teacher identifies a classroom intervention (Tier 1) and places a colored dot on the student's card that corresponds to a specific level. At these grade-level team meetings, the principal, literacy coach, and an intervention specialist participate to help promote collaboration, communication, and seamlessness across interventions. Based on the data, the team recommends diagnostic assessment (see Chapter 2) for students who need additional interventions. For each layer, a different colored dot is used on the student cards.

Immediately after all grade-level teams have met and the assessment wall is completely updated, an intervention team meeting is scheduled. The purpose is to continue the screening process and to collaborate among interventionists. Prior to the meeting, the literacy coaches prepare a list of students in the below or approaching categories, plus the students' layers of intervention as indicated on the data collection sheet. Students without intervention are highlighted, and the team requests another type of meeting (classified as As-Needed Intervention meeting) for discussing these students.

The As-Needed Intervention meetings are designed for problem solving around individual students and can be convened by anyone with a concern. All teachers bring their data and evidence, such as response logs, running records, reading and writing behavior checklists, and writing samples. The meeting begins with a review of the evidence, followed by collaborative planning for aligning the student's intervention across programs (see Chapter 1 for description of the intervention planner). Everyone receives a copy of the intervention plan, and a date for the next meeting is confirmed.

The fourth type of meeting is a vertical team meeting, during which all the grades and specialists across the school gather to review the assessment wall and discuss professional development goals. For example, the team noticed that students' writing was lagging behind their reading; consequently,

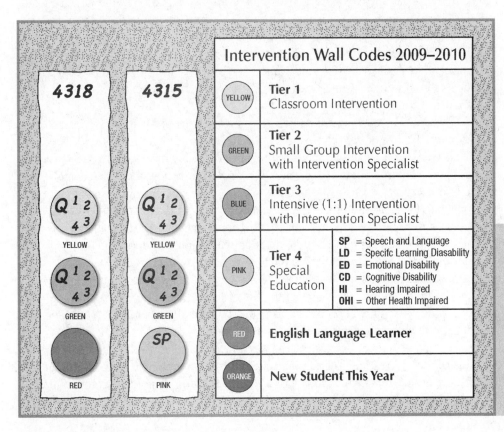

Teachers place colored dots on each student's card to indicate different tiers of intervention support. Teacher and student codes are used to protect identities.

the teachers initiated professional studies on the reading/writing connection. Vertical team meetings promote a systems approach to RtI, and occur once or twice per month when the students are released from school early.

Closing Thoughts

A comprehensive and systemic approach to RtI requires an assessment system for monitoring progress at both individual and system levels. The school's philosophy is grounded in four assessment principles: (1) assessment should involve multiple perspectives and sources of data; (2) assessment must be contextualized and provide evidence of students' learning, knowledge, and problem solving in connected texts; (3) assessment must reflect the curriculum and provide insights into effective instruction; and (4) team meetings provide teachers with a collaborative structure for providing responsive interventions to meet student needs. Within this multidimensional approach, teaching and learning are viewed as reciprocal processes, and the teacher is the agent of assessment.

School 3
Collaboration Teams for Decision Making

Anne Sullivan Elementary School is a large school (675 students, 120 staff members, 2 literacy coaches, and 14 interventionists) located in the Green Bay, Wisconsin, school district. The school has been implementing the CIM as its RtI method for two years. The school has a poverty index of 83 percent with an ethnically diverse student body: Hispanic (45%), Caucasian (34%), African American (9%), Asian (8%), and Native American (4%). Fifty-one percent of students are English language learners (ELLs) and 19 percent have an individualized education plan (IEP).

The Sullivan teachers are dedicated to meeting the needs of all students. However, the size of the school has required a creative approach for coordinating and managing its RtI method. In the past, Thursday mornings were reserved for As-Needed Intervention team meetings. After reflection, the coaches realized the meetings were only placement meetings: teachers brought data on the student and a decision to place the student into intervention was made. These meetings were not used to tailor the instruction for the student. In fact, once a student was receiving intervention, most collaboration was done "on the run." Time and space were not reserved during the day for the discussion around seamless instruction for the students. It was evident that the collaboration process should be restructured to meet the literacy requirements of the students.

A student-centered approach was needed where all stakeholders could work collaboratively, share accountability, and create incremental learning goals based on student data. Because of the size of the school, the staff needed to think of a way to efficiently monitor and tailor intervention for a large number of students. Teachers envisioned a process where multiple collaboration teams could meet simultaneously on a weekly basis. This would allow the literacy coaches to be available to support all collaboration meetings. Teachers would engage in brief, focused discussions around student data and collaborative interventions. In order for these discussions to be meaningful and student centered, an analysis of the student's literacy processing behaviors would have to occur.

Scheduling for Intervention Meetings

The first step in restructuring was to locate a space where simultaneous team meetings could take place. The library was selected because it had a large area with many tables, and each table could house a separate collaboration meeting. During meetings, the literacy coaches could move from table to table to offer support; and the 14 intervention teachers could facilitate the meetings to focus on four goals: (1) monitor time limits to ensure that all stakeholders contribute to the process; (2) keep the focus on what the child can do; (3) develop common goals and agree on common language to achieve the goal; and (4) set a date to reconvene the group to monitor and adjust goals.

A master list of all stakeholders who provided interventions was created, and all interventionists met in the library to plan the schedules. The interventionists agreed to meet with each team, and to focus on one or two grade levels each week. The collaboration meetings were scheduled to take place before classes began, and would last for 45 minutes with 15-minute sessions per team. With fourteen interventionists on staff, the school could potentially have forty-two different collaboration meetings weekly. Collaboration meetings were scheduled two weeks in advance, which allowed all stakeholders time to review and analyze student data prior to the meeting.

Using Data to Drive Instruction

Once the schedule was established, the staff identified the data sources to be examined during each intervention meeting. These included two running records, a writing sample, and anecdotal notes. The Literacy Collaboration Plan (see an example in Figure 7.2) was used to document a student's progress during interventions. Reading and writing interventions were tracked with the codes at each tier; reading levels were placed under the proper heading in the aligning grade; and a space for meeting dates documented the frequency of collaborations around the student. (See Appendix G4–G5 on pages 197–198 for reproducible forms).

The various reading, writing, and orthographic behavior checklists (see Appendix G6 on pages 199–202) provided teachers with tools for monitoring and recording literacy behaviors. The checklists describe essential, but overt behaviors, that indicate progression over time in literacy processing. The checklists were supported with evidence from running records and/or writing samples. Teachers recorded the date when a literacy behavior was observed and used this information to make decisions about instruction. The Collaboration Goal Sheet (see Appendix G5 on page 198) was used to summarize critical

FIGURE 7.2 Example of One Student's Literacy Collaboration Plan

Literacy Collaboration Plan

Student name: _____ Grade: __I__ Date: _3/31/10_

Classroom teacher: _____ Interventionist: _____

Other staff that works with the student: _N/A_ _____

Literacy related goal from I.E.P. ____N/A____ _____

Reading Interventions			Writing Interventions		
Code	Tier I Reading	Tier II Reading	Code	Tier I Writing	Tier II Writing
1:1 Rd	Additional 1:1 Conferences		1:1 W	Additional 1:1 Conferences	
WW	Additional Word Work		AW	Assisted Writing	Assisted Writing
GR+	Guided Reading Plus (20 min.)	Guided Reading Plus (30 min.)	PW	Process Writing	Process Writing
AW	Assisted Writing	Assisted Writing	CF		Comprehension Focus Group
RR		Reading Recovery	O	Oracy Group	Oracy Group

	Reading Levels				Use Codes from Above		Comments: Include if the child is making progress (MP) or no progress (NP) and any adjustment to intervention plan.
	Fall	Tri 1	Tri 2	Tri 3	Tier I	Tier II	
Kindergarten				B			
1st Grade	B	D	F			RR	MP. Entered RR in 2/10. Steady gains.
2nd Grade							
3rd Grade							
4th Grade							
5th Grade							

Next Meeting Date: _____ _____ _____ _____ _____ _____ _____ _____ _____ ___

behaviors from the collaborative analysis of student data. The interventionist made a copy of the goal sheet, and the original was placed in the student's intervention folder (see Figure 7.3).

Closing Thoughts

The staff at Anne Sullivan Elementary recognized the importance of restructuring the intervention meetings for greater communication. The collaboration meetings were designed to meet two goals: (1) align interventions across classroom and supplemental settings, and (2) promote open and frequent communication about student progress. The value of the meetings was captured in the comments from one first-grade teacher: "The collaboration meetings create seamlessness for the child and lessen confusion because the interventionist and I are using a common language. It is rewarding to know that I am helping the children transfer their knowledge from intervention into the classroom and to help them succeed in the long run."

FIGURE 7.3 Example of Collaborative Goal Sheet

Student name: _____ Date: 3/3/10 _____ Grade: 1 _____
Teachers: _____

Reading Behaviors   Guided Reading Level: 8IE

The student currently controls:	The student needs to control next:	Common language for teachers to use:
·Reading sounds phrased/fluent with great expression. ·Leads with Meaning/Structure upon difficulty	- Slow down to notice detail in print (L→R) -Look for parts in words -L→R scanning (seq. lapses)	-Does that look right? "-Something doesn't look right." -Can you find a part you know. +First letter first!

Writing Behaviors

The student currently controls:	The student needs to control next:	Common language for teachers to use:
-Generating a meaningful story with great detail/voice. -Writing HFW quickly (strong visual memory)	-use lowercase letters in writing -Listen to the sounds she hears (impulsive, seq. lapses)	(Giving her options of what looks right: E or e? Having her choose. -Say it slowly, what sounds can you hear?

Word Work: Circle All That Apply

The student currently controls:	The student needs to control next:	Common language for teachers to use:
Fast/L.I.D. Matching lwrcase/uppercase	-use analogies to help assist in reading/writing upon difficulty. -Letter formation (n,h,r)	Listen for the parts that sound the same in... "down, up, over • Look took book

x (ing) wordwork "say it slowly and make your finger

Oral Language Development: Circle All That Apply

The student currently controls:	The student needs to control next: match what you see!"
• Asks/answers questions to express understanding • Uses specific vocabulary to express ideas • Uses age appropriate grammar • Understands concepts used in verbal directions • Uses age appropriate speech sounds • Produces complete sentences	N/A

Please bring Literacy Folder with current running record and writing sample.

School 4
Aligning Classroom and Special Education

The Council Bluffs Community School District is located in southwest Iowa along the scenic Missouri River. With a preschool through twelfth grade student population of just over 9,200 students, Council Bluffs is the eighth largest district in the state of Iowa. Thirteen elementary schools have an average free and reduced lunch rate of 62 percent as compared to 67 percent districtwide. In addition to the thirteen elementary schools, there are two middle schools that serve grades six through eight and three high schools.

Last year, four elementary schools implemented the Partnerships in Comprehensive Literacy (PCL) model and the CIM. All four schools worked toward full implementation with literacy coaches, model classroom teachers, interventionists for general education students, special education interventionists, and external support from the district literacy coach, CIM coaches, and the special education strategic processing coach. Professional development followed each school's individual improvement plan, which was designed to support the aspects of the model and was monitored by the building principal through assessment wall analysis, daily observations, walkthroughs, and feedback. All professional development sessions were carefully planned with the end result of higher student achievement for all students.

As the state requirements for identifying special education students changed in Iowa, the need to design a seamless process for identifying students and monitoring student progress that would align with current work within the PCL model was critical. A systematic way of aligning general education with special education in the area of interventions was also needed. Coordinating the current use of the assessment wall with the state's new Child Find model involved a variety of stakeholders, which included district administrators, building principals, building literacy coaches, district coaches, and special education teachers. The initial plan was developed collaboratively by the district's supervisor of elementary education, supervisor of special education, district special education strategic processing coach, and district literacy coach. After an initial draft was created, it was presented to a small group of principals and literacy coaches who had been engaged in the model. After more input, the plan was presented to the special education interventionists for additional suggestions. The final draft was presented to building staff through site-based professional development, and the buildings began to pilot the process. The voices of each group were essential in order to design the best system for student identification and ongoing monitoring that would have the greatest impact on student achievement, yet provide a seamless process for all stakeholders.

The RtI Process

In order to provide a seamless approach for identification and intervention for all students, the assessment wall provided a natural starting point to determine intervention services for students. Our district termed the intervention process *Determining Appropriate Intervention Services (DAIS)*. As a result of the collaborative meetings mentioned previously, the district developed a flowchart (Figure 7.4) to illustrate the process of identifying students for interventions as well as monitoring their progress. The first step in the process was to make sure that common assessments were used to determine placement on the assessment wall. This was achieved through a district assessment matrix and was critical due to a high mobility rate. The plan had to ensure that students who were served in an intervention at one building would receive the same intervention at the next building so the student's instructional program would not be interrupted.

The leadership team determined which students would receive an intervention and which students would continue to make adequate progress through core instruction from the classroom teacher. The leadership team consisted of the building principal, building literacy coach, and a critical mass of teacher representatives.

FIGURE **7.4** Flowchart Determining Appropriate Intervention Services

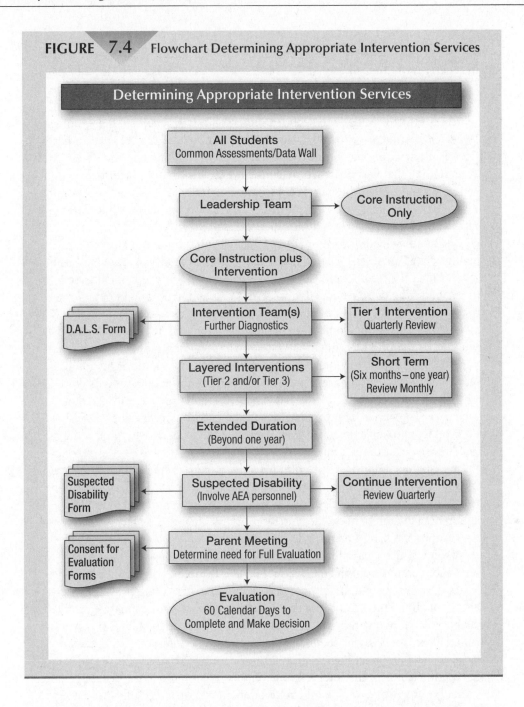

Determining Appropriate Intervention Services

Once the determination was made for students to receive an intervention, a separate team, which consisted of both regular and special education interventionists, a collection of classroom teachers, literacy coach, and building principal, then met to determine which students would be chosen to receive further diagnostic testing to determine appropriate intervention services. *It is important to note that the building principal was a key participant in both teams. As the instructional leader, the principal must have knowledge of the process and interventions in order to give suggestions and recommendations for placement of students.* The intervention team also must decide which students would be able to receive an intervention based on the available resources at the building. Every effort was made to secure an intervention for each student who was placed in either basic or below basic on the assessment wall. This was either a Tier 1 intervention that was provided by the classroom teacher or a Tier 2 or 3 intervention that was provided by an interventionist. After placements had been made and further diagnostic testing was completed within a few days, the intervention team was reconvened and all available data were used to determine the appropriate intervention.

During this meeting time, a DAIS form was used to record student interventions. The forms (see Appendix G7 on pages 203–206) were adapted from the RtI Plan for Aligning and Layering Interventions (Figure 1.4, Chapter 1). All teachers who were responsible for providing an intervention kept a form for each child to document the intervention and progress for the student. A student file was kept in a binder by the intervention team to update during monthly or quarterly meetings. This literacy intervention plan was completed by the entire group as the interventional groundwork was laid for the child. Not only did every student receive the universal program, but students who received an intervention also may have received more intensive instruction in the core. The classroom teacher was also responsible to provide the first tier of intervention. The teacher and team marked the areas where the student would receive additional services as well as record baseline data, discrepancy to peers, and the plan for monitoring the student's progress. The student status was also marked on the side of the page according to each quarterly move on the data (assessment) wall. During each move, the team completed the intervention plan to comment on the student progress, decide on a date to meet, and then recommend action on the intervention.

When the intervention team determined that a student was to receive a Tier 1 intervention from the classroom teacher, the team conducted a quarterly review of the student's progress during the next assessment wall move. During that time, the team again reviewed the assessment data and determined whether to continue with a Tier 1 intervention or provide an additional intervention, Tier 2 or 3. If a student needed an additional intervention, the team placed the student in an intervention group according to need and assigned an intervention teacher. The intervention could be a one-on-one intervention, such as Reading Recovery, or a small-group intervention such as Guided Reading Plus. Regardless of the type of support, any student who received either a Tier 2 or Tier 3 intervention was closely monitored until the first progress monitoring cycle had been completed and the interventionists, intervention team, and classroom teacher met to determine if the student would more than likely accelerate from the intervention within six months to a year or whether the student may need an extended intervention beyond a year.

If it was determined that the student needed an ongoing intervention, the team completed a state-mandated form that indicated the student may have a learning disability that could be interfering with his academic progress. *It is important to note that throughout the process, a student may be moved to a suspected disability form at any time based on the available data. Every effort should be made to provide an intervention to struggling students, but there may be some instances when the data indicate an immediate need for special education services.* If a disability was suspected, the student continued to receive an appropriate intervention throughout the entire process until a determination of program had been established.

During the suspected disability stage, the intervention team including the classroom teacher, AEA representative, and all teachers directly involved with the education of the student completed a state form. In this form, the team decided whether the student may have had a disability or if the student had other outside factors that may have been influencing the student's academic performance. The outside factors may include lack of quality instruction, English language proficiency, attendance problems, mobility, cultural expectations, and/or lack of prior knowledge. If it was determined that an outside factor was the root cause for poor academic performance, the team reviewed the progress of the student, analyzed the response to the intervention, continued with the intervention with necessary changes, and checked back again with the intervention team on a quarterly basis.

A student who had no outside factors influencing performance and showed little growth and limited response to the intervention continued to move through the process of determining an appropriate intervention. The parent was contacted and a meeting was scheduled so that everyone could discuss the student's progress. At that time, the team determined whether a full evaluation for special education services was warranted. If the parents and the team agreed to an evaluation, the consent for evaluation form was completed and the evaluation process began. The evaluation process did not interfere with the student's current intervention. The special education team conducted further testing outside of the intervention to gain additional information on the student's academic proficiency, while the student continued to receive an intervention. After 60 calendar days, the intervention team reconvened with the parents and shared data and progress. A decision was made to either place the student into special education or continue to serve the student in general education with additional interventions. This decision was based on collected data and progress in the current intervention.

If a student was placed in special education, the student continued to receive a high-quality intervention. *In our district, special education teachers have been trained in the interventions presented through CIM.* Because the student had been placed in a special education program, the student will likely receive the Tier 4 intervention either individually or in a smaller group, which may not have been possible in a Tier 2 or 3 intervention, which is delivered by a general education interventionist. All interventionists who provided either a Tier 2, 3, or 4 intervention documented progress on a literacy intervention plan. The supplemental teacher form (see

Appendix G7 on pages 203–206) was completed at the time of placement as the team made decisions on which intervention would best benefit the student. The interventionist recorded the type of intervention, baseline data, discrepancy to peers, and the intended plan for progress monitoring. In addition to this information, the interventionist and team determined the schedule for intervention, data that would be collected to share at the next intervention meeting, and any pertinent notes. On the reverse side of the plan, the interventionist summarized assessment information quarterly and recorded any changes made to the intervention as a result of student data analysis. The classroom teacher had a similar form that she completed while providing a Tier 1 intervention. The purpose of the forms not only served as documentation of the interventions, but they also held each teacher accountable for his/her part in the academic success of the child. The classroom teacher provided the first intervention for the student. Then as the interventions were layered onto the student, each interventionist did his/her part by meeting regularly with the teacher to discuss student progress and also meet with the intervention team to determine next steps.

Closing Thoughts

Each student who received an intervention had a team of teachers, interventionists, a literacy coach, and a principal monitoring his progress and adjusting the interventions to ensure he was receiving the best possible educational program that would translate into higher student achievement. The use of the assessment wall combined with a thoughtfully crafted plan for identifying students in need of assistance, intervening with tailored instruction, and systematically monitoring student progress resulted in an increase in student achievement for not only the general education population but the special education population as well.

School 5
Implementing a Comprehensive Plan for School Improvement

Spokane Public Schools is the largest school district in eastern Washington State, consisting of thirty-four elementary schools, six middle schools, six comprehensive high schools and a vocational skills center. Of the diverse population of 28,881 students, 50.7 percent qualify for free or reduced-price meals. English language learners (ELLs) in the district speak more than fifty different languages.

Four years ago, the district implemented the CIM as its RtI process. The plan was in reaction to district concerns on the overidentification of students to special education. This reality required a comprehensive and systemic plan for school improvement, including collaborative structures for changing teacher perceptions, instructional practices, and intervention approaches. The plan included four systemic goals: (1) reduce the number of students referred to special education; (2) increase the achievement level of students with learning disabilities; (3) provide specialized training in responsive interventions to special education teachers; and (4) create a seamless process between special education and general education programs.

The first step in the improvement process began with an examination of all programs and interventions within the district. The Special Programs Department, which included Title I and other federal and state compensatory programs, analyzed the existing interventions. Simultaneously, the curriculum directors and support staff analyzed the effectiveness of the district's core programs on student achievement. This information was presented to the district's administrative staff and to a joint committee reviewing the existing special education model.

At the intervention level, there was ample evidence documenting the success of the Reading Recovery program with the lowest 20 percent of first graders. Also, the small-group interventions within the CIM showed positive results for struggling readers in the primary grades. At the classroom level, the core program was designed to provide differentiated instruction within small groups. However, the data indicated that many students were at risk of reading failure; and special education had become the first intervention for those students.

After the district completed its analysis of programs, this information was used to create a districtwide RtI plan. The RtI goals focused on three areas of school improvement: (1) increase the quality of the classroom core with an emphasis on differentiated instruction to meet the needs of all students; (2) provide professional development in the CIM to intervention teachers; and (3) provide in-depth training to special education teachers in the Guided Reading Plus (GRP) and Comprehension Focus group interventions.

The CIM became the model for early intervening services in the district. A prereferral process was embedded in all elementary buildings to monitor early intervening services for any student not meeting the standards. The process included progress-monitoring data, intervention team meetings, and documentation of layered intervention support. Standardized procedures for monitoring progress and collecting data were initiated to measure achievement outcomes, as well as implementation integrity of the CIM relative to GRP. Teachers were given a checklist of specific teaching behaviors that were expected during GRP; coaches used this form during observations (see Appendix G8 on page 207). Also, the teachers used the checklist to plan small group instruction and to self-reflect on their own performance. Professional development was provided for building administrators regarding evidence of implementation of small-group intervention during instructional supervision.

The district's plan focused on implementing a comprehensive literacy design for school improvement. The process included six components: (1) identify the problem; (2) review the effectiveness of existing programs in the district; (3) provide classroom teachers with professional development on implementing a workshop framework; (4) train elementary interventionists in guided reading plus and assisted writing; (5) train upper level interventionists in comprehension focus groups; and (6) train special education teachers in the CIM. An important goal of the implementation plan was to develop congruency across classroom instruction, supplemental interventions, and special education programs, while building structures for teacher collaboration across the different contexts.

Closing Thoughts

The Spokane School District recognized the need for a comprehensive and systemic approach to RtI. Many of the problems associated with special education referrals were rooted in systemic issues. The CIM provided a professional development framework for increasing teachers' knowledge about reading interventions, thereby, preventing the reading failure of at-risk students and increasing the reading achievement of students with disabilities. Since its inception, thirty-seven literacy coaches, seventy elementary Special Education teachers, and twenty-one intervention teachers have received training in the intervention groups. In one year, the teachers had reduced the number of referrals to special education by more than 110 students. The next step in the district's plan is to train special education coaches, who will then be able to train special education teachers in the small-group interventions. As an RtI method, the CIM has provided a structure for aligning interventions, developing a common philosophy, and promoting collaboration across general education, Title I, and Special Education.

 **Putting It All Together**

In this final chapter, we have focused on the importance of teachers working together to support the struggling learner. Each school emphasized a decision-making model that used teacher collaboration as the heartbeat of the RtI method. Critical components of each school included: (a) developing expertise for teaching the struggling reader, (b) using assessment to inform and monitor student progress, (c) aligning instruction across programs, (d) providing interventions prior to referring a student for special education, and (e) implementing intervention teams to support student learning.

A central theme is that teams of teachers with a common philosophy and a united goal can accomplish more than the individual teacher working alone. This is especially important when teaching the struggling reader, since incongruent instruction can exacerbate the learner's confusions. All teachers must be knowledgeable about literacy processing and the changes that occur over time as a student progresses along a learning continuum. Equally important, teachers must understand the relationship of assessment to teaching and vice versa. If a student is not responding to instruction, the assessment could be inappropriate, thus providing the teacher with flawed data for planning (and monitoring) the best intervention to meet the student's needs. As a result, the referral process for special education may be grounded in a defective process, leading to the overidentification of students with disabilities.

Intervention teams provide teachers with a problem-solving structure for examining a student's learning across multiple contexts and for aligning instruction to promote the transfer of knowledge across these settings. Teachers use varied assessments to make decisions about how a student is responding to instruction; they establish progress-monitoring intervals for checking on the impact of interventions on student growth.

We end this book with a quote from an earlier text, *Apprenticeship in Literacy* (Dorn, French, & Jones, 1998), which continues to guide our philosophy of a comprehensive and systemic model for school improvement.

> Systemic change lies in our understanding of how children learn and in our ability to problem solve with colleagues who work with our children, who share our common experiences, and who speak our language of literacy (p. 160).

NOTES

1. The schools spotlighted in this chapter are part of the Partnerships in Comprehensive Literacy (PCL) network. The PCL model uses the Comprehensive Intervention Model as a system intervention. System interventions focus on increasing the expertise of teachers for meeting the unique needs of their struggling readers. This is in contrast to program interventions, which can be scripted or packaged, that are unable to respond to the individual characteristics of struggling readers. The five schools in this chapter provide examples of how educators can work together to improve schools. We owe a special acknowledgment to the literacy coaches and district leaders who contributed the case examples in this chapter.

2. The Environmental Scale for Assessing Implementation Levels (ESAIL) was developed by Dorn and Soffos in 2005 to provide schools with a measure for assessing literacy change at the systems level. The ESAIL is used at three points in time: beginning of year (baseline data), midyear (progress-monitoring data), and end-of-year (post data). At the initial level, the ESAIL is used for school planning with a focus on professional development in areas of growth. With a focus on patterns across the school (in contrast to individual teachers), the instrument provides a tool for promoting a shared vision, congruent practices, and collaboration among staff. Since its creation, the ESAIL has been used in approximately 200 schools as a critical component of school improvement.

3. The assessment wall was first discussed in *Shaping Literate Minds: The Development of Self-Regulated Learners* (Dorn & Soffos, 2001b). This concept was based on the original work of David Kerbow and colleagues (1999), who described how an assessment wall could be used to monitor students' growth over time on text reading levels. In PCL and CIM schools, this measure was used for several years; however, a text reading level by itself did not provide a comprehensive look at a student's learning. As a result, we recognized the importance of expanding the assessment system to include multiple and varied assessments (mostly formative) that would provide a more complete profile of a student's learning. Vicki Atland, a literacy coach in Arkansas, conceptualized the idea of a comprehensive assessment system as the basis of the current assessment wall (see Dorn & Soffos, in press; Dorn & Henderson, 2010; Meyer & Reindl, 2010 for more details).

Appendices

127

Appendix A1

RtI Plan for Aligning and Layering Literacy Interventions

Student Goal: Developing a Self-Regulated Learner

Student _____ Grade _____ Classroom Teacher _____ Date _____

DEGREES OF INTENSITY →

LAYERS OF SUPPORT/EXPERTISE ↔

		Individual	Small Group	Whole Class	Independent Work
Classroom: Tier 1	**Universal**	☐ Reading Conference ☐ Writing Conference	**Small Group (4–5)** ☐ Guided Reading Group ☐ Literature Discussion Group ☐ Reading and Writing Conferences ☐ Language Investigations ☐ Genre, Text, and Author Studies ☐ Tailored Minilessons	☐ Read Aloud ☐ Shared Reading ☐ Minilessons ☐ Spelling/Phonics ☐ Share Time	☐ Familiar/Easy Reading ☐ Writing Process ☐ Phonics or Vocabulary Tasks ☐ Literature Extensions ☐ Research Projects ☐ Internet Projects
Intervention Specialist	**Intervention**	**1:1 or Small Group (2–3)** ☐ Reading Conference ☐ Writing Conference	**Small Group (4–5)** ☐ Word Study (prior to Guided Reading) ☐ Writing about Reading (following Guided Reading) ☐ Assisted Writing Group ☐ Writing Process Group (push-in)	Plan/Monitoring/Duration	
	Tier 2	**Small Group (2–3)** ☐ Guided Reading Plus Group ☐ Comprehension Focus Group ☐ Assisted Writing Group ☐ Writing Process Group (push-in)	**Small Group (4–5)** ☐ Guided Reading Plus Group ☐ Comprehension Focus Group ☐ Assisted Writing Group ☐ Writing Process Group (push-in)	Plan/Monitoring/Duration	
	Tier 3	**1:1** ☐ Reading Recovery ☐ Targeted Intervention (beyond first grade)		Plan/Monitoring/Duration	
Special Education	**Tier 4**	**1:1** ☐ Targeted Intervention	**Small Group (2–5)** ☐ Guided Reading Plus Group ☐ Comprehension Focus Group ☐ Assisted Writing Group ☐ Writing Process Group (push-in)	Plan/Monitoring/Duration	

Team Members Present _____ Next Meeting: _____

Adapted and used with permission from *The Journal of Reading Recovery*.

Appendix A

Appendix B1

Progress Monitoring Form

Progress Monitoring **Grade 1**		Student:										Teacher:										
Book Level	Record Instructional Level																					
J																						
I																						
H																						
G																						
F																						
E																						
D																						
C																						
B																						
A																						
<A																						
Book Title, Accuracy Rate, Self-Correction Rate																						
Date of Progress Monitoring Interval																						
Week of Intervention	01			08					16					24					32	Post-test		
Tier 1																						
Tier 2																						
Tier 3																						
Tier 4																						

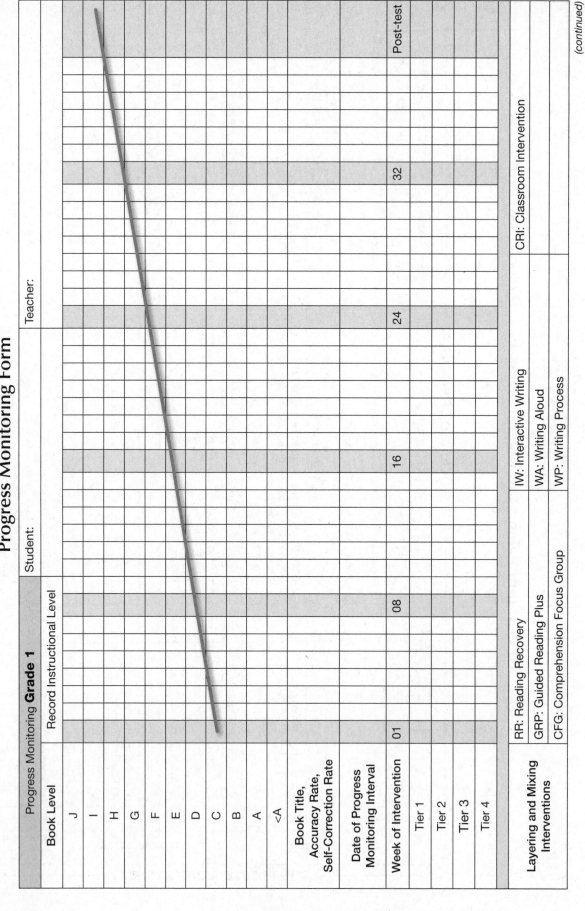

Layering and Mixing Interventions	RR: Reading Recovery	IW: Interactive Writing	CRI: Classroom Intervention
	GRP: Guided Reading Plus	WA: Writing Aloud	
	CFG: Comprehension Focus Group	WP: Writing Process	

(continued)

Progress Monitoring **Grade 2**

Student: Teacher:

Book Level	Record Instructional Level															
N																
M																
L																
K																
J																
I																
H																
G																
F																
E																
D																
C																
Book Title, Accuracy Rate, Self-Correction Rate																
Date of Progress Monitoring Interval																
Week of Intervention	01				08				16				24				32	Post-test
Tier 1																
Tier 2																
Tier 3																
Tier 4																

Layering and Mixing Interventions	GRP: Guided Reading Plus	IW: Interactive Writing	WP: Writing Process
	CFG: Comprehension Focus Group	WA: Writing Aloud	CRI: Classroom Intervention

(continued)

Appendix B1 (continued)

Progress Monitoring Grade 3

Student: _____   Teacher: _____

Book Level	Record Instructional Level																																
Q																																	
P																																	
O																																	
N																																	
M																																	
L																																	
K																																	
J																																	
I																																	
H																																	
G																																	
F																																	
Book Title, Accuracy Rate, Self-Correction Rate																																	
Date of Progress Monitoring Interval																																	
Week of Intervention	01							08							16								24								32			Post-test
Tier 1																																	
Tier 2																																	
Tier 3																																	
Tier 4																																	

Layering and Mixing Interventions		
GRP: Guided Reading Plus	IW: Interactive Writing	WP: Writing Process
CFG: Comprehension Focus Group	WA: Writing Aloud	CRI: Classroom Intervention

Appendix B2

Emergent Reading Behaviors: Attending to Print
(Assessing Processing Behaviors to Check on Teaching, Learning and Group Placement)
Guided Reading Levels: A–C

Student: _____ Date: _____

Book Title/Text Level: _____ Genre: _____

Accuracy Rate: _____ Self-Correction Ratio: _____

Reading Behaviors	Observed Unprompted *Behaviors Observed During Reading*	Not Observed Prompted *Behaviors Prompted for After Reading*
Uses meaning and language to read simple text.		
Points to words in a one-to-one match throughout two to three lines of text.		
Notices (self-monitors) on unknown words; searches for cues in picture and print.		
Rereads to cross check first letter with meaning and structure cues.		
Uses knowledge of some letter-sound relationships to initiate an action at point of difficulty; articulates first letter and attends to some endings.		
Reads known high-frequency words with fluency.		
Self-corrects using known high-frequency words and other print cues.		

Note: At the emergent level, teachers will not use the comprehension guide or oral fluency scale.

(continued)

Beginning Early Reading Processing Behaviors
(Assessing Processing Behaviors to Check on Teaching, Learning and Group Placement)
Guided Reading Levels: D–E

Student: _____ Date: _____

Book Title/Text Level: _____ Genre: _____

Accuracy Rate: _____ Self-Correction Ratio: _____

Reading Behaviors	Observed Unprompted *Behaviors Observed During Reading*	Not Observed Prompted *Behaviors Prompted for After Reading*
Reads without using finger to track print.		
Notices errors (self-monitors); *cross-checks* multiple sources of information to make self-correction (checks to be sure the reading makes sense, sounds right and looks right).		
Uses knowledge of letter-sound relationships to initiate an action at point of difficulty.		
Searches through unknown words in a left-right sequence; blends letters into sounds; repeats words to confirm. (*s-u-n, h-o-p*)		
Takes apart simple unknown words using simple word parts/patterns. (*s-un, h-op*)		
Reads known high-frequency words with fluency.		
Uses simple punctuation to regulate phrasing and fluency (prosody).		

Oral Reading Fluency Scale

Level 4	Reads primarily in larger, meaningful phrase groups. Although some regressions, repetitions, and deviations from text may be present, these do not appear to detract from the overall structure of the story. Preservation of the author's syntax is consistent. Some or most of the story is read with expressive interpretation.	
Level 3	Reads primarily in three- or four-word phrase groups. Some small groupings may be present. However, the majority of phrasing seems appropriate and preserves the syntax of the author. Little or no expressive interpretation is present.	
Level 2	Reads primarily in two-word phrases with some three- or four-word groupings. Some word-by-word reading may be present. Word groupings may seem awkward and unrelated to larger context of sentence or passage.	
Level 1	Reads primarily word by word. Occasional two-word or three-word phrases may occur, but these are infrequent and/or they do not preserve meaningful syntax.	

Source: U.S. Department of Education, Institute of Education Sciences, National Center for Education Statistics, National Assessment of Educational Progress (NAEP), 2002 Oral Reading Study.

(continued)

Late Early Reading Processing Behaviors
(Assessing Processing Behaviors to Check on Teaching, Learning and Group Placement)
Guided Reading Levels: F–G

Student: _____ Date: _____

Book Title/Text Level: _____ Genre: _____

Accuracy Rate: _____ Self-Correction Ratio: _____

Reading Behaviors	Observed Unprompted *Behaviors Observed During Reading*	Not Observed Prompted *Behaviors Prompted for After Reading*
Notices errors (self-monitors); initiates multiple attempts to self-correct; *integrates* multiple sources of information (checks to be sure the reading makes sense, sounds right and looks right).		
Self-monitors with greater ease; uses known words, word parts/patterns and inflectional endings to check on reading and self-corrects.		
Takes unknown words apart at the larger unit of analysis including onset and rime or at meaningful and logical units. (*out/side; wh-ite, g-ir-l-s*)		
Reads known high-frequency words with fluency.		
Uses simple punctuation to regulate phrasing and fluency (prosody).		

Oral Reading Fluency Scale

Level 4	Reads primarily in larger, meaningful phrase groups. Although some regressions, repetitions, and deviations from text may be present, these do not appear to detract from the overall structure of the story. Preservation of the author's syntax is consistent. Some or most of the story is read with expressive interpretation.	
Level 3	Reads primarily in three- or four-word phrase groups. Some small groupings may be present. However, the majority of phrasing seems appropriate and preserves the syntax of the author. Little or no expressive interpretation is present.	
Level 2	Reads primarily in two-word phrases with some three- or four-word groupings. Some word-by-word reading may be present. Word groupings may seem awkward and unrelated to larger context of sentence or passage.	
Level 1	Reads primarily word by word. Occasional two-word or three-word phrases may occur, but these are infrequent and/or they do not preserve meaningful syntax.	

Source: U.S. Department of Education, Institute of Education Sciences, National Center for Education Statistics, National Assessment of Educational Progress (NAEP), 2002 Oral Reading Study.

(continued)

Transitional Reading Processing Behaviors

(Assessing Processing Behaviors to Check on Teaching, Learning and Group Placement)

Guided Reading Levels: H–M

Student: _____ Date: _____

Book Title/Text Level: _____ Genre: _____

Accuracy Rate: _____ Self-Correction Ratio: _____

Reading Behaviors	Observed Unprompted *Behaviors Observed During Reading*	Not Observed Prompted *Behaviors Prompted for After Reading*
Orchestrates multiple sources of information (meaning, structure, and visual cues); reads texts with greater accuracy and more efficient self-correction.		
Takes apart multi-syllabic words; uses knowledge of syllables and word parts/ patterns to solve words quickly. (*far/mer, kit/chen*) Uses word meanings to solve problems (e.g., prefixes, suffixes, compound parts). Expands reading vocabulary; shows interest in unknown words.		
Reads complex high-frequency words with fluency and ease.		
Uses more complex punctuation to regulate phrasing and fluency (prosody).		

Oral Reading Fluency Scale

Level 4	Reads primarily in larger, meaningful phrase groups. Although some regressions, repetitions, and deviations from text may be present, these do not appear to detract from the overall structure of the story. Preservation of the author's syntax is consistent. Some or most of the story is read with expressive interpretation.	
Level 3	Reads primarily in three- or four-word phrase groups. Some small groupings may be present. However, the majority of phrasing seems appropriate and preserves the syntax of the author. Little or no expressive interpretation is present.	
Level 2	Reads primarily in two-word phrases with some three- or four-word groupings. Some word-by-word reading may be present. Word groupings may seem awkward and unrelated to larger context of sentence or passage.	
Level 1	Reads primarily word by word. Occasional two-word or three-word phrases may occur, but these are infrequent and/or they do not preserve meaningful syntax.	

Source: U.S. Department of Education, Institute of Education Sciences, National Center for Education Statistics, National Assessment of Educational Progress (NAEP), 2002 Oral Reading Study.

(continued)

Fluent Reading Processing Behaviors
(Assessing Processing Behaviors to Check on Teaching, Learning and Group Placement)
Guided Reading Levels: N–T

Student: _____ Date: _____

Book Title/Text Level: _____ Genre: _____

Accuracy Rate: _____ Self-Correction Ratio: _____

Reading Behaviors	Observed Unprompted *Behaviors Observed During Reading*	Not Observed Prompted *Behaviors Prompted for After Reading*
Orchestrates multiple sources of information (meaning, structure, and visual cues); reads texts with greater accuracy and more efficient self-correction. Reads longer text with specialized content and unusual words; learns new words daily. Applies knowledge about word meanings across different texts; makes predictions about word meanings and checks within texts; refines word knowledge.		
Takes apart multisyllabic words on the run and with flexibility; uses knowledge of syllables and more complex word parts/patterns to solve words quickly (*con/tain/er, ex/pl/an/a/tory*); makes excellent attempts at solving multisyllabic words.		
Reads complex high-frequency words with fluency and ease.		
Uses complex punctuation to regulate phrasing and fluency (prosody).		

Oral Reading Fluency Scale

Level 4	Reads primarily in larger, meaningful phrase groups. Although some regressions, repetitions, and deviations from text may be present, these do not appear to detract from the overall structure of the story. Preservation of the author's syntax is consistent. Some or most of the story is read with expressive interpretation.	
Level 3	Reads primarily in three- or four-word phrase groups. Some small groupings may be present. However, the majority of phrasing seems appropriate and preserves the syntax of the author. Little or no expressive interpretation is present.	
Level 2	Reads primarily in two-word phrases with some three- or four-word groupings. Some word-by-word reading may be present. Word groupings may seem awkward and unrelated to larger context of sentence or passage.	
Level 1	Reads primarily word by word. Occasional two-word or three-word phrases may occur, but these are infrequent and/or they do not preserve meaningful syntax.	

Source: U.S. Department of Education, Institute of Education Sciences, National Center for Education Statistics, National Assessment of Educational Progress (NAEP), 2002 Oral Reading Study.

Appendix B3

Comprehension Guide for Narrative Text

(Assessing *Literal Level* Comprehension on an Instructional Level Text)

Student: _____   Date: _____

Directions: After the student reads the instructional level text, the teacher uses the following prompt to stimulate a discussion. The teacher may use some sample prompts as needed to probe for further understanding.

Teacher's prompt: "Tell me in your own words about the story you just read."

Comprehension Behaviors	Unprompted	Sample Prompts to Probe for Further Understanding	Student's Response
Summarizes story in logical order. Uses some important details when describing events.		What happened first? What happened after that? What happened at the end?	
Identifies setting. Identifies main character. Describes main character. Describes how . . . changed over time.		Where did the story take place? Who was the main character in the story? Can you think of some words to describe . . . ? Describe how . . . changed over time. What was he/she like at the beginning, middle and end of the story?	
Identifies problem, goal, and/or solution.		What was the problem? What was the goal? Was the problem solved? If so, how was it solved?	
Asks questions (e.g., word meanings, characters actions, or an event).		Was there any vocabulary that the author used that you didn't understand? Do you have any questions about a specific character in the story? Do you have any questions about what happened in the story?	

(continued)

Appendix B3 *(continued)*

Comprehension Guide for Expository Text
(Assessing *Literal Level* Comprehension on an Instructional Level Text)

Student: _____ Date: _____

Directions: After the student reads the instructional level text, the teacher uses the following prompt to stimulate a discussion. The teacher may use some sample prompts as needed to probe for further understanding.

Teacher's prompt: "What did you learn about . . . from reading this book?"

Comprehension Behaviors	Unprompted	Sample Prompts to Probe for Further Understanding	Student's Response
States the main idea from text. Includes key points from text to support main idea.		What was this book mostly about? What were some important facts you learned about . . . ? Can you tell me more about . . . ?	
Uses some content specific vocabulary from text.		What language did the author use to teach you about . . . ? What language did the author use to describe the . . . ?	
Uses text features/aids to support understanding.		Why did the author include some text features in the book? Can you give me an example of how some of the features supported your understanding about . . . ?	
Identifies new learning. Compares previous understandings to new learning.		What was new information for you? How is what you learned today different from what you already knew?	
Asks questions (e.g., content, vocabulary, etc.).		Do you have any questions about any of the information presented in the book? Was there any vocabulary that the author used that you didn't understand?	

Appendix B4

Student:

Writing in Response to Reading for Emergent Intervention
(Guided Reading Levels A–C)
Check all behaviors observed without support.

Writing Behavior (Spelling Strategies and Writing Fluency)	Writes letters fluently and with correct formation.										
	Writes easy high-frequency words fluently. (*is, me, the, at*)										
	Says words slowly; hears and records beginning and ending consonants; at times, vowels may appear although they may not be correct.										
	Uses simple VC phonogram patterns to help spell words. (*c-up, c-at*)										
	Uses resources to help with writing letters and spelling words. (ABC Chart)										
	Uses a practice page to think strategically about writing letters and spelling unknown words.										
	Demonstrates movement from semi-phonetic to phonetic stage of spelling.										
Composing	Rehearses response; holds language in memory while transcribing message.										
	Uses the rereading strategy (returns to beginning of sentence) to remember the next word and to monitor meaning and language.										
Comprehension	Demonstrates understanding of text and prompt.										
	Incorporates some vocabulary that reflects attention to reading.										
Language Structure	Uses written language structures that reflect a shift from informal oral language structures to more conventional written language structures. • Composes simple sentences (noun + verb) • Uses prepositional phrases (*on the floor, in the bag*) • Uses conjunctions (*and*)										
Conventions	Controls left to right and top to bottom representation; leaves spaces between words.										
	Demonstrates some awareness of ending punctuation (periods) but over-generalizes (i.e., uses a period as a marker to separate words or designate the end of each line or page).										
	Progress Monitoring Date										
	Total Number of Observed Behaviors										

(continued)

Student:

Writing in Response to Reading for Beginning Early Intervention
(Guided Reading Levels D–E)
Check all behaviors observed without support.

Writing Behavior (Spelling Strategies and Writing Fluency)	Writes simple high-frequency words fluently. (*come, here, have*)											
	Uses a practice page to think strategically about writing letters and spelling unknown words.											
	Says words slowly; hears and records beginning and ending consonants and some middle consonants; includes a vowel in each word; spells three-letter words correctly. (*can, cat, ham*)											
	Uses known letters, familiar words and word parts to assist with spelling unknown words; uses word endings (*s, ing*) correctly; uses simple rime patterns (phonogram patterns) to spell unknown words. (*can, man*)											
	Demonstrates the phonetic stage of spelling development.											
Composing	Rehearses response; holds language in memory while transcribing message.											
	Uses the rereading strategy (rereads a phrase) to remember the next word and to monitor meaning and language.											
Comprehension	Response reflects understanding of the text and prompt.											
	Incorporates some vocabulary that reflects attention to reading; uses vocabulary appropriate for topic.											
Language Structure	Demonstrates use of language structures that reflect increasing complexity in language patterns. • Composes simple sentences (noun + verb) • Uses prepositional phrases (*on the floor, in the bag*) • Uses conjunctions (*and, but*)											
Conventions	Rereads writing and thinks about punctuation and capitalization. • Uses ending punctuation appropriately (periods and question marks) • Capitalizes sentence beginnings											
	Progress Monitoring Date											
	Total Number of Observed Behaviors											

(continued)

Appendix B4 *(continued)*

Student: _____

Writing in Response to Reading for Late Early Intervention
(Guided Reading Levels F–G)
Check all behaviors observed without support.

Writing Behavior (Spelling Strategies and Writing Fluency)	Writes more complex high-frequency words fluently. (*there, where, when*)										
	Uses a practice page to think strategically about spelling unknown words.										
	Says words slowly; hears and records beginning, ending, and middle consonants including blends, clusters, and diagraphs; spells most words using visual analysis. (*bike, stripe*)										
	Uses familiar words and word parts to spell unknown words; spells word endings (*s, ing, ed, es*) correctly; uses complex rime patterns (phonogram patterns) to spell unknown words. (*down-crown*)										
	Demonstrates movement from phonetic to the transitional stage of spelling development.										
Composing	Uses the rereading strategy (phrases, words, word) as needed to help with writing a meaningful response.										
	Response is longer and more complex; reflects fluency of thinking, fluency of encoding, and an increase in language control.										
Comprehension	Response reflects understanding of the text and prompt.										
	Incorporates a writing vocabulary that reflects attention to reading; uses vocabulary appropriate for topic.										
Language Structure	Demonstrates use of language structures that reflects increasing complexity in conventional language patterns; i.e., • Composes simple sentences (noun + verb) • Uses prepositional phrases (*on the floor, in the bag*) • Uses conjunctions (*and, but*) • Uses modifiers (*red* dress)										
Conventions	Rereads writing and thinks about punctuation and capitalization. • Uses ending punctuation appropriately (periods, exclamation marks, question marks) • Capitalizes sentence beginnings and proper names										
	Progress Monitoring Date										
	Total Number of Observed Behaviors										

(continued)

Appendix B4 *(continued)*

Student:

Writing in Response to Reading for Transitional Intervention
(Guided Reading Levels H–M)
Check all behaviors observed without support.

Writing Behavior (Spelling strategies and writing fluency)	Writes more complex high-frequency words fluently. (*because, once, knew*)									
	Uses complex rime patterns (phonogram patterns) to spell unknown words. (*down-crown*)									
	Breaks multi-syllabic words into parts and records new words in parts.									
	Uses transitional and/or conventional spelling for most words.									
Composing	Plans response (notes, outline, chart, web) on the planning page to organize thinking.									
	Uses the rereading strategy (phrases, words, word) as needed to help with writing a meaningful response.									
Comprehension	Response reflects understanding of the text and prompt.									
	Incorporates a writing vocabulary that reflects attention to reading; uses vocabulary appropriate for topic.									
Language Structure	Demonstrates use of language structures that reflects increasing complexity in conventional language patterns. • Uses modifiers (*red* dress) • Uses two phrases linked by a relative pronoun (*who, that, what, which*) • Uses two phrases linked by an adverb (*when, where, how, however, whenever, wherever*)									
Conventions	Rereads writing and thinks about punctuation. • Uses ending punctuation appropriately (periods, exclamation marks, question marks) • Uses additional forms of punctuation appropriately (quotation marks, apostrophes in contractions or possessives, commas to identify a series, ellipses to show pause) • Capitalizes sentence beginnings and proper names									
	Progress Monitoring Date									
	Total Number of Observed Behaviors									

Appendix B5

Emergent Writing Behaviors
(Assessing Writing Behaviors to Check on Teaching, Learning and Group Placement)

Student: _____   Date: _____   Genre: _____

Writing Behaviors	Observed Unprompted *Behaviors Observed During Writing*	Not Observed Prompted *Behaviors Prompted During Writing*
Establishes a relationship between print and pictures. Writes left to right across several lines of text; uses spaces between words with greater accuracy.		
Holds simple sentences in memory while encoding message; rereads to remember next word.		
Writes some alphabet letters fluently and with correct formation.		
Analyzes unknown words using slow articulation; records letters in word sequence. Uses a practice page to try out letters or word spellings. Uses resources for sound-letter link (e.g., ABC chart, name chart and/or letter books).		
Spells most unknown words phonetically drawing on phonemic awareness and sound–letter relationships. Writes easy high-frequency words fluently and accurately.		
Uses syntax of oral language; may include some book language and content specific vocabulary.		
Experiments with simple punctuation (e.g., uses punctuation as markers between words or to designate the end of each line or page).		

(continued)

Beginning Early Writing Behaviors

(Assessing Writing Behaviors to Check on Teaching, Learning and Group Placement)

Student: _____   Date: _____   Genre: _____

Writing Behaviors	Observed Unprompted *Behaviors Observed During Writing*	Not Observed Prompted *Behaviors Prompted During Writing*
Holds simple ideas in memory while encoding message.		
Rereads to remember next word or phrase; begins to reflect on meaning, sentence structures and word choice.		
Writes alphabet letters fluently and with correct formation.		
Analyzes unknown words using slow articulation; records letters in word sequence; spells grade level words conventionally (e.g., words comprised of short vowel patterns). Breaks unknown words into onset and rime or at meaningful and logical units; uses common spelling patterns to spell words conventionally. Uses known words as a base for adding simple inflectional endings (e.g., *s, ing, ed*). Writes grade level high-frequency words fluently and accurately.		
Uses a practice page to try out letters or word spellings. Uses resources less often for sound-letter link (e.g., ABC chart, name chart and/or letter books).		
Includes some words that reflect attention to vocabulary and word meanings from reading.		
Applies appropriate standard English grammar.		
Applies appropriate conventions of standard English (e.g., capitalization and punctuation appropriately).		

(continued)

Appendix B5 *(continued)*

Late Early Writing Behaviors
(Assessing Writing Behaviors to Check on Teaching, Learning and Group Placement)

Student: _____ Date: _____ Genre: _____

Writing Behaviors	Observed Unprompted *Behaviors Observed During Writing*	Not Observed Prompted *Behaviors Prompted During Writing*
Holds ideas in memory while encoding message. Rereads to remember next idea; reflects on meaning, sentence structures and word choice.		
Analyzes unknown words on the run; thinks visually about how words look; spells grade level words conventionally (e.g., words comprised of long vowel patterns). Breaks unknown words into syllables, onset, and rime, or at meaningful and logical units; uses common spelling patterns to spell words conventionally. Uses known words as a base for adding inflectional endings (e.g., *s, es, ing, ed*). Writes grade level high-frequency words fluently and accurately.		
Uses practice page to try out word spellings less often; analyzes unknown words on the run. Begins to use planning page for trying out word choice; begins to consider words and phrases from reading to support craft.		
Includes words that reflect attention to vocabulary and word meanings from reading.		
Applies appropriate standard English grammar.		
Applies appropriate conventions of standard English (e.g., capitalization and punctuation appropriately).		

(continued)

Transitional Writing Behaviors
(Assessing Writing Behaviors to Check on Teaching, Learning and Group Placement)

Student: _____   Date: _____   Genre: _____

Writing Behaviors	Observed Unprompted *Behaviors Observed During Writing*	Not Observed Prompted *Behaviors Prompted During Writing*
Holds more complex ideas in memory while encoding message. Rereads to remember next idea; reflects on meaning, sentence structure, and word choice.		
Analyzes unknown words quickly on the run. Breaks unknown words into syllables, syllables into onset and rime, or at meaningful and logical units; uses common and irregular spelling pattern knowledge to spell words conventionally. Uses known words as a base for adding inflectional endings (e.g., *s, es, ing, ed*). Uses word meanings to spell words conventionally (e.g., prefixes, suffixes and homophones). Writes grade level high-frequency words with fluency and accurately.		
Writing includes words that reflect attention to vocabulary and word meanings from reading. Uses planning page to try out crafting techniques (e.g., word choice, leads, endings, etc.).		
Applies appropriate standard English grammar.		
Applies appropriate conventions of standard English (e.g., capitalization and punctuation appropriately).		

Appendix B6

Recording Sheet for Guided Reading Plus Word Study

Group Members: _____ _____ _____

High–Frequency Words ✓ Can read and write fluently				Rime Patterns ✓ Taught and have been recorded on students' independent chart			
a*		at*		an		at	
am*		an*		am		ap	
and *		all		and		ash	
are		ask		ack		ank	
asked		after		all		ake	
away		be		ale		ame	
big		but		ain		ate	
by		back		ar		ay	
can*		car		aw			
come		did					
do*		day		et		ed	
for		from		est		ell	
go*		going		eat			
get		gets					
he*		had		in		ip	
has		have		ill		ick	
him		his		ink		ing	
here		her		ine		ice	
how		I*		ide		ight	
I'm		if		ir			
in*		into					
is*		it*		op		ock	
just		like*		oke		or	
look		little		ore			
me*		man					
my*		make		ug		uck	
mom		no*		ump		unk	
not*		now					
on		or					
of		one					
out		our					
over		put					
play		so*					
see*		she*					
saw		said					
to*		too					
the*		them					
than		that					
then		this					
their		there					
up*		us					
very		we*					
will		with					
went		was					
were		when					
what		where					
who		you					
your		zoo					

* Words that students should know at the end of kindergarten.

Kindergarten Scoring Guide for Writing Proficiency

Page 1

Student: _____   Date: _____

Proficiency Behaviors End of 1st Reporting Period	Proficiency Behaviors End of 2nd Reporting Period	Proficiency Behaviors End of 3rd Reporting Period	Proficiency Behaviors End of 4th Reporting Period
❑ Generates topic for writing by drawing a picture. ❑ Demonstrates awareness of where to begin writing and directional movement principle. ❑ Records strings of letters with little or no concept of space. ❑ Writes some letters with correct formation, mostly capital letters. ❑ Demonstrates limited knowledge of hearing and recording sounds in words by recording strings of letters. ❑ Writes name with correct formation using correct upper and lower case letters. ❑ Uses pre-communicative spelling. ❑ Uses label or simple drawings, along with random letters to communicate a written message. ❑ Edits by crossing out letters or words independently.	❑ Generates topic for writing with teacher assistance through conversation. ❑ Uses ABC chart, letter book and name chart to support sound-letter match with teacher assistance some of the time. ❑ Demonstrates understanding of where to begin writing and directional movement principle. ❑ Uses spaces between words some of the time. ❑ Writes some letters with correct formation. ❑ Edits by crossing out letters and uses practice pages for trying out letters. ❑ Segments words into individual phonemes with teacher assistance. ❑ Hears and records some consonant letter sounds, but not necessarily in sequential order.	❑ Generates topic for writing with teacher assistance through conversation. ❑ Uses ABC chart, letter book and name chart to support sound-letter match with or without teacher assistance some of the time. ❑ Uses spaces between words most of the time. ❑ Writes more letters with correct formation. ❑ Edits by crossing out letters and uses practice pages for trying out letters and experimenting with writing new words. ❑ Segments words into individual phonemes with or without teacher assistance some of the time. ❑ Hears and records some consonant letter sounds in sequential order and some easy to hear vowels may appear randomly.	❑ Generates topic for writing with or without teacher assistance. ❑ Uses ABC chart, letter book and name chart to support sound-letter match without teacher assistance some of the time. ❑ Uses spaces between words consistently. ❑ Writes more letters with correct formation. ❑ Edits by crossing out letters and uses practice pages for trying out letters and experimenting with writing new words. ❑ Segments words into individual phonemes without teacher assistance most of the time. ❑ Hears and records most consonant letter sounds and some easy to hear vowels may appear in sequential order.

(continued)

Kindergarten Scoring Guide for Writing Proficiency

Page 2

Proficiency Behaviors End of 1st Reporting Period	Proficiency Behaviors End of 2nd Reporting Period	Proficiency Behaviors End of 3rd Reporting Period	Proficiency Behaviors End of 4th Reporting Period
	❑ Writes a few simple high-frequency words accurately that reflect attention to print.	❑ Writes some high-frequency words accurately that reflect attention to print.	❑ Writes more high-frequency words accurately that reflect attention to print.
	❑ Uses rereading strategy with teacher assistance (prompting).	❑ Uses rereading strategy some of the time without teacher assistance.	❑ Uses rereading strategy most of the time without teacher assistance.
	❑ Uses precommunicative and some semiphonetic spellings.	❑ Uses pre-communicative and some semiphonetic spellings.	❑ Uses mostly semiphonetic and some phonetic spellings.
	❑ Writes a simple message (generally one sentence) that communicates the writer's purpose.	❑ Demonstrates some awareness of end punctuation (overgeneralizes placement).	❑ Demonstrates increased awareness of end punctuation (placement occurs at end of one sentence text and is misused when text contains more than one sentence).
		❑ Demonstrates some awareness of beginning capitalization (first word of text).	❑ Demonstrates increased awareness of beginning capitalization (first word of text).
		❑ Writes a simple message of one to two sentences that communicate the writer's purpose.	❑ Writes a simple message of one to three sentences that communicate the writer's purpose.

(continued)

First Grade Scoring Guide for Writing Proficiency

Page 1

Student: _____ Date: _____

Proficiency Behaviors End of 1st Reporting Period	Proficiency Behaviors End of 2nd Reporting Period	Proficiency Behaviors End of 3rd Reporting Period	Proficiency Behaviors End of 4th Reporting Period
❑ Generates topic for writing with teacher assistance through conversation. ❑ Creates an opening sentence or phrase that leads into the writing with teacher assistance some of the time (through conversation). ❑ Records series of 2–4 events in chronological order from beginning to end with teacher assistance. ❑ Demonstrates awareness of descriptive words, strong nouns, and muscular verbs with teacher assistance (through conversation and read aloud). ❑ Uses rereading strategy independently. ❑ Uses ABC chart, letter book and name chart to support sound-letter match without teacher assistance most of the time. ❑ Uses practice page for problem solving with teacher assistance (working on letters, word spellings and word fluency). ❑ Writes most letters with correct formation. ❑ Segments unknown words into individual phonemes independently.	❑ Generates topic for writing with or without teacher assistance some of the time through conversation. ❑ Creates an opening sentence or phrase that leads into the writing with or without teacher assistance some of the time (through conversation). ❑ Records series of events in chronological order from beginning to end (bed-to-bed) with or without teacher assistance some of the time. ❑ Demonstrates increased awareness of descriptive words, strong nouns, and muscular verbs with teacher assistance (through conversation, read aloud and "anchor" charts). ❑ Uses ABC chart, letter book and name chart to support sound-letter match independently. ❑ Uses resources to support spelling knowledge with teacher assistance (spelling trial page, teacher and student created "anchor" charts). ❑ Uses practice page for problem solving with or without teacher assistance some of the time (working on letters, word spellings, trying out different spellings and word fluency).	❑ Generates topic for writing without teacher assistance most of the time. ❑ Creates an opening sentence or phrase that leads into the writing without teacher assistance most of the time. ❑ Records series of events in chronological order from beginning to end (bed-to-bed) without teacher assistance most of the time. ❑ Demonstrates understanding of descriptive words, strong nouns, and muscular verbs with or without teacher assistance some of the time (through conversation, read aloud and "anchor" charts). ❑ Uses writing checklist to reflect on writing process with or without teacher assistance some of the time. ❑ Uses resources to support spelling knowledge with or without teacher assistance some of the time (spelling trial page, teacher and student created "anchor" charts). ❑ Uses practice page for problem solving without teacher assistance most of the time (working on letters, word spellings, trying out different spellings and word fluency).	❑ Generates topic for writing independently. ❑ Creates an opening sentence or phrase that leads into the writing independently. ❑ Develops and maintains an idea throughout the piece and the ideas are in logical order. ❑ Demonstrates understanding of descriptive words, strong nouns, and muscular verbs without teacher assistance most of the time. ❑ Uses writing checklist to reflect on writing process with or without teacher assistance some of the time. ❑ Uses resources to support spelling knowledge without teacher assistance most of the time (teacher and student created "anchor" charts). ❑ Uses practice page for problem solving independently (working out word spellings, trying out different spellings of words and word fluency). ❑ Segments unknown words using larger units of sound without teacher assistance most of the time (visual patterns are in sequential order).

(continued)

First Grade Scoring Guide for Writing Proficiency

Page 2

Proficiency Behaviors End of 1st Reporting Period	Proficiency Behaviors End of 2nd Reporting Period	Proficiency Behaviors End of 3rd Reporting Period	Proficiency Behaviors End of 4th Reporting Period
❏ Hears and records all consonant letter sounds and some easy to hear vowels in sequential order. ❏ Edits by crossing out letters or words independently. ❏ Revises message by using a caret to add a new word or two to the text with teacher assistance. ❏ Writes a few simple high-frequency words accurately. ❏ Demonstrates understanding of closing punctuation with teacher assistance. ❏ Demonstrates understanding of beginning capitalization with teacher assistance (rule is overgeneralized when editing independently). ❏ Uses mostly phonetic spelling. ❏ Demonstrates awareness of different genre writing (text structure) with teacher assistance.	❏ Writes all letters with correct formation. ❏ Segments unknown words into individual phonemes and attends to visual patterns in words with teacher assistance (may overgeneralize visual letter placement). ❏ Edits by circling a few words that do not look right and attempts to self-correct with teacher assistance. ❏ Revises message by using a caret to add a word or two to the text with or without teacher assistance some of the time. ❏ Writes some basic high-frequency words accurately. ❏ Demonstrates understanding of closing punctuation with or without teacher assistance some of the time (placement is overgeneralized when punctuating independently). ❏ Demonstrates understanding of beginning capitalization with or without teacher assistance some of the time (rule is overgeneralized when editing independently). ❏ Uses phonetic spelling and some transitional spelling. ❏ Demonstrates increased awareness of different genre writing (text structure) with teacher assistance.	❏ Segments unknown words into individual phonemes and attends to visual patterns in words with or without teacher assistance some of the time (visual patterns are in sequential order some of the time). ❏ Edits by circling a few words that do not look right and attempts to self-correct with or without teacher assistance some of the time. ❏ Revises message by using a caret to add new words or ideas to the text without teacher assistance most of the time. ❏ Writes more basic high-frequency words accurately. ❏ Demonstrates understanding of closing punctuation with or without teacher assistance some of the time (placement is more accurate when punctuating independently). ❏ Demonstrates understanding of beginning capitalization with or without teacher assistance some of the time (rule is overgeneralized when editing independently). ❏ Uses phonetic spelling and some transitional spelling. ❏ Demonstrates increased awareness of different genre writing (text structure) with or without teacher assistance some of the time.	❏ Edits by circling some words that do not look right and attempts to self-correct without teacher assistance most of the time. ❏ Revises message by using a caret to add new words or ideas to the text independently. ❏ Revises message by deleting some words and using proofreading techniques (drawing a line through unwanted text) without teacher assistance most of the time. ❏ Writes most basic high-frequency words accurately. ❏ Demonstrates understanding of closing punctuation with or without teacher assistance most of the time (placement is more accurate when punctuating independently). ❏ Demonstrates understanding of beginning capitalization with or without teacher assistance some of the time (rule is overgeneralized when editing independently). ❏ Uses some phonetic spelling, some transitional spelling, and some conventional spelling. ❏ Demonstrates understanding of different genre writing (text structure) without teacher assistance most of the time.

(continued)

Second Grade Scoring Guide for Writing Proficiency

Page 1

Student: _____ Date: _____

Proficiency Behaviors End of 1st Reporting Period	Proficiency Behaviors End of 2nd Reporting Period	Proficiency Behaviors End of 3rd Reporting Period	Proficiency Behaviors End of 4th Reporting Period
❑ Generates topic for writing and expresses ideas using teacher or peer assistance. ❑ Writes in different modes with some understanding (letters, reports, lists, directions, notes, recipes, labels . . . see appropriate rubrics). ❑ Uses prewriting strategies to plan and organize ideas (talk, questioning, sharing of ideas or graphic organizers). ❑ Writing includes an opening phrase or sentence (Did you know the sun is a huge ball of fire?). ❑ Setting is identified in narrative writing. ❑ Characters are identified in narrative writing. ❑ Writing is in logical, sequential order. ❑ Writes complete sentences most of the time. ❑ Uses a variety of sentence structures and lengths. ❑ Rereads to clarify message by adding or deleting information. ❑ Writing includes some "good word choice" to create mind pictures (e.g., muscular verbs, adjectives, adverbs, dialogue).	❑ Generates topic for writing using teacher or peer assistance. ❑ Writes in different modes with some understanding (letters, reports, lists, directions, notes, recipes, labels . . . see appropriate rubrics). ❑ Uses prewriting strategies to plan and organize ideas (talk, questioning, sharing of ideas or graphic organizers). ❑ Writing includes an opening with more than one sentence. ❑ Setting is identified in narrative writing. ❑ Characters are identified in narrative writing. ❑ Ideas are logically ordered and clustered into groups. ❑ Writes complete sentences most of the time. ❑ Uses a variety of sentence structures and lengths. ❑ Rereads to clarify message by adding or deleting information. ❑ Revises word choices by substituting richer vocabulary to create mind pictures with teacher assistance (e.g., muscular verbs, adjectives, adverbs, dialogue).	❑ Generates topic for writing independently. ❑ Writes in different modes with more understanding (letters, reports, lists, directions, notes, recipes, labels . . . see appropriate rubrics). ❑ Uses prewriting strategies to plan and organize ideas (talk, questioning, sharing of ideas or graphic organizers). ❑ Writing includes an opening with more than one sentence. ❑ Setting is established. ❑ Main character(s) are clearly introduced. ❑ Ideas are logically ordered and clustered into groups. ❑ Writes complete sentences most of the time. ❑ Uses more complex sentence structures. ❑ Rereads to clarify message by adding or deleting information. ❑ Revises word choices by substituting richer vocabulary to create mind pictures with teacher assistance (e.g., muscular verbs, adjectives, adverbs, dialogue). ❑ Uses similes and/or metaphors with some understanding of their usefulness.	❑ Generates topic for writing independently. ❑ Writes in different modes with greater understanding (letters, reports, lists, directions, notes, recipes, labels . . . see appropriate rubrics). ❑ Uses prewriting strategies to plan and organize ideas (talk, questioning, sharing of ideas or graphic organizers). ❑ Writing includes an opening that moves smoothly into the body of the writing. ❑ Setting is established and somewhat described. ❑ Main character(s) are clearly introduced and somewhat described. ❑ Ideas are logically ordered and clustered into groups. ❑ Writes complete sentences most of the time. ❑ Uses more complex sentence structures. ❑ Rereads to clarify message by adding or deleting information. ❑ Revises word choices by substituting richer vocabulary to create mind pictures. ❑ Uses similes and/or metaphors with more understanding of their usefulness.

(continued)

Appendix C *(continued)*

Second Grade Scoring Guide for Writing Proficiency

Page 2

Proficiency Behaviors End of 1st Reporting Period	Proficiency Behaviors End of 2nd Reporting Period	Proficiency Behaviors End of 3rd Reporting Period	Proficiency Behaviors End of 4th Reporting Period
❏ Begins to use similes and/or metaphors with limited understanding.	❏ Uses similes and/or metaphors with some understanding.	❏ Writing includes a sense of closure.	❏ Writing includes a sense of closure.
❏ Writing includes a sense of closure (It was fun! I had a great time at the zoo.).	❏ Writing includes a sense of closure (It was fun! I had a great time at the zoo.).	❏ Demonstrates more accurate use of end punctuation.	❏ Demonstrates more accurate use of end punctuation.
❏ Demonstrates some accurate use of closing punctuation.	❏ Demonstrates more accurate use of closing punctuation.	❏ Demonstrates more accurate use of capitalization at the beginning of sentences and proper nouns.	❏ Demonstrates more accurate use of capitalization at the beginning of sentences and proper nouns.
❏ Demonstrates some accurate use of beginning capitalization.	❏ Demonstrates more accurate use of beginning capitalization.	❏ Writes more high-frequency words correctly.	❏ Writes more high-frequency words correctly.
❏ Writes some high-frequency words correctly.	❏ Writes more high-frequency words correctly.	❏ Uses more transitional spelling and some conventional spelling.	❏ Uses more transitional spelling and some conventional spelling.
❏ Uses phonetic and some transitional spelling.	❏ Uses phonetic and more transitional spelling.	❏ Uses resources to check his or her writing (dictionary, checklist).	❏ Uses resources to check his or her writing (dictionary, checklist).
❏ Uses resources to check his or her writing (dictionary, checklist).	❏ Uses resources to check his or her writing (dictionary, checklist).		

(continued)

Third Grade Scoring Guide for Writing Proficiency
Page 1

Student: _____   Date: _____

Proficiency Behaviors End of 1st Reporting Period	Proficiency Behaviors End of 2nd Reporting Period	Proficiency Behaviors End of 3rd Reporting Period	Proficiency Behaviors End of 4th Reporting Period
❑ Records ideas with some fluency. ❑ Uses prewriting strategies to plan and organize ideas (talk, questioning, sharing of ideas or graphic organizers). ❑ Generates topics for writing independently. ❑ Writes in different modes with some understanding (letters, lists, directions, notes, recipes, labels, paragraph reports, persuasive, process writing . . . see appropriate rubrics). ❑ Writing includes an opening that moves smoothly into the body of the writing and somewhat grabs the audience's attention. ❑ Setting is established and somewhat described. ❑ Main character(s) are clearly introduced and somewhat described. ❑ Ideas are logically ordered and clustered into groups and use more complex transition words some of the time. ❑ Writes complete sentences most of the time. ❑ Uses more compound and complex sentence structures some of the time.	❑ Records ideas with some fluency. ❑ Uses prewriting strategies to plan and organize ideas (talk, questioning, sharing of ideas or graphic organizers). ❑ Generates topics for writing independently. ❑ Writes in different modes with some understanding (letters, lists, directions, notes, recipes, labels, paragraph reports, persuasive, process writing . . . see appropriate rubrics). ❑ Writing includes an opening that moves smoothly into the body of the writing and somewhat grabs the audience's attention. ❑ Setting is established and somewhat described. ❑ Main character(s) are clearly introduced and somewhat described. ❑ Ideas are logically ordered and clustered into groups and use more complex transition words some of the time. ❑ Writes complete sentences most of the time. ❑ Uses more compound and complex sentence structures some of the time.	❑ Records ideas fluently. ❑ Uses prewriting strategies to plan and organize ideas (talk, questioning, sharing of ideas or graphic organizers). ❑ Generates topics for writing independently. ❑ Writes in different modes with more understanding (letters, lists, directions, notes, recipes, labels, paragraph reports, persuasive, process writing . . . see appropriate rubrics). ❑ Writing includes an opening that moves smoothly into the body of the writing and grabs the audience's attention. ❑ Setting is established and described more. ❑ Main character(s) are clearly introduced and described more. ❑ Ideas are logically ordered and clustered into groups and use more complex transition words most of the time. ❑ Writes complete sentences all of the time. ❑ Uses more compound and complex sentence structures some of the time. ❑ Rereads to clarify message by adding or deleting information.	❑ Records ideas fluently. ❑ Uses prewriting strategies to plan and organize ideas (talk, questioning, sharing of ideas or graphic organizers). ❑ Generates topics for writing independently. ❑ Writes in different modes with greater understanding (letters, lists, directions, notes, recipes, labels, paragraph reports, persuasive, process writing . . . see appropriate rubrics). ❑ Writing includes an opening that moves smoothly into the body of the writing and grabs the audience's attention. ❑ Setting is established and well described. ❑ Main character(s) are clearly introduced and well described. ❑ Ideas are logically ordered and clustered into groups and use more complex transition words. ❑ Writes complete sentences all of the time. ❑ Uses more compound and complex sentence structures some of the time. ❑ Rereads to clarify message by adding or deleting information.

(continued)

Appendix C *(continued)*

Third Grade Scoring Guide for Writing Proficiency

Page 2

Proficiency Behaviors End of 1st Reporting Period	Proficiency Behaviors End of 2nd Reporting Period	Proficiency Behaviors End of 3rd Reporting Period	Proficiency Behaviors End of 4th Reporting Period
❏ Rereads to clarify message by adding or deleting information.	❏ Rereads to clarify message by adding or deleting information.	❏ Revises word choices by substituting richer vocabulary to create mind pictures.	❏ Revises word choices by substituting richer vocabulary to create mind pictures.
❏ Revises word choices by substituting richer vocabulary to create mind pictures.	❏ Revises word choices by substituting richer vocabulary to create mind pictures.	❏ Uses similes and/or metaphors with more understanding of their usefulness.	❏ Uses similes and/or metaphors with greater understanding of their usefulness.
❏ Uses similes and/or metaphors with some understanding of their usefulness.	❏ Uses similes and/or metaphors with more understanding of their usefulness.	❏ Uses literary structure (book language, specialized vocabulary, or structures from text) with some understanding.	❏ Uses appropriate literary structure (book language, specialized vocabulary, or structures from text).
❏ Begins to use literary structure (book language, specialized vocabulary, or structures from text) with some understanding.	❏ Uses literary structure (book language, specialized vocabulary, or structures from text) with some understanding.	❏ Writing includes a sense of closure that begins to tie the story together with some understanding.	❏ Writing includes a sense of closure that is interesting and ties the story together.
❏ Writing includes a sense of closure that begins to tie the story together with some understanding.	❏ Writing includes a sense of closure that begins to tie the story together with some understanding.	❏ Uses subject/verb agreement some of the time.	❏ Uses subject/verb agreement.
❏ Uses subject/verb agreement some of the time.	❏ Uses subject/verb agreement some of the time.	❏ Uses correct pronouns some of the time.	❏ Uses correct pronouns.
❏ Uses correct pronouns some of the time.	❏ Uses correct pronouns some of the time.	❏ Demonstrates accurate use of end punctuation and uses other punctuation with some accuracy.	❏ Demonstrates accurate use of end punctuation and uses other punctuation with more accuracy.
❏ Demonstrates accurate use of end punctuation.	❏ Demonstrates accurate use of end punctuation.	❏ Demonstrates accurate use of capitalization at the beginning of sentences and proper nouns most of the time.	❏ Demonstrates accurate use of capitalization at the beginning of sentences and proper nouns all of the time.
❏ Demonstrates accurate use of capitalization at the beginning of sentences and proper nouns some of the time.	❏ Demonstrates accurate use of capitalization at the beginning of sentences and proper nouns most of the time.	❏ Writes most high-frequency words correctly.	❏ Writes all high-frequency words correctly.
❏ Writes most high-frequency words correctly.	❏ Writes most high-frequency words correctly.	❏ Uses transitional spelling and some conventional spelling.	❏ Uses transitional spelling and some conventional spelling.
❏ Uses transitional spelling and some conventional spelling.	❏ Uses transitional spelling and some conventional spelling.	❏ Uses resources to check his or her writing (dictionary, checklist, and thesaurus).	❏ Uses resources to check his or her writing (dictionary, checklist, and thesaurus).
❏ Uses resources to check his or her writing (dictionary, checklist, and thesaurus).	❏ Uses resources to check his or her writing (dictionary, checklist, and thesaurus).		

Guidesheet for Interactive Writing
Phase One: Reading

1. **Reread Familiar Text (Big Books, Songs, Nursery Rhymes or Poetry):** The goal is for the students to develop knowledge of written and oral language.

   - The teacher uses a familiar text to demonstrate how the four language systems—meaning (semantic), structure (syntactic), auditory (phonological), and visual (orthographic)—work. The teacher:
     - Rereads the text with prosody with the students.
     - Discusses with the students specific literary aspects of text and responds personally to the text (e.g., story structure, concepts about print, letter and word knowledge).
     - Uses the text experience to develop phonological and phonemic awareness.
     - Directs the student's attention to various aspects of the text, including the awareness of sounds in connection with the visual features of words.
     - Engages the students in explicit word analysis (e.g., high-frequency words, saying words slowly, connecting letters to sounds).

2. **Phonological and Phonemic Awareness:** The goal is for students to develop awareness of sound patterns that can be used to learn about words. The teacher:

   - Provides an opportunity for the students to develop phonological and phonemic awareness (e.g., manipulate individual sounds and sound patterns).
   - Gives explicit instruction in hearing syllables, recognizing rhyming words, generating rhyming words, and segmenting and blending onset and rime to say new words (phonological).
   - Shows students how to hear and manipulate individual phonemes in different ways (phonemic).

3. **Shared Reading of ABC Chart**
   ABC Chart: The goal is for the students to acquire letter-sound alphabet cues to be used during reading and writing. (see Figure 4.4). The teacher:

   - Says the name of each upper and lowercase letter fluently, with the students, and points to the adjacent picture that begins with that letter.
   - Provides an opportunity for the students to fluently read the ABC chart in a variety of ways to develop print knowledge.

4. **Phonics: Letter/Word Work:**

   Letter Work: The goal is for students to develop letter knowledge (i.e., become familiar with letters, features of letters, and relate letters to sounds). The teacher:

   - Provides explicit instruction in letter learning by helping students learn how to look at letters, for example directing the students' attention to the features of letters by providing them with an opportunity to trace over letters (sandpaper, magnetic letters, salt, shaving cream) and describing the path of movement.
   - Engages students in kinesthetic experiences (salt, sandpaper, shaving cream) to help the students learn the directionality principle, features of letters and letter names.
   - Gives the students the opportunity to feel the features of the letters as they trace over the letters.
   - Explains letter learning explicitly so that students can learn to make to make links between letters and sounds.
   - Provides an opportunity for students to make links between letters and sounds by reading letter books.
   - Encourages students to link letter learning to a key word by using their ABC chart and name chart.
   - Provides an opportunity for the students to become fluent and flexible with letter knowledge.
   - Helps students with identifying letters (e.g., pull down letters and say letter names quickly) so that students will become fluent with letter indentification.
   - Provides an opportunity for students to become fluent with writing letters (e.g., write the letter "h" on your board quickly).

   AND/OR

   (continued)

5. **Word Work:** The goal is for the students to develop knowledge of how words work and to use their phonological and orthographic knowledge to develop systems for learning words. The teacher:

   ■ Provides explicit and systematic instruction to help students learn how words work (e.g., helping the students learn that letters in words occur in a left-to-right order; showing students the directionality principle by building their name, new words or known words; encouraging students to recognize the link between known sounds and letters by building simple one-syllable (CVC) words; building, writing, and locating high-frequency words in print, and promoting fluent word knowledge by prompting the students to write known or partially known words for fluency).

   ■ Provides explicit and systematic instruction in breaking known words into larger parts (onset and rime) (e.g., prompting students to build a known word; encouraging students to apply their orthographic knowledge to break the word into onset and rime; supporting students as they generate other words that sound the same; helping the students to change the onset to make new words; allowing students to read the new words; recording the word pattern and generated words that contain that pattern on a chart and the students read the words fluently).

6. **Personal Dictionary:** The goal is for the students to acquire a core of high frequency words to be used in reading and writing. The teacher:

   ■ Provides an opportunity for the students to record known high-frequency words in their personal dictionary.

   ■ Supports the students as they read their recorded words from several pages in their dictionary for word fluency practice.

   Pattern Chart: The goal is for the students to acquire knowledge of spelling patterns to be used in reading and writing. The teacher:

   ■ Provides the students with a resource that helps them make connections across words (e.g., providing an opportunity for students to notice simple word patterns; prompting the students to use a known word from a prior word work experience to notice patterns in words.

7. **Introduce a New Text (Poem, Song, Nursery Rhyme, Shared Text or Interactive Read-Aloud):** The goal is for the student to develop ways of thinking about texts, extend their linguistic structures, and build vocabulary through a supportive and engaging contexts.

   Orientation New Text
   The teacher:

   ■ Introduces the text by reading the title and author; discusses genre.

   ■ Activates background knowledge through a discussion about the title and pictures and allows for predictions to be made based on the summary statement or the major theme of the book, story, or poem.

   ■ Sets the purpose for reading and/or listening comprehension.

   During Reading
   The teacher:

   ■ Reads the text with prosody and at times encourages the students to make predictions, ask questions, or make inferences.

   ■ Allows for ongoing discussions at strategic places as the meaning unfolds.

   ■ Encourages students to join in on repetitive parts if applicable.

   ■ Rereads the text with prosody with the students if applicable.

   After Reading
   The teacher:

   ■ Provides an opportunity for the students to deepen their level of understanding of the text by engaging in a lively and meaningful discussion.

   ■ Encourages the students to go deeper with their understanding of the text by facilitating and scaffolding a discussion about the text (e.g., the author's message or theme and relate text message or theme to the world, respond personally to text and form opinions, make further predictions and inferences, discuss characters' actions and outcomes, retell or summarize the text, or discuss new learning gained from nonfiction reading).

(continued)

Guidesheet for Interactive Writing
Phase Two: Writing

1. **Types of Writing:** The goal is for the students to apply strategies for writing across different genres. The teacher:

   ■ Thinks critically about the type of writing the students need to learn more about (e.g., informational/explanatory, opinion, narrative or respond to piece of previously read literature).

   ■ Records the type of writing for the lesson.

2. **Resources to Support Group Writing:** The goal is for the students to use resources to assist them in writing. The teacher:

   ■ Provides each student with a small copy of the ABC chart and their personal dictionary that houses previously learned high-frequency words.

   ■ Makes available a large group co-constructed word pattern chart to be referred to during the writing lesson.

   ■ Prompts the students to use their phonological and word pattern knowledge to write words fluently.

3. **Interactive Writing Lesson:** The goal is for the students to acquire strategies for writing across different genres.

   Negotiate and Generate Group Message
   The teacher:

   ■ Prompts the students to engage in a conversation around a common experience (e.g., a text that has been previously read and discussed or some new learning).

   ■ Listens carefully to the students' ideas and converses with them about their ideas.

   ■ Captures an idea/s from the conversation and gently shifts the conversation to "Could we write that?"

   Record Generated Message
   The teacher:

   ■ Records the partial or entire message on lesson planner while the students rehearse the message or part of the message.

   Co-Construction of Message
   The teacher:

   ■ Makes a quick decision based on students' knowledge of encoding which letters and/or words to take to fluency, which words to use as a tool for helping the students learn how to create links between sounds, letters, and words (sound analysis), which processes to demonstrate, and which letters, or words to be written by teacher.

   ■ Shares the responsibility of transcribing the message with the students.

   ■ Prompts the students to apply writing strategies while encoding message (e.g., reread to

think about what word to write next, say words slowly and record letters, use ABC chart, pattern chart and dictionary as resources and reflect on message; that is, does our writing make sense, sound right and look right so far?).

   ■ Models and encourages the students to use their practice page to think more metacognitively about word solving.

   Reflect on Group Message
   The teacher:

   ■ Guides the students to use a simple writing checklist to reflect on their problem-solving processes while transcribing the message.

4. **Independent Writing:** The goal is is for the students to apply writing startegies. The teacher:

   ■ Holds a genuine but short conversation with each student about a picture they have drawn in relationship to the previously read text (e.g., a personal experience, an opinion about a specific aspect of story or poem, or some new learning from a nonfiction text).

   ■ Supports the students as they rehearse their message and provides language scaffolds as needed.

   ■ Makes sure the language comes from the students.

   ■ Provides an opportunity for the students to write their message in a journal that includes a blank practice page at the top for applying problem-solving strategies as needed.

5. **Individual Conferences:** The goal is for the students to learn from teacher assistance. The teacher:

   ■ Prompts the students to apply rereading strategies to prepare for the next move.

   ■ Encourages the students to apply visual processing strategies within their zone of proximal development.

   ■ Assists individual students to initiate problem-solving actions needed to complete a specific task.

   ■ Celebrates each student's completed message by inviting the student to reread his or her message.

   ■ Provides explicit praise by placing a light checkmark over the student's contributions and writes the message at the bottom of the page.

   ■ Gives the students an opportunity to read their message that has been written conventionally.

   ■ Records anecdotal notes of each student's problem-solving strategies.

Dorn, L., & Soffos, C. (2013, in process). *Interventions that Work: Assisted Writing.* Boston, MA: Pearson.

Writing Checklist

❑ Did you start in the right place?

❑ Did you leave spaces between words to make it easier to read?

❑ Did you say the words slowly and write the letters that make those sounds?

❑ Did you use the alphabet chart to help you with letters and sounds?

❑ Did you reread to help you know the next word to write?

❑ Did you use your practice page to help you work on the hard parts?

❑ Did your story make sense?

❑ Did you use a ? or ! or . at the end of each sentence?

Planner for Assisted Writing: Interactive Writing

Phase One: Reading

Date: _____ Week: _____ Lesson: _____

Group Focus: _____

Shared Reading of Familiar Text, Phonological Awareness, and Word Study	Introduce and Read New Poem, Shared Text, or Interactive Read-Aloud Text
Familiar Text (Poem, Song, Nursery Rhyme or Shared Text): Title of Text:	**New Text:** (consider an option below): ❑ Read Poem, Song, Nursery Rhyme ❑ Read Big Book ❑ Read-Aloud Text (Narrative or Nonfiction)
Phonological/Phonemic Awareness:	**Orientation to New Text:** ❑ Title:
	❑ Author:
Shared Reading of ABC Chart (consider an option below): ❑ Read entire ABC chart with fluency ❑ Read every other letter ❑ Read consonants or vowels	❑ Genre:
	Before Reading: (Activate background knowledge and set a purpose for reading and/or listening comprehension)
Phonics: Letter Work and/or Word Work: ❑ Letter Learning:	
	During Reading: (Identify critical stopping places to support comprehension) ❑ Page numbers and language prompts:
❑ Word Work:	
	Discussion after Reading: (Language prompts to promote deeper comprehension)
Personal Dictionary and/or Pattern Chart: (consider an option below): ❑ Add _____ word to dictionary ❑ Read words from _____ page(s) ❑ Create pattern chart ❑ Read pattern chart	

Dorn, L., & Soffos, C. (2013, in process). *Interventions that Work: Assisted Writing.* Boston, MA: Pearson.

Appendix D3 *(continued)*

Planner for Assisted Writing: Interactive Writing

Phase Two: Writing

Group Focus: Date: Week: Lesson:

Planning for Writing Before Co-Construction of Message	During Co-Construction of Group Message and after the Co-Construction of Group Message
Planning for Writing: **Type of Writing:** ❑ Informational/Explanatory ❑ Opinion ❑ Narrative ❑ Response to Literature **Resources to Support Group Writing:** ❑ ABC chart ❑ Personal dictionary ❑ Pattern chart **Before Co-construction of Message:** **Negotiate and Generate Group Message:** ❑ Engage in a genuine and rich conversation around a particular element of a previously read text or topic to be described or explained. **Generated Group Message:**	**During Co-Construction of Message:** **Early Concepts of Print:** ❑ CAP: **Fluent Writing:** ❑ Letter(s): ❑ Word(s): **Letters and/or Words to Teach a Process:** ❑ Letters: ❑ Word(s): **Writing Strategies:** ❑ Reread to think about next word ❑ Reread to check on meaning, structure, and language ❑ Say words slowly ❑ Hear individual sounds and record corresponding letters ❑ Use resources to assist with sound-letter match **After Writing Group Message:** ❑ Use writing checklist to check on strategies used during writing **Independent Writing:** ❑ Rehearse individual message ❑ Write a meaningful message **Individual Conferences:** (Record notes on labels) ❑ Conduct one-to-one conferences; validate message and problem-solving processes and prompt student to apply writing strategies

Dorn, L., & Soffos, C. (2013, in process). *Interventions that Work: Assisted Writing.* Boston, MA: Pearson.

Appendix D4

Personal Narrative Text Map and Writing Guide

Name: _____   Date: _____

Title:	Author:

Introduction (Who, What, When, Where):

Event:

Elaboration:

Event:

Elaboration:

Event:

Elaboration:

Event:

Elaboration:

Event:

Elaboration:

Event:

Elaboration:

Conclusion:

(continued)

Appendix D4 *(continued)*

Narrative Story Text Map and Writing Guide

Name: _____   Date: _____

Title:			
Who:	What:	When:	Where:

Introduction:

Major Events
Event 1:   Elaboration:
Event 2:   Elaboration:
Event 3:   Elaboration:

Conclusion:

(continued)

Expository Sequential Text Map and Writing Guide
(Sequence)

Name: _____   Date: _____

Title:	Author:	Topic:

Introduction:

Event 1: Elaboration:	Event 2: Elaboration:

Event 3: Elaboration:	Event 4: Elaboration:

Event 5: Elaboration:	Event 6: Elaboration:

Conclusion:

(continued)

Appendix D4 *(continued)*

Expository Sequential Text Map and Writing Guide
(How To—Instructions or Recipes)

Name: _____ Date: _____

How To:

Introduction :

Step 1:

Step 2:

Step 3:

Step 4:

Step 5:

Conclusion:

(continued)

Expository Descriptive Text Map and Writing Guide

Name: _____ Date: _____

Title:	Author:
Introduction:	

Sub-Topic

Topic

Sub-Topic

Details/Elaboration

Sub-Topic

Details/Elaboration

Details/Elaboration

Conclusion:

(continued)

Appendix D4 *(continued)*

Persuasive Text Map and Writing Guide

Name: _____   Date: _____

Title:	Author:

Position/Claim:

Introduction:

Argument:	Evidence/Support:
Argument:	Evidence/Support:
Argument:	Evidence/Support:

Conclusion/Clincher:

Appendix D5

Guidesheet for Writing Aloud
Phase One: Reading

1. **Reread Shared Poetry:** The goal is for the students to experience the rhythm, rhyme, and cadence of language by rereading poetry over and over again. Reading poetry leads to increased participation and discovery. The teacher:

   - Provides an opportunity for the students to experience language by reading aloud a poem with fluency and prosody.

   - Discusses the poem and encourages the students to respond personally to the text.

   - Uses poetry to direct students' attention to the awareness of sounds in connection with the visual features of words.

   - Engages the students in explicit word analysis

2. **Phonics (Word Work):** The goal is for students to develop knowledge of how words work and to use their phonological and orthographic knowledge to develop a system for learning about words. The teacher:

   - Provides explicit and systematic instruction to help students learn how words work (i.e., helping the students to develop a larger core of more complex site words—contains more complex word patterns using their knowledge of how words work; providing an opportunity for the students to develop a core of more complex high-frequency words; and assisting students as they recognize the link between sound and word patterns).

   - Provides explicit and systematic instruction to help students break known words at meaningful and logical units. The following represent some *possibilities* for expanding their orthographic system. The teacher:

     - Teaches the students a new and important word that would expand their repertoire of known words and support efficient processing during reading and writing.

     - Directs the students' attention to a word pattern and the teacher and students highlight or underline the pattern.

     - Prompts the students to build a known word; prompts the students to break the word at meaningful and logical units; draws the students' attention to the word pattern within the word.

     - Prompts the students to generate other words that have the same sound and visual pattern; prompts the students to categorize the words according to sound and visual patterns.

     - Prompts the students to build two known words; after the teacher asks the student to build two known words, prompts the students to take the onset of one word and the rime from another word and read the new word.

     - Provides the students with an unknown word (written on a card) and prompts them to take the word apart and read the new word; asks the students to draw lines to represent how they took the word apart.

3. **Orientation to New Text (Poem or Interactive Read Aloud):** The goal is for the students to develop ways of thinking about texts, extend their linguistic structures, and to build vocabulary through a supportive and engaging context.

   Orientation to New Text
   The teacher:

   - Introduces the text by reading the title and author.

   - Encourages the students to identify the genre.

   - Activates and builds background through a discussion.

   - Invites students to ask questions and make predictions.

   - Draws the students' attention to the illustrations including charts, graphs, maps, etc.

   - Sets the purpose for reading.

   During Reading
   The teacher:

   - Reads the text with fluency and prosody.

   - Allows for ongoing discussions at strategic places as the meaning unfolds.

   - Stops at strategic places and prompts the students to think about a word meaning, make connections, summarize information thus far, and check on their understanding.

   After Reading
   The teacher:

   - Provides an opportunity for the students to go deeper with their understanding of the text by facilitating and scaffolding a discussion about the text (e.g., the author's message or theme in relation to the world, respond personally to text or form opinions, make further predictions and inferences, discuss characters actions and outcomes, retell or summarize the text, or discuss new learning gained from nonfiction reading).

(continued)

Guidesheet for Writing Aloud
Phase Two: Writing (across subsequent days)

1. **Writing-Aloud Lesson (teacher's message may be modeled over several days):** The goal is for students to acquire knowledge of the writing process through a supportive and engaging context.

Prior Planning for the Writing-Aloud Lesson
The teacher:

- Considers genre and plans accordingly.
- Composes entire message on paper prior to the writing-aloud lesson.
- Records composing, revising, word-solving, and editing strategies to be demonstrated or modeled at strategic times over the next few days.

Day One: Planning the Message
The teacher:

- Tells the students that the purpose for the writing is to create a message that others will enjoy and/or learn from.
- Orally shares his or her message with students.
- Organizes his or her thinking on a writing guide related to author's purpose and genre.

Subsequent Days
The teacher:

- Orally reviews writing guide.
- Considers the part of the pre-planned message to be modeled for this lesson (e.g., introduction, paragraph [events or section] or conclusion).
- Considers all writing strategies needed to be modeled in today's lesson.
- Invites the students to assist her as she composes her message, adds details, and applies spelling strategies.
- Focuses on composing a meaningful message as she models the conventions of writing and spelling strategies.
- Transcribes the message and invites the students to engage in the problem-solving processes throughout the composition of the message.
- Composes her message over several days.
- Completes message and teacher and the students engage in the revision and editing processes.
- Uses a thesaurus or dictionary to reflect on word spellings.
- Guides students to use a writing checklist to reflect on the writing process.

2. **Independent Writing (student's message is written on over several days):** The goal is for the students to apply knowledge of the writing process across genre. The teacher:

- Supports students in choosing a topic to write about (related to the genre and structure the teacher used as a model).
- Provides an opportunity for the students to orally rehearse their message.
- Supports the students if needed as they rehearse their message.
- Gives the students an opportunity to plan their writing using an appropriate writing guide or outline.
- Has students write their message using lined paper and also provides a blank practice/planning page for applying problem-solving strategies while composing.
- Makes available a dictionary for the students to use to look up word spellings during the editing process.
- Supplies each student with a writing checklist daily to check on where they are in the writing process.

3. **Individual Conferences:** The goal is for the students to learn from teacher assistance. The teacher:

- Supports students with selecting a topic, completing a writing guide or outline for composing their message.
- Prompts students to apply rereading strategies to prepare for next move and to think about meaning and language.
- Encourages students to use resources to support craft.
- Prompts students to apply visual processing strategies within their zone of proximal development.
- Suggests that individual students initiate problem-solving actions needed to complete a specific task.
- Celebrates each student's completed message by allowing the student to reread his or her message.
- Records anecdotal notes on each student's understanding of the planning, crafting, and problem-solving processes used during the writing of the message.

Dorn, L., & Soffos, C. (2013, in process). *Interventions that Work: Assisted Writing.* Boston, MA: Pearson.

Appendix D6

Lesson Planner for Assisted Writing: Writing Aloud
Phase One: Reading

Group Focus: _____ Date: _____ Week: _____ Lesson: _____

Shared Reading of Poetry and Word Work	Introduce New Poem or Read-Aloud Text
Reread a Familiar Poem: Title of Poem: **Word Work:**	**New Text** (consider an option below): □ Read poem □ Read Aloud Text (Fiction or Nonfiction) **Orientation to New Text:** Title: Author: Genre: □ Narrative □ Expository (nonfiction) □ Poetry **Before Reading:** (Build and/or activate background knowledge and set a purpose for listening comprehension) **During Reading:** (Identify critical stopping places to support comprehension beyond the text, e.g., revisit purpose for listening and comprehending) □ Page numbers and language prompts: **Discussion after Reading:** (Language prompts to promote deeper comprehension beyond the text, e.g., revisit purpose for listening and comprehending) **Build or Add to Language Chart Using Examples from Text:** □ Text Structure □ Author's Craft Including Text Features □ Vocabulary Charts (words instead of . . . , examples used to describe being sad and etc.) □ Language Use and Conventions (Grammar, Spelling, Punctuation)

Dorn, L., & Soffos, C. (2013, in process). *Interventions that Work: Assisted Writing.* Boston, MA: Pearson.

(continued)

Appendix D6 (continued)

Lesson Planner for Assisted Writing: Writing Aloud
Phase Two: Writing

Group Focus: _____   Date: _____ Week: _____ Lesson: _____

Planning and Introducing Writing	During the Co-Construction of Message
Planning: **Type of Writing:** ☐ Informational/Explanatory ☐ Opinion ☐ Narrative ☐ Response to Literature **Resources to Support Writing:** ☐ Mentor text(s) ☐ Co-constructed language charts ☐ Writing checklist **Before Writing Aloud Lesson:** **Introduce Lesson:** ☐ Explain author's purpose: ☐ Genre: (narrative, informational/explanatory or persuasive) ☐ Complete writing guide to support organization OR ☐ Revisit previous day's writing ☐ Review, as a writer, where you are in the writing process and set purpose for today's composition **Message for This Lesson:**	**Draw Students' Attention to Writing Strategies During the Composition:** ☐ Composing Strategies: ☐ Word-Solving Strategies: ☐ Revising and/or Editing Strategies: **After Writing Group Message:** ☐ Use writing checklist to check on strategies used during writing **Independent Writing:** ☐ Rehearse individual message ☐ Write a meaningful message **Individual Conferences** ☐ Conduct one-to-one conferences; validate message and prompt student to apply writing strategies

Dorn, L., & Soffos, C. (2013, in process). *Interventions that Work: Assisted Writing*. Boston, MA: Pearson.

Writing Checklist
For Grades 1–2

PREWRITING

❑ Plan your story.

DRAFTING

❑ Write your story.

❑ Reread often to think about the next word.

REVISING

❑ Reread your story quietly to make sure it makes sense.

❑ Add to your story or take out what you don't want.

❑ Check for precise language (adjectives and strong verbs) and use the thesaurus as a resource.

EDITING

❑ Read your story and check for correct punctuation (periods, questions marks, commas, etc.)

❑ Check your writing for capital letters at the beginning of sentences and proper nouns.

❑ Circle words that do not look right and look up the circled words in the dictionary.

PUBLISHING

❑ Decide if this will be a piece you wish to publish now or place in your writing portfolio.

(continued)

Writing Checklist
For Grades 3–4

PREWRITING

❑ Plan your story.

DRAFTING

❑ Begin writing your story.

❑ Reread your story often to make sure it makes sense and sounds right and to help you think about the next word, phrase or idea.

REVISING

❑ Read your story to make sure it makes sense and sounds right. (subject–verb agreement, consistent verb tense throughout piece)

❑ Add to your story or take out what you don't want.

❑ Check for precise language and use the thesaurus as a resource. (strong verbs, adjectives, onomatopoeia, similes, metaphors)

EDITING

❑ Circle words that do not look right and look up the circled words in the dictionary.

❑ Read your story and check for correct punctuation. (periods, questions marks, commas, etc.)

❑ Check your writing for capital letters at the beginning of sentences and proper nouns.

PUBLISHING

❑ Decide if this will be a piece you want to publish now or place in your writing portfolio.

Appendix E1

Guidesheet for Guided Reading Plus Groups
Phase One

1. **Fluent Writing:** The goal is for the students to write fluently a large core of high-frequency words. The teacher:

   - Selects one or two partially known high-frequency words for the students to write fluently.

2. **Phonological Awareness:** The goal is for the students to hear and manipulate larger units of sound (e.g., word boundaries); hear, say and generate rhyming words; hear and manipulate smaller phonemes within words, (e.g., phoneme segmentation, deletion, addition, and blending [Phonemic Awareness]). The teacher:

   - Provides explicit instruction in hearing and manipulating the sounds of language.

   - Provides explicit instruction in identifying word boundaries, hearing, and generating rhyming words, segmenting onset and rhyme, and syllables.

   - Provides explicit instruction in hearing and manipulating individual phonemes.

   AND/OR

3. **Phonics (Letter/Word Work):** The goal is for the students to become familiar with letters and features of letters and to connect letters and sounds; build a core of high-frequency words to be read quickly; use word-solving strategies fast, fluently, and flexibly while processing in continuous text. The teacher:

   - Provides explicit instruction in letter learning.

   - Provides explicit and systematic phonics instruction to help students learn how words work.

   - Provides explicit and systematic instruction in breaking words into parts (e.g., onset and rime or at meaningful and logical units).

   - Provides explicit and systematic instruction in how to use known words and known word parts to build, read and write unknown words.

   - Provides an opportunity for the students to use known words and word patterns to read and write new words.

4. **Personal Dictionary:** The goal is for the students to acquire a core of high-frequency words that can be used in reading and writing. The teacher:

   - Provides an opportunity for the students to record known high-frequency words in their personal dictionary.

   - Provides the students with an opportunity to read their recorded words from a few pages in their dictionary for word fluency practice.

   OR

5. **Pattern Chart:** The goal is for the students to acquire knowledge of spelling patterns to be used in reading and writing. The teacher:

   - Provides the students with a resource that helps them make connections across words (e.g., provides an opportunity to notice simple word patterns, prompts to use known words from a prior word work experience to notice patterns in words).

6. **Guided Reading**

   Orientation to New Book: The goal is for the students to apply their knowledge of content, language, and reading strategies to prepare for the text reading. During the discussion, the teacher:

   - Provides an overview of the text and the teacher and the students co-construct meaning by discussing the pictures.

   - Uses specific language structures that will enable the students to predict the language during reading.

   - Discusses relevant or new vocabulary that will help the students read the text with understanding.

   - Guides the students to locate known and/or unknown words using their knowledge of letters and sounds.

   - Points out important features within text (e.g., illustrations, text structure [organization] and/or text features to support comprehension).

   During Reading of New Book: The goal is for the students to use meaning, structure and visual information in an orchestrated way to read fluently and with comprehension. The teacher:

   - Holds one-to-one conferences, listens to the student read orally and notes his/her reading fluency, word solving strategies, and checks on comprehension through a brief discussion.

   - Prompts the student to think about the text meaning, structure, and/or initiate problem-solving strategies.

   After Reading New Book: The goal is for the students to engage in a meaningful discussion and to reflect on their problem-solving and comprehending strategies. The teacher:

   - Discusses the book at the meaning level with the students (e.g., theme, new learning, and personal responses to the text).

   - Validates processing strategies used during reading.

   - Explicitly teaches for strategy development if processing strategies were neglected.

(continued)

Guidesheet for Guided Reading Plus Groups
Phase Two

1. **Reading Assessment:** The goal is for the teacher to code, score and analyze the students's reading behaviors and to use the data to plan for instruction. The teacher:

   - Takes a running record on two or more students using the guided reading text from the previous day's lesson.
   - Analyzes the behaviors used and/or neglected during reading.
   - Uses language to validate and/or activate processing during reading.

2. **Independent Reading:** The goal is for students to read texts with high levels of efficient processing and with comprehension. The teacher:

   - Provides an opportunity for students to read easy or familiar texts from their independent reading boxes.

3. **Writing about Reading**

   Writing about Reading Lesson: The goal is for the students to extend their understanding of text and apply fluent transcription processes to encode their thinking about the text. The teacher:

   - Provides the students with an oral prompt to promote deeper thinking about the text.
   - Supports the students in thinking about the text (e.g., supports the planning, encoding and problem-solving processes).
   - Models and/or prompts for word-solving strategy use.
   - Engages students in problem-solving processes on their individual wipe-off boards, if applicable.
   - Prompts the students to use known letters, sounds and words to write unknown words.

   OR

Writing Prompt: The goal is for students to extend their understanding of text by thinking about the text at higher levels and by using efficient problem-solving writing strategies to transcribe their message fluently. The teacher:

   - Provides students with a comprehension prompt that stimulates deeper thinking.
   - Supports the students in composing messages in response to prompt.
   - Prompts students to rehearse their response before writing and provides support if needed.
   - Invites the students to use their practice page to problem-solve on unknown letters or words.
   - Encourages the students to use a planning page to organize their thinking before responding and to experiment with word choice, language phrases and creating techniques during composing.

Individual Conferences: The goal is for students to initiate writing strategies (composing and transcription) independently. The teacher:

   - Prompts students to apply rereading strategies to prepare for next move and to initiate visual processing strategies while encoding their thinking.

4. **Reading and Writing Analysis:** The goal is for the teacher to use data across reading and writing to check on reading and writing and plan next lessons. The teacher:

   - Reflects on focus for lessons.
   - Uses reading and writing data to validate progress.
   - Uses reading and writing data to prepare a new focus and writes predictions of progress.

Dorn, L., & Soffos, C. (2009). *Interventions that Work: Guided Reading Plus.* Boston, MA: Pearson.

Appendix E2

Planner for Guided Reading Plus
Phase One

Group Focus: _____   Date: _____ Week: _____ Lesson: _____

Group Members:

Fluent Writing, Phonological Awareness, and Phonics	Orientation to New Book	Orientation to New Book	After Reading New Book
Word/s for Fluent Writing:	New Book: Title: _____ Level: _____ Orientation to New Book:	Unfamiliar Language Structures:	Discussion Prompts:
Phonological/Phonemic Awareness:		Relevant Vocabulary:	
Phonics (Letter/Word Work):			
Personal Dictionary or Word Pattern Chart:		New and Important Word/s:	

Appendix E2 *(continued)*

Planner for Guided Reading Plus
Phase Two

Group Focus: _____   Date: _____   Week: _____   Lesson: _____

Assessment: Running Record	Writing About Reading	Reading & Writing Group Analysis
Book Title:	Writing About Reading Lesson or Writing Prompt:	
Book Level:		
Student's Name:		
Accuracy Rate:		
SC Ratio: 1:		
Student's Name:		
Accuracy Rate:		
SC Ratio: 1:		

Dorn, L., & Soffos, C. (2009). *Interventions that Work: Guided Reading Plus.* Boston, MA: Pearson.

Appendix F1

Path of Movement for Learning about Letters

A slant down, slant down, across

B down, up around, around

C over, around and open

D down, up, around

E down, across, across, across

F down, across, across

G over, around, across

H down, down, across

I down, across, across

J down, curve, across

K down, slant in, slant out

L down, across

M down, slant down, slant up, down

N down, slant down, up

O over, around, close

P down, up, around

Q over, around, close, slant out

R down, up, around, slant out

S over, around, curve

T down, across

U down, curve up

V slant down, slant up

W slant down, slant up, slant down, slant up

X slant down, slant across

Y slant down, slant up, down

Z across, slant down, across

a over, around and down

b down . . . n, up and around

c over, around and open

d over, around u . . . p and down

e across, over, around and open

f over, dow . . . n, across

g over, around, dow . . . n and curve

h dow . . . n, up and over

i down, dot

j down, curve, dot

k dow . . . n, slant in, slant out

l dow . . . n

m down, up, over, up, over

n down, up, over

o over, around, close

p dow . . . n, up, around

q over, around, down

r down, up, curve

s over, around and curve

t down, across

u down, curve up, down

v slant down, slant up

w slant down, slant up, slant down, slant up

x slant down, slant across

y slant down, slant dow . . . n

z across, slant down, across

Appendix F2

Becoming Aware of the Phonological and Orthographic Systems
Emergent Processing Level
Guided Reading Levels: A–C

Possibilities for Strategic Letter Work

- Reads ABC chart chorally; reads in a variety of ways (reads consonants, reads vowels, every other letter).
- Reads letter books chorally.
- Develops knowledge for how to learn letters (describes path of movement).
- Recognizes and sorts distinguishable features of letters.
- Recognizes and names all upper- and lower-case letters fluently.
- Writes most upper- and lowercase letters fluently.

Possibilities for Strategic Word Work
(Building word knowledge and supporting visual searching processes)

- Builds name letter by letter in left-to-right order using a model and without a model; breaks word (name) letter by letter; rebuilds word (name) letter by letter; reads word (name) with fluency.

- Builds, breaks, and reassembles grade-level, simple high-frequency words letter by letter in a left-to-right order; reads words with fluency.
- Builds simple one-syllable CVC words in left-to-right order; breaks words letter by letter and blends letter sounds back together to say words (*cat, c-a-t, cat, run, r-u-n, run*); reads words with fluency (*is, at, am*).
- Builds simple one-syllable CVC words in a left-to-right order; distinguishes between similarly spelled words by identifying the sounds of the letters that are different (*bat, sat; cat, can; hit, hot*); reads words.
- Records simple high-frequency words or CVC words in personal dictionary using first letter; reads recorded words with fluency.
- Builds known words with CVC pattern; breaks words using onset and rime; blends parts back together; reads words with fluency.
- Builds known words with a CVC pattern; breaks words using onset and rime; rebuilds words; generates other words that sound the same (*h-am, f-an*); manipulates onset to make new words; reads new words with fluency.

(continued)

Increasing Awareness of the Phonological and Orthographic Systems
Beginning Early Processing Level
Guided Reading Levels: D–E

Possibilities for Strategic Letter Work

- Reads ABC chart chorally.
- Reads letter books chorally.
- Develops knowledge for how to form letter (describe path of movement).
- Recognizes and categorizes distinguishable features of letters.
- Identifies and categorizes letters by vowels and consonants.
- Recognizes and names all upper- and lower-case letters fluently.
- Writes most upper- and lowercase letters fluently.

Possibilities for Strategic Word Work

(Building word knowledge and supporting visual searching processes)

- Builds, breaks, and reassembles simple grade-level high-frequency words letter by letter in a left-to-right order (*w-e-n-t, went*); reads words with fluency.
- Writes simple high-frequency words (grade appropriate) in a personal dictionary using first letter; reads recorded words with fluency.
- Builds simple VC words in left-to-right order; breaks words letter by letter and rebuilds words; reads words with fluency (*is, at, am*).

- Builds simple one-syllable CVC words in left-to-right order; breaks words letter by letter and rebuilds words; reads words with fluency (*cat, c-a-t, cat; run, r-u-n, run*).
- Builds simple one-syllable CVC words in left-to-right order; manipulates consonants or vowels in the beginning, middle, or ending position to make new words (*cat, hat; hot, hit; stop, step*); reads new words with fluency.
- Builds known words with a CVC pattern; breaks words using onset and rime; generates other words that sound the same (*h-am, f-an*); manipulates onset to make new words; reads words with fluency.
- Builds known words with a CVCe pattern in left-to-right order; breaks words letter by letter; rebuilds words letter by letter; reads words with fluency (*have, h-a-v-e*).
- Builds known words in a left-to-right order; adds inflectional endings (*s, ing, ed*) to make new words (*looks, looking, looked*); reads words with fluency.
- Builds words in left-to-right order with consonant clusters and diagraphs in beginning, and ending position; breaks words using onset and rime patterns (*st-ep, f-ish*) or at meaningful and logical units (*sh-i-p, f-i-sh*); builds words; reads words with fluency.

(continued)

Gaining Control of the Phonological and Orthographic Language Systems
Late Early Processing Level
Guided Reading Levels: F–G

Possibilities for Strategic Letter Work

- Develops speed, fluency, and ease in identifying and writing all upper- and lowercase letters.

Possibilities for Strategic Word Work
(Building word knowledge and supporting visual searching processes)

- Builds, breaks, and reassembles grade level high-frequency words letter by letter in left-to-right order (*w-h-e-n, when; a-w-a-y, away*); reads words with fluency.

- Reads regularly spelled one-syllable words with fluency using knowledge of word patterns (*much, bake, bring*).

- Reads two-syllable words; breaks words (using basic pattern and syllable knowledge); reads words with fluency (*rab-bit, stop-ping*).

- Reads irregularly spelled words (*said, their, there, none, both*); forms generalizations about words; reads words with fluency.

- Builds base words in a left-to-right order and adds inflectional endings (*-ing, -ed*) (*stop-stopped, stopping*); forms generalizations about word ending; reads words with fluency.

- Builds base words in a left-to-right order; adds (*-s* or *-es*) to base word to form plurals; forms generalizations about word meanings; reads words with fluency (*balls, glasses*).

- Reads regularly spelled, one-syllable short and long vowel words; distinguishes between short (CVC: *cat*) and long vowels (CVCe: *bike*; CVVC: *steep*).

- Builds words with long vowel patterns (vowel teams) in a left-to-right order; breaks words at meaningful and logical units (*sh-e-e-t* or *sh-ee-t* or *sh-eet*; *s-e-a-t* or *s-ea-t* or *s-eat*); attends to vowel word patterns; rebuilds words; reads words with fluency.

- Builds words with long vowel patterns (vowel teams); generates other words that sound the same and look the same; forms generalizations of long vowel word patterns; reads words with fluency.

- Builds words with consonant diagraphs (beginning or ending position) in left-to-right order; breaks words at meaningful and logical units (*sh-ir-t; sh-irt; fish, wash*); attends to diagraphs in beginning or ending position; reads words with fluency.

- Uses known patterns or word parts to build and read new words; reads words with fluency (*stop + day = stay*).

- Builds words with *r* controlled vowels in a left-to-right order; breaks words at meaningful and logical units (*c-a-r* or *c-ar; st-a-r-t* or *st-ar-t* or *st-art*); blends parts back together to read words; notices diphthong patterns; generates other words that have the same sound and look the same.

- Builds words with diphthongs in a left-to-right order; breaks words at meaningful and logical units (*h-o-u-s-e* or *h-ou-s-e* or *h-ouse; fl-o-w-e-r* or *fl-ow-er*); blends parts back together to read words; attends to diphthong patterns; generates other words that have the same sound and look the same.

- Reads compound words; breaks words at meaningful and logic units (*out-side, sun-shine*); forms generalizations about words.

- Builds two known words (*I, am*); removes a letter or letters to form a contraction (*I'm*); forms generalizations about words; reads words with fluency.

- Reads unknown words by breaking words into syllables; uses knowledge that every syllable contains a vowel sound to determine the number of syllables in a printed word; reads words with fluency, (e.g., *can/dy*).

(continued)

Developing Control of the Phonological and Orthographic Language Systems
Transitional Processing Level
Guided Reading Levels: H–M

Possibilities for Strategic Word Work
(Building word knowledge and supporting visual searching processes)

- Builds, reads, and writes many high-frequency words with fluency.

- Builds and reads words with long vowel patterns (vowel teams) with fluency.

- Builds words with additional common vowel patterns (vowel teams); breaks words at meaningful and logical units (*l-ou-d, h-oo-p, sn-ow, b-oy, s-oi-l, c-or-n, c-ar-t*); rebuilds words; attends to additional vowel patterns (vowel teams); reads words with fluency.

- Builds and reads words with consonant blends and digraphs in beginning, medial, and ending positions with fluency (*bathtub, spend, splash, chair, whale*).

- Builds regularly spelled two-syllable words with long vowels; uses knowledge of word patterns to make words; breaks words at meaningful and logical units; forms additional generalizations about word patterns; reads words with fluency.

- Builds base words; makes new words by changing letters and adding common prefixes and derivational suffixes; forms generalizations about word meanings (*do* vs. *undo*; *help* vs. *helpful*); reads words with fluency.

- Builds base words; makes new words by adding common prefixes and derivational suffixes (*un, re, mis, ful, less, able*); forms generalizations about base words and changes in meaning when adding or deleting prefixes or suffixes; reads words with fluency.

- Builds base words; makes new words by adding common Latin suffixes (*-tion/sion; -ity, -ment*); forms generalizations about base words and changes in word meaning when adding Latin suffixes; reads words with fluency.

- Builds base words; makes new words by adding suffixes that form comparatives (*high/ higher/highest*); forms generalization about base words and changes in meaning when adding a comparative suffix; reads words with fluency.

- Builds words with silent consonants; breaks words at meaning and logical units; forms additional generalizations about word patterns; reads words with fluency (*sight, know*).

- Builds and reads a range of contractions (*that's, won't, they're, you've*) with fluency.

- Builds and reads grade-level appropriate irregularly spelled words; forms generalizations about words; reads words with fluency (*through, eyes, busy, people*).

- Builds base words; makes new words by changing and/or adding letter(s) (*s, es*) to form plurals; forms generalizations about word meanings; reads words with fluency (*boys, boxes, stoves*).

- Builds and reads base words; adds inflectional endings (*-ing, -ed*) (*stop-stopped, stopping; lunch, lunches*); forms generalizations about words; reads words with fluency.

- Builds homophones (same pronunciation, but different spelling) or homographs (same spelling, different meanings, and sometimes different pronunciations) using meaning as the basis for building the correct words; forms generalizations about word meanings; reads words with fluency.

- Uses known patterns or word parts to build and read multisyllabic words; reads words with fluency (*whisper, mistake, invention*).

Appendix F3

Word/Spelling Patterns

Note: It is important to remember that children DO NOT need to learn every word or spelling pattern in isolation. Once they understand there are patterns in words and learn how to look for them, they will discover more for themselves.

(*Represents 37 common rime patterns)

Short-Vowel Patterns — One Syllable Words

Short-a patterns	
-at*	cat, sat, at, mat, that
-an*	can, man, an, ran, fan
-am*	am, jam, ham, clam
-ad	had, bad, mad, sad, glad
-ag	bag, flag, drag, brag
-ap*	map, snap, clap, strap
-ack*	back, black, pack, sack
-and*	and, sand, hand, stand
-ank*	bank, sank, drank, tank
-ash*	dash, rash, flash, sash
Short-e Patterns	
-ed	bed, red
-ell*	tell, well, yell
-en	ten, men, when
-et*	get, let, pet, set, wet, yet
-end	end, send, bend
-ent	cent, went, sent
-est*	best, nest, rest
Short-i patterns	
-it*	it, sit
-in*	in, win, skin
-ill*	will, hill
-id	did, hid, kid
-ig	big, pig, dig
-ing*	ring, sing, thing, bring
-ip*	ship, trip, slip
-ick*	pick, sick trick
-ish	dish, fish, wish
-ink*	wink, sink, link, stink

Long-Vowel Patterns — One Syllable Words

Long-a patterns	
-ake*	cake, take, wake, shake
-ame*	came, name, same, game
-ate,* -ait	ate, date, late, hate; wait
-ave	gave, save, wave, brave
-ade, -aid	made, grade; paid
-ace	face, race, place
-age	age, page, cage
-ale,* -ail	whale; tail, sail, mail
-ain,* -ane	rain, train; plane, crane
-ay*	day, may, say, stay, play
Long-e patterns	
-e, ee,	he, me, she; see, free, tree, three
-eep	keep, sleep, jeep, sheep
-een, -ean	green; mean, clean
-eet, -eat*	feet, meet, sweet; heat
-eel, eal	feel; meal, real
-ead, -eed	read; need, feed
-eam	dream, cream, stream
Long-i patterns	
-ie, igh	pie, lie; high
-ight*	night, light, might, right
-ike	bike, like, hike
-ide*	ide, ride, side, wide
-ime	time, dime, lime
-ine	nine, line, mine, shine
-ice*	ice, nice, rice
-ile	mile, smile, while
-ife	life
-ite	bite, white
-y	my, cry, sky, why, fly

R-Vowel and Other-Vowel Patterns — One Syllable Words

R-vowel patterns	
-ar*	car, far, jar, star
-ark	park, bark, dark
-arm	arm, farm, harm
-art	part, start; heart
-air, -are, -ere	hair, pair, chair; care, share, scare; where, there
-or, -ore, -oor	for, more, tore, wore, store; door, poor
-orn	born, corn, horn, torn
-ir, -ur, -er	sir, stir; fur; her
-urn, -earn	burn, turn; earn, learn
-ird, -ord, -eard	bird, third; word; heard
-ear, -eer	ear, dear, fear, hear, near; steer
aw patterns	
-all*	all, ball, call, fall, tall, small
-aw*	saw, draw
-alk	walk, talk, chalk
-aught, -ought	caught, taught; ought, bought
-ost	cost, lost
-ong	long, song, strong, wrong
oo patterns	
-oo	zoo, too; moon, noon, soon
-new, ue	new, flew, grew; blue, true
-oot, uit	boot, shoot; fruit, suit
-ool	cool, fool, pool, school
-oom	boom, broom, room
-ook	book, took, look, shook
-ood, -ould	stood, wood, good; could, would, should
-ull	pull
-ush	push, bush

(continued)

Appendix F3 *(continued)*

	Short-o patterns		**Long-o patterns**		**ow patterns**
-op*	hop, top, shop	-o; -oe	no, go, so, toe	-ow	cow, how, now
-ot*	lot, hot, not, spot	-ow	low, grow, show, slow, know	-own	down, town, brown, clown
-ock*	block, clock	-oat	goat, boat, coat; note, wrote	-ound	found, sound, round, pound
		-oad	toad, load, road	-oud, -owd	loud, cloud, proud; crowd
		-ole, -oll	hole, pole; roll	-out	out, shout
		-old*	old, gold, cold, hold, sold, told	-ouse	house, mouse
		-oke*	woke, joke, broke, spoke		
		-ose	nose, rose, chose, close, those		
		-one	bone, alone		
		-ore*	store, chore		

	Short-u patterns		**Long-u patterns**		**oy patterns**
-ug*	bug, rug, hug	-ule	mule	-oy	boy, toy, joy
-un	fun, run, sun	-use	use	-oil	oil, boil
-ut	but, cut, shut	-uge	huge		
-up	up, cup	-ute	flute		
-ub	cub, rub, tub	-ew	few		
-ump*	bump, jump, dump				
-unk*	junk, skunk, trunk				
-us	us, bus				
-ust	must, just				
-uck*	truck, luck				

Gunning, BUILDING WORDS, Table 9.3, "Spelling Patterns" pp. 234–235, © 2001 by Pearson. Reproduced by permission of Pearson Education, Inc.

Appendix F3 (continued)

Syllable Patterns

High-frequency patterns		Other vowel Patterns	
Compound words	someone, sometime, something, anyone, anything, outside, inside	al, au, aw	also, although, always; autumn, author; awful, drawing
Schwa-a	ago, away, alone, about, around, along, across, again, against, asleep	-oi, -oy	noisy; enjoy, destroy, loyal, voyage
		-ou, -ow	around, about, announce; flower, allow, power
-en	open, happen, twenty, plenty	-oo, -u = oo	balloon, cartoon; super, student, truly, tuna
-er	over, under, ever, never, other, brother, mother	-ook	book, bookstore
-ar	garden, farmer	-oot	football
-at	matter	-ood	neighborhood, goodness
-it	kitten, kitchen	-ful	thankful, careful
-in	winter, dinner, finish	-tion , -sion	action, addition, invention, information, question, mention, confusion, occasion
-is (s)	sister, mistake, whisper		
-un	under, until, hundred		
be-	became, below, begin, belong		
re-	report, receive		
-or	before, morning, forty		
-a	paper, baby, famous		
y = e	sunny, funny, money		
-i	tiger, tiny, spider, Friday		
-ur	hurry, purple		

Short-vowel patterns		Long-vowel patterns	
-ic(k)	chicken, nickel, pickle	-ea, -ee = long e	season, reason, easily, eaten, repeat, leader; beetle, indeed, succeed, agree
-et	letter, lettuce, settle, metal	-ide	beside, divide, decide
-im	limit, improve, simple	-ise	surprise
-ab	absent, cabin	-ail, -ale	detail, female
-ad	shadow, ladder, address	-ain	contain, explain, obtain
-ag	magazine, magnet	-ate	hesitate, appreciate
-ang	sang, angry	-ope	envelope, telescope
-am	hammer	-oke	broken, spoken
-an	candy	-ope	envelope
-ap	happy, happen, captain, chapter	-u, -ture	future, nature adventure, creature
-ent	event, prevent		
-el (l)	yellow, elbow, jelly, welcome		
-il (l)	middle, hidden, midnight		
-oc	doctor, chocolate,		
--op	copy, popular, opposite		
-ot	bottom, bottle, robot		
-ub	rubber, stubborn		
-uck	lucky, chuckle		
-ud	sudden, study		
-ug	struggle		
-up	puppy, supper, upper		
-us	muscle, discuss		
-ut	butter		

Environmental Scale for Assessing Implementation Levels (ESAIL)
Descriptions of Ten Criteria
Developed by L. Dorn & C. Soffos (2005)

The ESAIL instrument is designed to assess a school's level of implementation in a comprehensive literacy model, specifically the Partnerships in Comprehensive Literacy (PCL) model. Schools can use the ESAIL for multiple purposes, including: 1) a pre-assessment to determine a school's readiness for implementing a comprehensive literacy model; 2) a periodic assessment to study a school's growth over time on one or more literacy criteria, and 3) a post-assessment to measure a school's improvement over the academic year. Schools can use the ESAIL to guide and monitor school-wide efforts, including professional development in particular areas. All PCL schools must include the results from the ESAIL in annual reports and school plans.

Criterion 1: Creates a Literate Environment

Teachers create a literate environment by providing a wide variety of reading experiences, including rich and diverse opportunities for students to read, discuss, and write texts across the curriculum. Students' learning at various stages in the reading and writing process is celebrated and displayed on walls within and outside classrooms. Classrooms are arranged to promote whole and small group problem-solving discussions. Inquiry-based learning is evident, including relevant and purposeful talk. Respectful talk and attitudes are promoted and used among students, and students' questions are valued by providing additional opportunities for clarifying and seeking information through research.

Criterion 2: Organizes the Classroom

Teachers organize the classroom to meet the needs of diverse learners, including selecting appropriate materials and working with whole group, small group, and individual learners. Other features include an emphasis on establishing classroom norms that support the children's ability to self-regulate their literate behaviors for different purposes and across changing contexts, including staying on-task, working independently, assuming responsibility for classroom materials, and respecting the rights of others. Teachers' workspace and materials, including assessment notebooks, are organized and used to document learning and plan for instruction. Students' workspace and materials, including students' logs, are organized and easily accessible. Classroom libraries are well organized and contain an abundant amount of reading material across genres, authors and topics.

Criterion 3: Uses Data to Inform Instruction and to Provide Research-Based Interventions

Teachers use assessments to inform instruction and to monitor students' learning. A range of summative and formative assessments are used, including portfolio assessments, conference notes, constructed response measures, observations, anecdotal notes, running records, logs, and norm- and criterion-referenced tests. Data are used to tailor interventions that provide multiple layers of support for the most needy students, including a comprehensive intervention model with Reading Recovery in first grade and small group interventions across the grades. The specialty teachers collaborate and plan with the classroom teachers to ensure consistency of interventions across the school day.

Criterion 4: Uses a Differentiated Approach to Learning

Teachers use a workshop approach to learning across the curriculum, including reading, writing, language, and content workshops. Small group reading and writing instruction is provided to meet the needs of diverse learners; and explicit minilessons are tailored to meet the needs of the majority of students across the curriculum. Daily one-to-one conferences are scheduled with students during the workshop framework. Teaching prompts are used to promote problem-solving strategies, higher-order thinking processes, and deeper comprehension. Quality literature is read, enjoyed, and analyzed across the various workshops. A writing continuum is used to meet student needs, plan instruction, and monitor student progress. Writing is taught as a process, including drafting, revising, editing, and publishing processes. Mentor texts and notebooks are used as resources across genres; and inquiry-based learning is promoted and arranged across the content areas.

(continued)

Criterion 5: Uses Assessment Wall for School-wide Progress Monitoring

Schools use common assessments across grade levels for measuring student achievement. Data on the assessment/intervention wall are used for monitoring program effectiveness and to ensure struggling students are receiving appropriate interventions.

Criterion 6: Uses Literacy Coach to Support Teacher Knowledge and Reflective Practice

Coach follows guidelines for coordinating, monitoring, and assessing school change: 50%-60% of time coaching and supporting teachers in the classroom, and planning and implementing literacy team meetings and other professional learning opportunities for teachers; 20%-40% of time teaching struggling readers in intervention groups; and 10%-20% of time coordinating and supervising the school's literacy program, including meeting with administrators, designing curriculum, analyzing and reporting data for school improvement, and spotlighting the school's literacy program. Coach applies scaffolding techniques through coaching cycles that use a gradual release model to promote self-regulated teachers. Coach coordinates an assessment team, collects school-wide data, assists in data analysis for continuous school improvement, and uses results for school planning.

Criterion 7: Builds Collaborative Learning Communities

Coach plans and coordinates teachers' professional study groups, grade level planning, and peer observations. Coach creates a climate for collaborative problem-solving and reflective practice. Teachers use reflection logs to reflect on learning during and after team meetings, conferences, cluster visits, and other professional learning experiences.

Criterion 8: Creates and Uses School Plans for Promoting Systemic Change

Coach and teachers collaboratively identify strengths and needs of current literacy practices and create a plan of action, including school plan with timelines and persons responsible for executing the plan. Coach and teachers share with stakeholders and gain support for school improvement initiatives. Coach compiles data into a school report and shares results with stakeholders.

Criterion 9: Uses Technology for Effective Communication

Coach and teachers network with other professionals through the use of technology including list servers and discussion boards. They use technology to collect, analyze, and store student data and keep current with research and best practices. Coach models effective use of technology through well-designed Powerpoint presentations, Internet searches, and research. Teachers provide opportunities for students to use technology for real world purposes, including word processing, research, and presenting information.

Criterion 10: Advocates and Spotlights School's Literacy Program

Stakeholders, including parents, are informed and engaged in accomplishments of the school's literacy goals. Coach and teachers invite the community into the classrooms and recruit volunteers to assist with the school's literacy initiatives. Coach disseminates information (e.g., brochures, school reports, newsletters) on the school's literacy program to various audiences.

(continued)

ESAIL: Environmental Scale for Assessing Implementation Levels

Criterion 1: Creates a Literate Environment	Proficiency Levels		
	Meeting	Approaching	Below
1. Reading responses through writing are displayed on walls and in hallways.			
2. Writing is taught as a process and published version is displayed on walls and in hallways.			
3. Diverse reading materials are enjoyed, discussed and analyzed across the curriculum.			
4. Co-constructed language charts embrace student language and are displayed on walls and in students' notebooks.			
5. Tables, clusters of desks and/or areas are arranged to promote collaborative learning and problem-solving.			
6. Problem-solving is collaborative (pairs or groups) and talk is purposeful.			
7. Engagement is maintained by meaningfulness and relevance of the task.			
8. Respectful talk and attitudes are promoted and used among all learners.			
9. Elaborated discussions around specific concepts are promoted and students' thinking is valued and discussed.			
10. Classroom environment is conducive to inquiry based learning and learners are engaged in constructive interactions around purposeful literacy events.			

Criterion 2: Organizes the Classroom	Proficiency Levels		
	Meeting	Approaching	Below
1. Routines and procedures are clearly established.			
2. Classroom is designed for whole group, small group and individual teaching and learning.			
3. Teachers' workspace and instructional materials are organized for teaching and learning.			
4. Students' materials are organized and easily accessible.			
5. Students' logs are organized and reflect integrated learning across the curriculum.			
6. Classroom libraries contain an abundant amount of reading material across genres, authors and topics.			
7. Literature for daily instruction is organized and accessible.			

(continued)

Criterion 2: Organizes the Classroom (continued)	Proficiency Levels		
	Meeting	Approaching	Below
8. Books in classroom library are organized and labeled according to genre, topic and/or by author.			
9. Literacy tasks are organized and are designed to meet the needs of groups and individual learners.			
10. Summative and formative assessments are organized for instructional purposes and documentation.			

Criterion 3: Uses Data to Inform Instruction and to Provide Research-Based Interventions	Proficiency Levels		
	Meeting	Approaching	Below
1. Summative and formative assessments are used to determine where to begin instruction and to provide interventions.			
2. Data are used across the curriculum to monitor student progress and to guide and plan instruction.			
3. Summative and formative assessments are used to tailor in-class interventions to meet the needs of struggling learners.			
4. Data are used to plan a Comprehensive Intervention Model (CIM), including one-to-one and small groups in grades K–8.			
5. Teachers collaborate with intervention teacher/s around student/s progress and collaboratively develop a plan of action.			

Criterion 4: Uses a Differentiated Approach to Learning	Proficiency Levels		
	Meeting	Approaching	Below
1. Instruction includes a workshop approach to learning across the curriculum.			
2. Explicit minilessons are tailored to meet the needs of the majority of students across the curriculum.			
3. Daily small group reading and writing instruction is provided to meet the diverse needs of students.			
4. Daily one-to-one reading and writing conferences are scheduled with students.			
5. Prompts are used to activate successful problem-solving strategies, higher order thinking, and deeper comprehension.			
6. Writing is taught as a process, including composing, drafting, revising, editing, and publishing.			
7. A writing continuum is used to meet student needs, plan instruction, and monitor progress over time.			
8. Quality literature is read, enjoyed and analyzed across the curriculum.			

(continued)

Criterion 4: Uses a Differentiated Approach to Learning (continued)	Proficiency Levels		
	Meeting	Approaching	Below
9. Mentor texts and notebooks are used as resources across genres.			
10. Inquiry based learning opportunities are promoted and arranged across the curriculum.			

Criterion 5: Uses Assessment Wall for School-wide Progress Monitoring	Proficiency Levels		
	Meeting	Approaching	Below
1. Common assessments are developed and used across grade levels for measuring student achievement.			
2. Data on the assessment/intervention wall are used for progress monitoring school-wide program effectiveness.			
3. Data on the assessment/intervention wall are used to ensure struggling students are receiving appropriate interventions.			

Criterion 6: Uses Literacy Coaches to Support Teacher Knowledge and Reflective Practice	Proficiency Levels		
	Meeting	Approaching	Below
1. Coach supports teachers in classrooms; teaches groups of struggling learners, networks with other coaches; plans team meetings; meets weekly with principal; and coordinates the school's literacy program.			
2. Coach uses coaching cycles and scaffolding techniques in a gradual release model to promote self-regulated teachers.			
3. Coach collects data from teachers and organizes and assists in data analysis for assessing program effectiveness in the school.			
4. Coach guides teachers in analyzing data for assessing teaching and learning across various curricular areas.			
5. Coach organizes an assessment team in the school to assess new students and discusses data with teachers.			

Criterion 7: Builds Collaborative Learning Communities	Proficiency Levels		
	Meeting	Approaching	Below
1. Administrator and coach plan and coordinate teacher professional study groups, grade level planning, and peer observations.			
2. Administrator and coach create a climate for collaborative problem-solving and reflective practice.			
3. Teachers use reflection logs to reflect on learning during and after team meetings and to engage in problem-solving discussions.			

(continued)

Appendix G1 *(continued)*

Criterion 8: Creates and Uses School Plans for Promoting Systemic Change	Proficiency Levels		
	Meeting	Approaching	Below
1. Coach, teachers, and administrators collaboratively identify strengths and needs of current literacy practices and create a plan of action (school plan with timelines and persons responsible for executing the plan).			
2. Coach, teachers, and administrators share plan with stakeholders and gain support for school improvement initiatives.			
3. Coach compiles data into a school report and shares results with stakeholders.			

Criterion 9: Uses Technology for Effective Communication	Proficiency Levels		
	Meeting	Approaching	Below
1. Coach and teachers network with other professionals through the use of technology including list serves and discussion boards.			
2. Coach and teachers use technology to collect, analyze and store student data and keep current with research and best practices.			
3. Coach models effective use of technology through well-designed presentations, Internet searches, research, etc.			
4. Teachers provide opportunities for students to use technology for real world purposes, including word processing, research and presenting information.			

Criterion 10: Advocates and Spotlights School's Literacy Program	Proficiency Levels		
	Meeting	Approaching	Below
1. Stakeholders, including parents, are informed and engaged in accomplishments of the school's literacy goals.			
2. Coach and teachers invite the community into the classrooms and recruit volunteers to assist with the school's literacy initiatives.			
3. Coach disseminates information on the school's literacy program to various audiences (brochures, school reports, newsletters, etc.).			

Washington School for Comprehensive Literacy Assessment System 2009–2010

Bold Assessments are for all students. Italic Assessments are for Below and Approaching Students on the Intervention Wall (Stages I–III on the OLAI)

Grade	Beginning-of-Year — Sep 28–30: Intervention Wall Placement		First Quarter — Nov 6: First Quarter Ends / Nov 16–18: Update Intervention Wall		Second Quarter — Jan 21: Second Quarter Ends / Jan 25–27: Update Intervention Wall		Third Quarter — Mar 26: Third Quarter Ends / April 6–7: Update Intervention Wall		End-of-Year — Jun 1–2: Update Intervention Wall / Jun 9: Fourth Quarter Ends	
	Summative (Formal)	Formative (Informal)	Summative (Formal)	Formative (Informal)	Summative (Formal)	Formative (Informal)	Summative (Formal)	Formative (Informal)	Summative (Formal)	Formative (Informal)
Kindergarten	Observation Survey (Letter ID; CAP; Writing Vocabulary; Sentence Dictation; DRA)	2-Week Reading Observation	Letter ID	Reading Conference Notes	Benchmark Book • 90–94% Accuracy • NAEP Fluency • Comprehension • SC Rate	Reading Conference Notes	Benchmark Book* • 90–94% Accuracy • NAEP Fluency • Comprehension • SC Rate	Reading Conference Notes	Observation Survey (Letter ID; CAP; Writing Vocabulary; Sentence Dictation; DRA)	Reading Conference Notes
		2-Week Writing Observation	Concepts About Print (CAP)	Writing Conference Notes	Letter ID	Writing Conference Notes	Letter ID	Writing Conference Notes	Clay Writing Assessment	Writing Conference Notes
			Clay Writing Assessment	Quarterly Writing Checklist	Concepts About Print (CAP)	Running Records	Concepts About Print (CAP)	Running Records	Gentry Spelling Assessment	Running Records
			Gentry Spelling Assessment			Quarterly Writing Checklist		Quarterly Writing Checklist	*Oral Language Acquisition Inventory*	Quarterly Writing Checklist
	Oral Language Acquisition Inventory				*Oral Language Acquisition Inventory*					
1st Grade	Spring DRA from Assessment Folder • 90–94% Accuracy • NAEP Fluency • Comprehension • SC Rate	2-Week Reading Observation	Benchmark Book • 90–94% Accuracy • NAEP Fluency • Comprehension • SC Rate	Reading Conference Notes	Benchmark Book • 90–94% Accuracy • NAEP Fluency • Comprehension • SC Rate	Reading Conference Notes	Benchmark Book • 90–94% Accuracy • NAEP Fluency • Comprehension • SC Rate	Reading Conference Notes	DRA Level • 90–94% Accuracy • NAEP Fluency • Comprehension • SC Rate	Reading Conference Notes
	Personal Narrative Writing Prompt	2-Week Writing Observation	Genre Writing Prompt	Writing Conference Notes	Gentry Spelling Assessment	Writing Conference Notes	Genre Writing Prompt	Writing Conference Notes	Personal Narrative Writing Prompt	Writing Conference Notes
	Gentry Spelling Assessment	2-Week Spelling Observation		Running Records	Genre Writing Prompt	Running Records		Running Records	Gentry Spelling Assessment	Running Records
	Benchmark Book • 90–94% Accuracy • NAEP Fluency • Comprehension • SC Rate			Independent Reading Rubric	*Oral Language Acquisition Inventory*	Independent Reading Rubric		Independent Reading Rubric	*Oral Language Acquisition Inventory*	Independent Reading Rubric
	Oral Language Acquisition Inventory			Writing Portfolio Rubric		Writing Portfolio Rubric		Writing Portfolio Rubric	Independent Reading Rubric	Writing Portfolio Rubric

(continued)

Pages 193–195 reprinted with the permission of the International Reading Association, from *RtI in Literacy: Responsive and Comprehensive* (2010), Johnston, P.H., pp. 137–142.

Appendix G2 (continued)

Grade										
2nd Grade	Spring DRA from Assessment Folder • 90–94% Accuracy • NAEP Fluency • Comprehension • SC Rate	2-Week Reading Observation	Benchmark Book • 90–94% Accuracy • NAEP Fluency • Comprehension • SC Rate	Reading Conference Notes	Benchmark Book • 90–94% Accuracy • NAEP Fluency • Comprehension • SC Rate	Reading Conference Notes	Benchmark Book • 90–94% Accuracy • NAEP Fluency • Comprehension • SC Rate	Reading Conference Notes	DRA Level • 90–94% Accuracy • NAEP Fluency • Comprehension • SC Rate	Reading Conference Notes
	Spring Writing Prompt from Assessment Folder	2-Week Writing Observation	Genre Writing Prompt	Writing Conference Notes	Words Their Way Spelling Assessment	Writing Conference Notes	Genre Writing Prompt	Writing Conference Notes	Personal Narrative Writing Prompt	Writing Conference Notes
	Words Their Way Spelling Assessment	2-Week Spelling Observation		Thoughtful Log Entry Rubric	Genre Writing Prompt	Literature Discussion Rubric		Literature Discussion Rubric	Words Their Way Spelling Assessment	Literature Discussion Rubric
	Benchmark Book • 90–94% Accuracy • NAEP Fluency • Comprehension • SC Rate			Independent Reading Rubric	*Oral Language Acquisition Inventory*	Thoughtful Log Entry Rubric		Thoughtful Log Entry Rubric	*Oral Language Acquisition Inventory*	Thoughtful Log Entry Rubric
	Oral Language Acquisition Inventory			Writing Portfolio Rubric		Independent Reading Rubric		Independent Reading Rubric		Independent Reading Rubric
						Writing Portfolio Rubric		Writing Portfolio Rubric		Writing Portfolio Rubric
3rd Grade	Spring DRA from Assessment Folder • 90–94% Accuracy • NAEP Fluency • Comprehension • SC Rate	2-Week Reading Observation	Benchmark Book • 90–94% Accuracy • NAEP Fluency • Comprehension • SC Rate	Reading Conference Notes	Benchmark Book • 90–94% Accuracy • NAEP Fluency • Comprehension • SC Rate	Reading Conference Notes	Benchmark Book • 90–94% Accuracy • NAEP Fluency • Comprehension • SC Rate	Reading Conference Notes	DRA Level • 90–94% Accuracy • NAEP Fluency • Comprehension • SC Rate	Reading Conference Notes
	Spring Writing Prompt from Assessment Folder	2-Week Writing Observation	Genre Writing Prompt	Writing Conference Notes	Genre Writing Prompt	Writing Conference Notes	Genre Writing Prompt	Writing Conference Notes	Personal Narrative Writing Prompt	Writing Conference Notes
	Spring Words Their Way Spelling from Assessment Folder			Literature Discussion Rubric	Words Their Way Spelling Assessment	Literature Discussion Rubric		Literature Discussion Rubric	Words Their Way Spelling Assessment	Literature Discussion Rubric
	Oral Language Acquisition Inventory			Thoughtful Log Entry Rubric	*Oral Language Acquisition Inventory*	Thoughtful Log Entry Rubric		Thoughtful Log Entry Rubric	*Oral Language Acquisition Inventory*	Thoughtful Log Entry Rubric
	Benchmark Book • 90–94% Accuracy • NAEP Fluency • Comprehension • SC Rate			Independent Reading Rubric		Independent Reading Rubric		Independent Reading Rubric		Independent Reading Rubric
				Writing Portfolio Rubric		Writing Portfolio Rubric		Writing Portfolio Rubric		Writing Portfolio Rubric

(continued)

Grade									
4th Grade	Spring DRA from Assessment Folder • 90–94% Accuracy • NAEP Fluency • Comprehension • SC Rate 2-Week Reading Observation Spring Writing Prompt from Assessment Folder 2-Week Writing Observation Spring Words Their Way Spelling from Assessment Folder 2-Week Spelling Observation Oral Language Acquisition Inventory Benchmark Book • 90–94% Accuracy • NAEP Fluency • Comprehension • SC Rate	Benchmark Book • 90–94% Accuracy • NAEP Fluency • Comprehension • SC Rate Genre Writing Prompt Writing Portfolio Rubric	Reading Conference Notes Writing Conference Notes Literature Discussion Rubric Thoughtful Log Entry Rubric Independent Reading Rubric Writing Portfolio Rubric	Benchmark Book • 90–94% Accuracy • NAEP Fluency • Comprehension • SC Rate Words Their Way Spelling Assessment Genre Writing Prompt Oral Language Acquisition Inventory	Reading Conference Notes Writing Conference Notes Literature Discussion Rubric Thoughtful Log Entry Rubric Independent Reading Rubric Writing Portfolio Rubric	Benchmark Book • 90–94% Accuracy • NAEP Fluency • Comprehension • SC Rate Genre Writing Rubric	Reading Conference Notes Writing Conference Notes Literature Discussion Rubric Thoughtful Log Entry Rubric Independent Reading Rubric Writing Portfolio Rubric	DRA Level • 90–94% Accuracy • NAEP Fluency • Comprehension • SC Rate Personal Narrative Writing Prompt Words Their Way Spelling Assessment Oral Language Acquisition Inventory	Reading Conference Notes Writing Conference Notes Literature Discussion Rubric Thoughtful Log Entry Rubric Independent Reading Rubric Writing Portfolio Rubric
5th Grade	Spring DRA from Assessment Folder • 90–94% Accuracy • NAEP Fluency • Comprehension • SC Rate 2-Week Reading Observation Spring Writing Prompt from Assessment Folder 2-Week Writing Observation Spring Words Their Way Spelling from Assessment Folder 2-Week Spelling Observation Oral Language Acquisition Inventory Benchmark Book • 90–94% Accuracy • NAEP Fluency • Comprehension • SC Rate	Benchmark Book • 90–94% Accuracy • NAEP Fluency • Comprehension • SC Rate Genre Writing Prompt Writing Portfolio Rubric	Reading Conference Notes Writing Conference Notes Literature Discussion Rubric Thoughtful Log Rubric Independent Reading Rubric Writing Portfolio Rubric	Benchmark Book • 90–94% Accuracy • NAEP Fluency • Comprehension • SC Rate Words Their Way Spelling Assessment Genre Writing Prompt Oral Language Acquisition Inventory	Reading Conference Notes Writing Conference Notes Literature Discussion Rubric Thoughtful Log Rubric Independent Reading Rubric Writing Portfolio Rubric	Benchmark Book • 90–94% Accuracy • NAEP Fluency • Comprehension • SC Rate Genre Writing Prompt	Reading Conference Notes Writing Conference Notes Literature Discussion Rubric Thoughtful Log Rubric Independent Reading Rubric Writing Portfolio Rubric	DRA Level • 90–94% Accuracy • NAEP Fluency • Comprehension • SC Rate Personal Narrative Writing Prompt Words Their Way Spelling Assessment Oral Language Acquisition Inventory	Reading Conference Notes Writing Conference Notes Literature Discussion Rubric Thoughtful Log Rubric Independent Reading Rubric Writing Portfolio Rubric

Appendix G3

Data Collection Sheet

Washington School for Comprehensive Literacy

Teacher:													Grade:				
Students		Reading							Writing				Interventions Third Quarter				
Last Name, First Name	Card #	Guided Reading or Lit Discussion Level and Proficiency	Benchmark Book Level and Proficiency	Reading Conference Notes	Independent Reading Rubric	Thoughtful Log Rubric	Literature Discussion Rubric	Intervention Wall Placement	Quarterly Writing Portfolio Rubric	Genre Rubric Understands Structure Y or N	Writing Conference Notes	Intervention Wall Placement	Tier 1: Classroom Intervention	Tier 2: Intervention Specialist	Tier 3: 1:1 or Reading Recovery	Tier 4: Special Education	
		/	/														1
		/	/														2
		/	/														3
		/	/														4
		/	/														5
		/	/														6
		/	/														7
		/	/														8
		/	/														9
		/	/														10
		/	/														11
		/	/														12
		/	/														13
		/	/														14
		/	/														15
		/	/														16
		/	/														17
		/	/														18
		/	/														19
		/	/														20
		/	/														21
		/	/														22
		/	/														23

GR+=Guided Reading Plus
AW=Assisted Writing
EIG=Emergent Intervention Group
CFG=Comprehension Focus Group
CONF=Additional Conferences
RR=Reading Recovery
TC=Task Cards
OR=Oracy
SP=Speech/Language
LD=Learning Disability

Appendix G4

Literacy Collaboration Plan

Student Name: _____   Grade: _____   Date: _____

Classroom teacher: _____   Interventionist: _____

ELL Staff: _____   Is the child a monitor or universal? _____   ELL level _____   See attached for IEP goals _____

Other staff that works with the student: _____

Reading Interventions

Code	Tier 1 Reading	Tier 2/3/4 Reading
1:1 Rd	Additional 1:1 Conferences	
WW	Additional Word Work	
GR+	Guided Reading Plus (20 min.)	Guided Reading Plus (30 min.)
AW	Assisted Writing	Assisted Writing
RR		Reading Recovery
SE		Special Education

Writing Interventions

Code	Tier 1 Writing	Tier 2/3/4 Writing
1:1 W	Additional 1:1 Conferences	
AW	Assisted Writing	Assisted Writing
PW	Process Writing	Process Writing
CF		Comprehension Focus Group
O		Oracy Group
SE		Special Education

Use Codes from Above

Tier 1 Read	Tier 1 Writing	Tier 2/3 Read	Tier 2/3 Writing	Tier 4 Read	Tier 4 Writing

Comments: Include if the child is making progress (MP) or no progress (NP) and any adjustment to intervention plan.

Reading Levels

	Fall	Tri 1	Tri 2	Tri 3
Kindergarten				
1st Grade				
2nd Grade				
3rd Grade				
4th Grade				
5th Grade				

Next Meeting Date:

Appendix G5

Collaborative Goal Sheet

Student Name: _____ Date: _____ Grade: _____

Teachers: _____

Reading Behaviors   Guided Reading Level: _____

The student currently controls:	The student needs to control next:	Common language for teachers to use:

Writing Behaviors

The student currently controls:	The student needs to control next:	Common language for teachers to use:

Word Work

The student currently controls:	The student needs to control next:	Common language for teachers to use:

Oral Language Development: Circle All That Apply

The student currently controls:	The student needs to control next:
• Asks/answers questions to express understanding • Uses specific vocabulary to express ideas • Uses age-appropriate grammar • Understands concepts used in verbal directions • Uses age-appropriate speech sounds • Produces complete sentences	

Please bring Literacy Continuum with current running record and writing sample.

Next Meeting Date:

Emergent Level (Levels A–C)
Literacy Collaboration

Student Name: _____ Grade:_____

Classroom Teacher:_____ Interventionist:_____

Check all behaviors below that the student uses consistently.

Reading Behaviors: Teaching for Transfer and Self-Regulation

	Date											
Emergent	Attends to print using known words											
	Points to works with 1–1 matching on 1 and 2 lines of text											
	Fluently reads some high-frequency words											
	Articulates first letter in unknown words											
	Notices unknown words and searches for cues in picture and print											
	Uses a special key word from ABC chart or letter book to help with solving words											
	Rereads to cross-check first letter with meaning and structure cues											
	Total	/7	/7	/7	/7	/7	/7	/7	/7	/7	/7	/7

Other notes:

Writing Behaviors: Teaching for Transfer and Self-Regulation

	Date											
Emergent	Uses known letter with correct formation											
	Uses spaces between words with greater accuracy											
	Recognizes link between known sounds and related letters; slowly articulates word with blended sounds											
	Uses ABC chart or letter book as resource for sound-letter links											
	Writes a few high-frequency words with accuracy; begins to acquire a writing vocabulary that reflects attention to reading											
	Uses first part of known words to help write parts of unknown words											
	Includes new words from reading experiences in writing											
	Total	/7	/7	/7	/7	/7	/7	/7	/7	/7	/7	/7

Other notes:

Orthographic Behaviors: Teaching for Transfer and Self-Regulation

	Date											
Emergent	Analyzes letter features; identifies letters based on discriminating features											
	Knows concept of word; constructs single-syllable words in left-to-right order											
	Builds familiar words using slow articulation and direct letter-sound match in single-syllable words											
	Notices relationship between known letters and sounds as they relate to special key words											
	Constructs high-frequency words in left-to-right order; says word slowly and coordinates letter-sound match											
	Compares and categorizes words by initial sound and basic rhyming patterns											
	Sorts words according to meaning classifications; expands word knowledge by noting meaningful relationships											
	Total	/7	/7	/7	/7	/7	/7	/7	/7	/7	/7	/7

Other notes:

From *Shaping Literate Minds: Developing Self-Regulated Learners* by Linda J. Dorn and Carla Soffos, copyright © 2001, reproduced with permission of Stenhouse Publishers. www.stenhouse.com <http://www.stenhouse.com>

(continued)

Appendix G6 *(continued)*

Early Level (Levels D–G)
Literacy Collaboration

Student Name: _____ Grade:_____

Classroom Teacher:_____ Interventionist:_____

Check all behaviors below that the student uses consistently.

Reading Behaviors: Teaching for Transfer and Self-Regulation												
	Date										
Early — Self-monitors reading with greater ease; uses known words and patterns to check on reading												
Searches through words in a left-to-right sequence; blends letters into sounds; repeats word to confirm												
Takes words apart at the larger unit of analysis												
Reads high-frequency words fast, fluently, and automatically												
Becomes faster at noticing errors and initiates multiple attempts to selfcorrect												
Total	/5	/5	/5	/5	/5	/5	/5	/5	/5	/5	/5

Other notes:

Writing Behaviors: Teaching for Transfer and Self-Regulation												
	Date										
Early — Begins to notice common misspellings; circles words that do not look right; uses a simple dictionary to self-correct; uses resources to check work; acquires a writing vocabulary that reflects reading												
Analyzes sequences of sounds and records corresponding letters; segments and blends sounds in words with greater ease												
Constructs words using the larger units of sound-to-letter patterns for writing unknown words												
Applies knowledge of onset and rime patterns for writing unknown words												
Notices similarities between word patterns												
Total	/5	/5	/5	/5	/5	/5	/5	/5	/5	/5	/5

Other notes:

Orthographic Behaviors: Teaching for Transfer and Self-Regulation												
	Date										
Early — Spells most unknown words phonetically, including embedded sounds in two- or three-syllable words; later, moves into transitional spelling, noticing common patterns from reading and writing; letter knowledge fast and automatic												
Knows that letters come together in a left-to-right sequence; says words slowly to match letters to sounds; acquires knowledge of interletter relationships from building familiar words (sh/she; th/the)												
Notices relationship between letter patterns and clusters of sounds; uses known words as a base for adding inflections												
Uses known patterns (onset and rime) to build unknown words												
Manipulates letters to form simple analogies												
Total	/5	/5	/5	/5	/5	/5	/5	/5	/5	/5	/5

Other notes:

From *Shaping Literate Minds: Developing Self-Regulated Learners* by Linda J. Dorn and Carla Soffos, copyright © 2001, reproduced with permission of Stenhouse Publishers. www.stenhouse.com <http://www.stenhouse.com>

(continued)

Transitional Level (Levels H–M)
Literacy Collaboration

Student Name: _____ Grade:_____

Classroom Teacher:_____ Interventionist:_____

Check all behaviors below that the student uses consistently.

Reading Behaviors: Teaching for Transfer and Self-Regulation												
	Date											
Transitional	Expands reading vocabulary; shows interest in unfamiliar words read											
	Solves multisyllabic words by noticing parts within words											
	Quickly takes words apart at the larger unit of analysis											
	Uses word meanings to solve word problems (prefixes, suffixes, roots, compound parts, etc.)											
	Reads longer texts with greater accuracy and fluency; preprocesses error before mistake is made											
	Total	/5	/5	/5	/5	/5	/5	/5	/5	/5	/5	/5

Other notes:

Writing Behaviors: Teaching for Transfer and Self-Regulation												
	Date											
Transitional	Expands writing vocabulary; includes new and unusual words											
	Attends to syllables when writing words; problem-solves with greater ease and fluency											
	Writes increasingly longer texts with greater ease and speed											
	Shows flexibility with word choice; tries out different ways of saying a message with the same meaning; revises word choice in writing process; uses a thesaurus as a resource											
	Uses dictionaries, editing checklists, and other resources to self-correct writing											
	Total	/5	/5	/5	/5	/5	/5	/5	/5	/5	/5	/5

Other notes:

Orthographic Behaviors: Teaching for Transfer and Self-Regulation												
	Date											
Transitional	Analyzes unknown words with greater efficiency and speed											
	Uses syllable breaks to spell longer words											
	Uses more complex analogies to analyze words											
	Analyzes parts of words (inflectional endings, rimes, contractions)											
	Classifies words according to meaningful parts											
	Spells words with greater accuracy; shows evidence of transitional spelling of words with more unusual patterns											
	Total	/6	/6	/6	/6	/6	/6	/6	/6	/6	/6	/6

Other notes:

(continued)

Fluent Level (Levels N–Z)
Literacy Collaboration

Student Name: _____ Grade:_____

Classroom Teacher:_____ Interventionist:_____

Check all behaviors below that the student uses consistently.

Reading Behaviors: Teaching for Transfer and Self-Regulation												
	Date										
Fluent Has an extensive reading vocabulary; reads longer texts with specialized content and unusual words; learns new words daily												
Applies knowledge of word meaning to reading texts with more complex language structures												
Responds to reading at many different levels; applies knowledge about word meanings across different texts; makes predictions about word meanings and checks within texts; refines word knowledge												
Total	/3	/3	/3	/3	/3	/3	/3	/3	/3	/3	/3

Other notes:

Writing Behaviors: Teaching for Transfer and Self-Regulation												
	Date										
Fluent Has an extensive writing vocabulary; writes longer texts with good word choice; uses new words from reading												
Uses figurative language (similes, metaphors) and descriptive phrases to enhance message												
Uses a range of resources, including thesaurus, dictionary, encyclopedia, and other research materials to plan and inform writing												
Total	/3	/3	/3	/3	/3	/3	/3	/3	/3	/3	/3

Other notes:

Orthographic Behaviors: Teaching for Transfer and Self-Regulation												
	Date										
Fluent Has flexible control of spelling patterns; knows when words do not look right; can spell most words with minimal attention												
Classifies words according to word meanings, including figurative and descriptive language												
Notices multiple meanings of words; acquires a mental dictionary of word meanings												
Total	/3	/3	/3	/3	/3	/3	/3	/3	/3	/3	/3

Other notes:

Determining Appropriate Intervention Service (DAIS)
Literacy Intervention Plan

Supplemental Teacher Form

Student: _____ Grade: _____ Classroom Teacher: _____

Date: _____

Student Status

Initial Placement	
Reading	**Writing**
☐ Advanced	☐ Advanced
☐ Proficient	☐ Proficient
☐ Basic	☐ Basic
☐ Below Basic	☐ Below Basic

End Quarter 1	
Reading	**Writing**
☐ Advanced	☐ Advanced
☐ Proficient	☐ Proficient
☐ Basic	☐ Basic
☐ Below Basic	☐ Below Basic

End Quarter 2	
Reading	**Writing**
☐ Advanced	☐ Advanced
☐ Proficient	☐ Proficient
☐ Basic	☐ Basic
☐ Below Basic	☐ Below Basic

End Quarter 3	
Reading	**Writing**
☐ Advanced	☐ Advanced
☐ Proficient	☐ Proficient
☐ Basic	☐ Basic
☐ Below Basic	☐ Below Basic

End Quarter 4	
Reading	**Writing**
☐ Advanced	☐ Advanced
☐ Proficient	☐ Proficient
☐ Basic	☐ Basic
☐ Below Basic	☐ Below Basic

Degrees of Intensity →

Layers of Support/Expertise

Plan/Monitoring/Duration	Tier II Intervention Group (3-5)	Tier III: Individual or 1:2
Baseline	☐	☐
Discrepancy to Peers		
Progress Monitoring		

Teacher — Tier II & III / Tier IV Supplemental

Intervention Specialist / Special Education

Intervention Schedule: _____

Data to collect for next meeting: _____

Teaching Notes: _____

CBCSD │ DAIS
Supplemental

Adapted and used with permission from *The Journal of Reading Recovery.*
(continued)

Appendix G7 (continued)

Quarter 1

Date of meeting:

Summary of assessment information:

Changes to intervention:

Quarter 2

Date of meeting:

Summary of assessment information:

Changes to intervention:

Quarter 3

Date of meeting:

Summary of assessment information:

Changes to intervention:

Quarter 4

Date of meeting:

Summary of assessment information:

Changes to intervention:

(continued)

Determining Appropriate Intervention Service (DAIS)
Literacy Intervention Plan

Student File Form

Student: _____ Grade: _____ Classroom Teacher: _____ Date: _____

Student Status

	Initial Placement		End Quarter 1		End Quarter 2		End Quarter 3		End Quarter 4	
	Reading	Writing	Reading	Writing	Reading	Writing	Reading	Writing	Reading	Writing
	☐ Advanced ☐ Proficient ☐ Basic ☐ Below Basic	☐ Advanced ☐ Proficient ☐ Basic ☐ Below Basic	☐ Advanced ☐ Proficient ☐ Basic ☐ Below Basic	☐ Advanced ☐ Proficient ☐ Basic ☐ Below Basic	☐ Advanced ☐ Proficient ☐ Basic ☐ Below Basic	☐ Advanced ☐ Proficient ☐ Basic ☐ Below Basic	☐ Advanced ☐ Proficient ☐ Basic ☐ Below Basic	☐ Advanced ☐ Proficient ☐ Basic ☐ Below Basic	☐ Advanced ☐ Proficient ☐ Basic ☐ Below Basic	☐ Advanced ☐ Proficient ☐ Basic ☐ Below Basic

Degrees of Intensity

Layers of Support/Expertise

Layer		Individual or 1:2	Small Group	Whole Class	Independent Work
Tier I Classroom	Universal Program	☐ Reading Conference ☐ Writing Conference	☐ Guided Reading ☐ Literature Discussion ☐ Response Logs ☐ Language Investigations	☐ Read Aloud ☐ Shared Reading ☐ Mini-Lessons ☐ Share Time	☐ Familiar/Easy Reading ☐ Writing Process ☐ Phonics or Vocabulary Tasks ☐ Literature Extensions/Research Project
	Classroom Intervention	**Individual or 1:2** ☐ Additional Reading Conference ☐ Additional Writing Conference	**Intervention Group (3–5)** ☐ Tailored Word Study ☐ Writing About Reading ☐ Oracy Group or Emergent Literacy Group ☐ Task Card Group: ☐ Phonic Vocabulary ☐ Assisted Writing Group ☐ Interactive Writing Aloud	**Plan/Monitoring/Duration** Baseline Discrepancy to Peers Progress Monitoring	
Tier II & III/ Tier IV Supplemental	Intervention Specialist Special Education Teacher	**Tier III: Individual or 1:2** ☐ Reading Recovery (1:1) ☐ Intervention Group (1:2)	**Tier II Intervention Group (3–5)** ☐ Guided Reading Plus Group ☐ Comprehension Focus Group ☐ Oracy Group or Emergent Literacy Group ☐ Writing Process Group (push-in) ☐ Assisted Writing Group: ☐ Interactive Writing Aloud	**Plan/Monitoring/Duration** Baseline Discrepancy to Peers Progress Monitoring	

CBCSD |DAIS
Student File

Adapted and used with permission from *The Journal of Reading Recovery.*
(continued)

Appendix G

Appendix G7 (continued)

Quarter 1

People Present at Meeting:

Date of meeting:

Comments:

Date to re-meet:

Team Recommends
☐ Continue Current Intervention ☐ Modify Intervention ☐ Discontinue Intervention ☐ Complete Suspected Disability ☐ Other

Quarter 2

People Present at Meeting:

Date of meeting:

Comments:

Date to re-meet:

Team Recommends
☐ Continue Current Intervention ☐ Modify Intervention ☐ Discontinue Intervention ☐ Complete Suspected Disability ☐ Other

Quarter 3

People Present at Meeting:

Date of meeting:

Comments:

Date to re-meet:

Team Recommends
☐ Continue Current Intervention ☐ Modify Intervention ☐ Discontinue Intervention ☐ Complete Suspected Disability ☐ Other

Quarter 4

People Present at Meeting:

Date of meeting:

Comments:

Date to re-meet:

Team Recommends
☐ Continue Current Intervention ☐ Modify Intervention ☐ Discontinue Intervention ☐ Complete Suspected Disability ☐ Other

Appendix G8

Look-Fors in Small-Group Intervention
Guided Reading Plus

Goals	Criteria	1 Rarely	2 Sometimes	3 Frequently	4 Consistently
Schedule	Teacher meets with group four to five days a week.				
Materials	Teacher and students' materials are organized and easily accessible. Students use their materials efficiently (magnetic letters, wipe-off boards, erasers, alphabet chart).				
Assessments	Teacher uses ongoing summative (formal) and formative (informal) assessments to make decisions about each student's progress within the intervention.				
Components	Teacher teaches all components of Guided Reading Plus.				
Phase One Word Study	Teacher selects appropriate words to teach an appropriate word learning principle. Teacher engages the students in applying phonological, phonemic, and phonetic processes for learning how words work (sound analysis, visual analysis, pattern analysis, analogies, meaning). Teacher links the word learning processes to reading and writing.				
Guided Reading	Teacher selects a book that matches the students' instructional level, containing a few challenging features to promote efficient problem solving. Teacher builds prior knowledge needed to comprehend the text. Teacher introduces the book, giving an overview of the text and sets the purpose for reading. Teacher engages the students in the co-construction of meaning. Teacher uses unfamiliar words or phrases that students need to have in their listening vocabulary. Teacher provides individual reading time.				
Conferences	Teacher holds individual conferences. Teacher records student's processing behaviors and applies contingent scaffolding to lift the student's processing.				
Discussion	Teacher conducts a discussion of the meaning of the text. Teacher prompts students to locate a problem area of the text. Teacher uses these opportunities to teach for strategy use.				
Phase Two Progress Monitoring	Teacher provides an opportunity for students, to read familiar and independent text to promote fluency, apply efficient problem-solving strategies and to foster deeper comprehension.				
Writing in Response to Reading	Teacher provides a writing strategy lesson or provides a prompt to deepen comprehension through writing. Teacher provides opportunities for students to rehearse their response. Teacher provides students' individual writing time and individual conferences.				
Conferring with Students	Teacher records students processing behaviors (reading prompt and understanding academic vocabulary, fluency of thinking while rehearsing, organizing for response, using writing strategies, and fluency of encoding response) while writing. Teacher applies contingent scaffolding to lift the student's processing.				

References

Aaron, P. G. (1997). The impending demise of the discrepancy formula. *Review of Educational Research, 67(4)*, 461–502.

Adams, M. (1990). *Beginning to read: Thinking and learning about print*. Cambridge, MA: MIT Press.

Allington, R. L. (2002). Research on reading/learning disability interventions. In A. E. Farstrup & S. Samuels (Eds.), *What research says about reading instruction* (3d ed., pp. 261–290). Newark, DE: International Reading Association.

Allington, R. L. (1983). Fluency: The neglected reading goal in reading comprehension. *The Reading Teacher, 36*, 556–561.

Clay, M. M. (1987). Learning to be learning disabled. *New Zealand Journal of Educational Studies, 22*, 155–173.

Clay, M. M. (1991). *Becoming literate: The construction of inner control*. Portsmouth, NH: Heinemann.

Clay, M. M. (1993). *Reading Recovery: A guidebook for teachers in training*. Portsmouth, NH: Heinemann.

Clay, M. M. (2001). *Change over time in children's literacy development*. Portsmouth, NH: Heinemann.

Clay, M. M. (2002, 2006). *An observation survey of early literacy achievement*. Portsmouth, NH: Heinemann.

Clay, M. M. (2005). *Literacy lessons designed for individuals: Part two, teaching procedures*. Portsmouth, NH: Heinemann.

Clay, M. M. (2007). *Record of oral language*. Portsmouth, NH: Heinemann.

Dole, J., Brown, K., & Trathen, W. (1996). The effects of strategy instruction on the comprehension performance of at-risk students. *Reading Research Quarterly, 31*, 62–88.

Dorn, L. J., & Allen, A. (1995). Helping low-achieving first-grade readers. A program combining Reading Recovery tutoring and small-group instruction. *ERS Spectrum: Journal of School Research and Information, 13(3)*, 16–24.

Dorn, L. J., French, C., & Jones, T. (1998). *Apprenticeship in literacy: Transitions across reading and writing*. Portland, ME: Stenhouse.

Dorn, L. J., & Henderson, S. C. (2010a). A comprehensive intervention model: A systems approach to Response to Intervention. In M. Wixon & K. Lipson (Eds.), *Approaches to Response to Intervention (RTI): Evidence-based frameworks for preventing reading failure*. Newark, DE: International Reading Association.

Dorn, L. J., & Henderson, S. C. (2010b). A comprehensive assessment system as a response to intervention process. In P. H. Johnston (Ed.), *RtI in Literacy: Responsive and comprehensive*. Newark, DE: International Reading Association.

Dorn, L. J., & Schubert, B. (2010). A comprehensive intervention model for reversing reading failure: A Response to Intervention approach [Reprint *from Journal of Reading Recovery, 7(2)*, 29–41]. In P. H. Johnston (Ed.), *RTI: Responsive and comprehensive*. Newark, DE: International Reading Association.

Dorn, L. J., & Schubert, B. (2008, spring). A comprehensive intervention model for reversing reading failure: A Response to Intervention approach. *Journal of Reading Recovery, 7(2)*, 29–41.

Dorn, L. J., & Soffos, C. (2009a). *Interventions that work: Guided reading plus*. [Computer Software]. Boston: Allyn & Bacon.

Dorn, L. J., & Soffos, C. (2009b). *Interventions that work: Comprehension focus groups*. [Computer Software]. Boston: Allyn & Bacon.

Dorn, L. J., & Soffos, C. (2009c). *Small group intervention: Linking word study to reading and writing*. [Computer Software]. Portland, ME: Stenhouse.

Dorn, L. J., & Soffos, C. (2005a). The environmental scale for assessing levels of implementation: ESAIL. Unpublished instrument. University of Arkansas–Little Rock.

Dorn, L. J., & Soffos, C. (2005b). *Teaching for deep comprehension: A reading workshop approach*. Portland, ME: Stenhouse.

Dorn, L. J., & Soffos, C. (2001a). *Scaffolding young writers: A writers' workshop approach*. Portland, ME: Stenhouse.

Dorn, L. J., & Soffos, C. (2001b). *Shaping literate minds: Developing self-regulated learners.* Portland, ME: Stenhouse.

Duffy, G. G. & Israel, S. E. (2009). Where to from here? Themes, trends, and questions. In Israel,S. E. & Duffy, G. G. (Eds). Handbook of Research in Reading Comprehension. New York:Routledge. pp. 668-675.

Dunn, M. (2007). Diagnosing reading disability: Reading Recovery as a component of a Response to Intervention assessment method. *Learning Disabilities: A Contemporary Journal, 5(2),* 31–47.

Farstrup A., & Samuels, S. J. (2006). *What research has to say about reading instruction.* Newark, DE: International Reading Association.

Gentile, L. M. (2004). *The oral language acquisition inventory.* Boston: Pearson.

Gersten, R., Fuchs, L., Williams, P., & Baker, S. (2001). Teaching reading comprehension strategies to students with learning disabilities: A review of research. *Review of Educational Research, 71,* 279–320.

Gindis, B. (2003). Remediation through education: Sociocultural theory and children with special needs. In A. Kizlulin, B. Gindis, V. S. Ageyev, & S. M. Miller (Eds.), *Vygotsky's educational theory in cultural context* (pp. 200–221). New York: Cambridge University Press.

Goldenberg, C. (1992). Instructional conversations: Promoting comprehension through discussion. *Reading Teacher, 46,* 316–326.

Graham, S., & Harris, K. R. (2005). Improving the writing performance of young struggling writers: Theoretical and programmatic research from the Center on Student Learning. *Journal of Special Education, 39*(1), 19–33.

Harris, K., & Pressley, M. (1991). The nature of cognitive strategy instruction: Interactive strategy construction. *Exceptional Children, Vol. 57,* 392–404.

Harrison, L. (2003). A study of the complementary effects of Reading Recovery and small group literacy instruction. Unpublished educational specialist thesis, University of Arkansas–Little Rock.

International Reading Association & National Council of Teachers of English. (2009). *Standards for the assessment of reading and writing* (Rev. ed.). Newark, DE; Urbana, IL: Authors. Retrieved February 3, 2010 from www.ncte.org/library/NCTEFiles/Resources/Books/Sample/StandardsDoc.pdf

James, K. (2005). Reading Recovery and small group intervention: A layered approach for comprehensive literacy. Unpublished educational specialist thesis, University of Arkansas–Little Rock.

Johnston, P. H. (2010). *RTI: Responsive and comprehensive.* Newark, DE: International Reading Association.

Kozulin, A. (1998). *Psychological tools: A sociocultural approach to education.* Cambridge, MA: Harvard University Press.

Kerbow, D. J., Gwynne, J., & Jacob, B. (1999). Evaluation of achievement gains at the primary level. Paper presented at American Educational Research Association Meeting. Montreal, Canada, April.

Kuhn, M. R., Schwanenflugel, P. J., & Meisinger, E. B. (2010). Aligning theory and assessment of reading fluency: Automaticity, prosody, and definitions of fluency. *Reading Research Quarterly, 45*(2), 230–251.

Kuhn, M. R., & Stahl, S. A. (2003). Fluency: A review of developmental and remedial practices. *Journal of Educational Psychology, 95,* 3–21.

Lidz, C., & Gindis, G. (2003). Dynamic assessment of the evolving cognitive functions in children. In A. Kozulin, B. Gindi, V. Ageyev, & S. Miller (Eds.), *Vygotsky's educational theory in cultural context* (pp. 83–116). New York: Cambridge University Press.

Lipson, M. Y., & Wixson, K. K. (2010). *Successful approaches to RtI: Collaborative practices for improving K–12 literacy.* Newark, DE: International Reading Association.

Luria, A. R. (1980). *Higher cortical functions in man.* New York: Basic Books.

Meyer, K., & Reindl, B. (2010). Spotlight on Comprehensive Intervention Model: The case of Washington School for Comprehensive Literacy. In M. Wixson & K. Lipson (Eds.), *Approaches to Response to Intervention (RTI): Evidence-based frameworks for preventing reading failure.* Newark, DE: International Reading Association.

Meichenbaum, D., & Biemiller, A. (1998). *Nurturing independent learners: Helping students take charge of their learning.* Cambridge, MA: Brookline Books.

McKeough, A., Lupart, J., & Marini, A. (1995). *Teaching for transfer: Fostering generalization in learning.* Hillsdale, NJ: Lawrence Erlbaum.

Paris, S., Lipson, M. Y., & Wixson, K. (1994). Becoming a strategic reader. In Ruddell, R. D., Ruddell, M. R., & Singer, H. (Eds.), *Theoretical models and processes of reading* (4th ed., pp. 788–810). Newark, DE: International Reading Association.

Pedhazur, E. J., & Schmelkin, L. P. (1991). *Measurement,*

design, and analysis: An integrated approach. Hillsdale, NJ: Lawrence Erlbaum.

Pinnell, G. S., Pikulsik, J. J., Wixson, K. K., Campbell, J. R., Gough, P. B., & Beatty, A. S. (1995). *Listening to children read aloud.* Washington, DC: Office of Educational Research and Improvement, U.S. Department of Education.

Samuels, S. J., & Farstup, A. (2006). *What research has to say about fluency.* Newark, DE: International Reading Association.

Saunders, W. M., & Goldenberg, C. (1999). *The effects of instructional conversations and literature logs on story comprehension and thematic understanding of English proficient and limited English proficient students.* Research Report No. 6. Center for Research on Education, Diversity & Excellence. University of California, Santa Cruz.

Scanlon, D., & Anderson, K. (2010). Using the interactive strategies approach to prevent reading difficulties in an RtI context. In *Successful approaches to RtI: Collaborative practices for improving K–12 literacy.* Newark, DE: International Reading Association.

Spear-Swerling, L., & Sternberg, R. (1996). *Off track: When poor readers become learning disabled.* Bolder, CO: Westview Press.

Vellutino, X., & Scanlon, D. (2002). The interactive strategies approach to reading intervention. *Contemporary Educational Psychology, 27,* 573–635.

Vygotsky, L. S. (1978). *Mind in society: The development of higher psychological processes* (M. Cole, V. John-Steiner, S. Scribner, & E. Souberman, Eds. & Trans.). Cambridge, MA: Harvard University Press.

Zull, J. (2002). *The art of the changing brain: Enriching the practice of teaching by exploring the biology of teaching.* Sterling, VA: Stylus Publishing.

Index